SKETCHES by SHIGERU BAN

建築家・坂　茂　スケッチ集

光村推古書院

SKETCHES by **SHIGERU BAN**

First Edition November 2024
Published by Culture Convenience Club Co., Ltd.
Sale by Mitsumura Suiko Shoin Publishing Co., Ltd.
407-2 Shimomaruya-cho Kawaramachi Sanjo Nakagyou-ku, Kyoto 604-8006 Japan

Author: Shigeru Ban

Publisher: Kazuki Yamashita

All rights reserved. No part of this publication may be reproduced or used in any form or by any means, graphic, electronic, or mechanical, including photocopying, recording, taping, or information storage and retrieval systems, without written permission of the publisher.

© 2024 Shigeru Ban
Printed in Japan
ISBN978-4-8381-0627-1

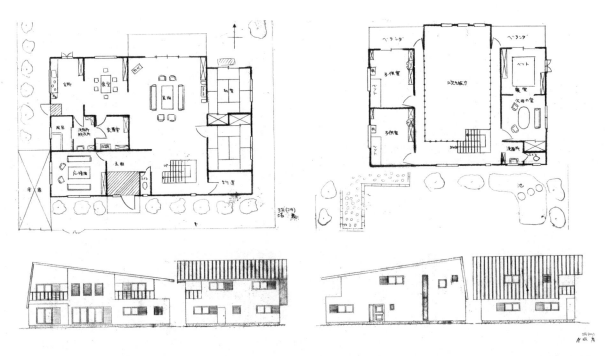

Sketches drawn by Shigeru Ban at the age of 13.
13歳の時に描いたスケッチ。

心 の 表 現 と し て の ス ケ ッ チ
坂 茂

　スケッチを手で描く行為は、僕にとって建築を作る作業です。 建築現場では、我々建築家は実際に手を出すことはできないので、スケッチを描き、自分の中に満ち溢れるアイディアを紙の上に表現し、建築を作っています。ですから、スケッチを作ることで、建築作業の半分は終わっていると言えます。つまりスケッチに描いたのとほぼ同じものが、現実にでき上がるからです。

　僕は建築のフォームを作る前に、構造の素材やシステムを考え、構造のディティールを考えます。形はそのシステムに適したフォームが自然に生まれます。そんなスケッチを描いている時間は、自分にとって最も楽しく幸せな時で、スケッチができ上がった瞬間は最高の充実感を味わいます。

　旅（ほとんど出張）する時は、いつもスケッチブックに列車の中でも飛行機の中でもスケッチを描きます。以前、飛行機の中でスケッチ

をしていたらキャビン・アテンダントの方に、「お上手ですね！」と褒められました。

そしてベッドに入り、寝入るまでのときも建築のアイディアを考えています。夢でもデザインの夢をよく見て、起きて枕元に置いてあるメモ帳にメモします。しかし夢で時々、自分では絶対にデザインしない極彩色の、とてもデコラティブな建築空間を見ることがあります。僕は普段はできる限りシンプルなデザインを考えますが、自分の深層心理の中ではそのようなデコラティブな建築を考え、将来作る潜在性があるのかもしれません。

最後に、2014年にプリツカー賞をいただいた時、セレモニーの後の記者会見で、僕があまりデジタルテクノロジーに頼らないことを知っている記者の方から、意地悪（？）な質問として、僕はいかにコンピューターで設計をしているか聞かれました。僕は全て手描きのスケッチ（図面）しか作りませんが、当然スタッフはそれをもとにCAD図面を書き、構造家がコンピューターで解析し建築を実現していきます。そんな質問をされた時、僕の横にいた尊敬する友人の中国人建築家 王澍（ワン・シュー）が、その質問を僕の代わりに答えてくれました。"コンピューターで図面を書くときは、その行為は直接脳につながっている。しかし手でスケッチをするときは、その行為は直接自分の心に繋がっている 。"

本書は私が何十年も書き溜めたスケッチの一部を選んで編集しました。旅の時のスケッチブック上のスケッチ以外の全てのスケッチは、事務所でA4コピー用紙の裏紙に書いたものです。何故か真新しい紙に描くより、"もったいない"と思わず躊躇なく描けるのです。そんな"もったいない"という精神が、再生紙の紙管建築の開発につながったのだと思います。

Sketching as an Expression of My Heart

Shigeru Ban

The act of drawing sketches by hand is, for me, the process of creating architecture. Since we architects cannot actually do anything with our hands at the construction site, we create architecture by drawing sketches on paper to express the ideas that fill our minds. Therefore, it can be said that by making sketches, half of the architectural work is finished. In other words, what is built in reality is almost the same as whatever was drawn in the sketch.

Before I create the architectural form, I first think about the structural system, materials and the structural details. The appropriate form will naturally arise from the system. The time I spend drawing such sketches is the most enjoyable and blessed time for me, and the moment the sketch is completed, I experience the greatest sense of fulfillment.

Whenever I travel (mostly for work), I always draw sketches in my sketchbook, either on the train or on the airplane. Once, when I was sketching on an airplane, I was praised by a cabin attendant, "You are very good."

I think about architectural ideas when I go to bed and just before falling asleep. I also often dream about design in my sleep, and I wake up and jot them down in a notepad that I keep by my pillow. Sometimes I dream about extremely colorful decorative architectural spaces that I would never design. I think of designs that are as simple as possible, but maybe in my deepest psyche I have the potential to think about and create such decorative architecture in the future.

Finally, when I received the Pritzker Architecture Prize in 2014, at the press conference after the ceremony, I was asked a (mean?) question by a reporter who knew that I do not rely much on digital technology. He asked me how much I design with the aid of computers. I only make hand-drawn sketches (drawings), but of course my staff create CAD drawings based on the sketches,

and the structural engineer analyzes them on the computer to realize the architecture. When I was asked this question, my friend Wang Shu, a Chinese architect who I respect, was next to me and answered the question for me. He said, "When you draw using a computer, this act is directly connected to your brain, but when you sketch by hand, it is directly connected to your heart."

This book was compiled from a selection of sketches I have made over several decades. All of the sketches, except for the ones I draw in my sketchbook during my travels, were done in my office on the back of used A4 printing paper. For some reason, I can draw without hesitation and without thinking "what a waste" compared to drawing on a brand new piece of paper. I believe it was this spirit of "mottainai" that led to the development my paper tube architecture using recycled paper.

Odawara Festival Main Hall East Gate of Odawara Festival
小田原パビリオン　メイン会場東ゲート

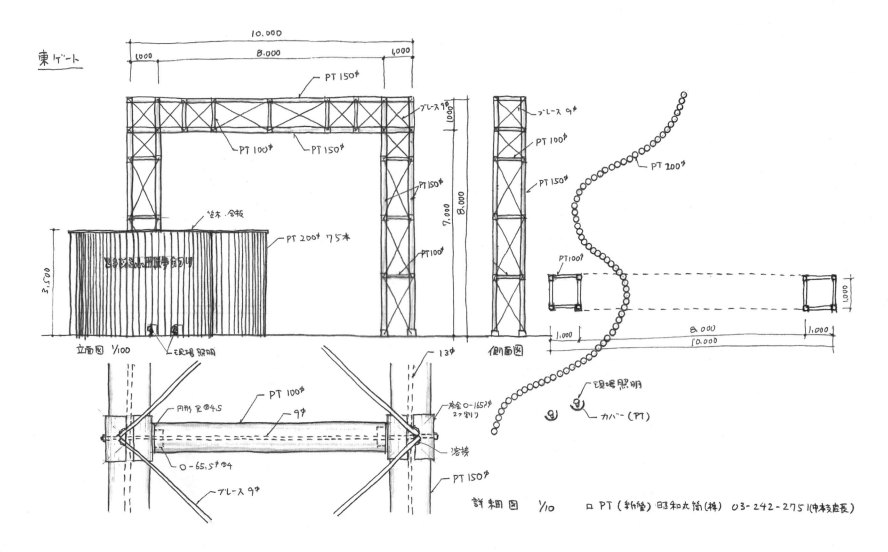

Odawara Festival Main Hall
小田原パビリオン

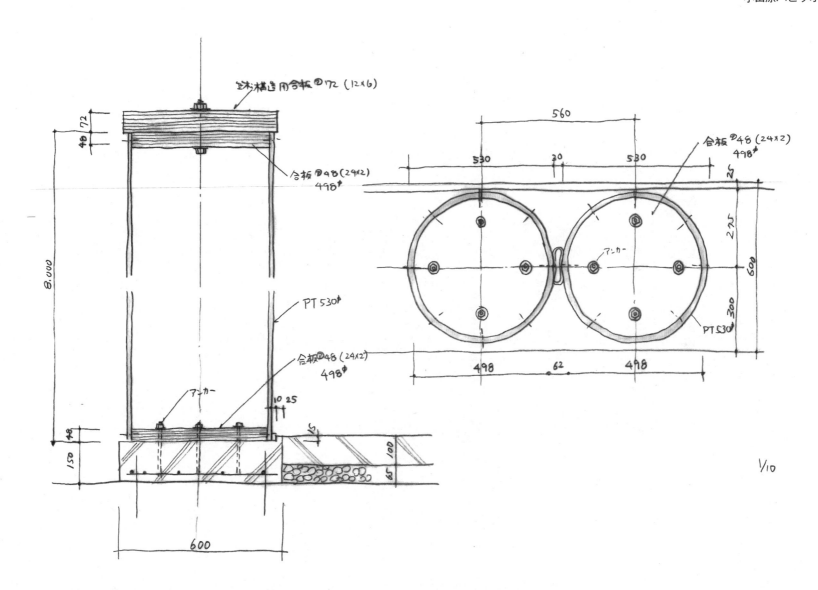

Library of a Poet
詩人の書庫

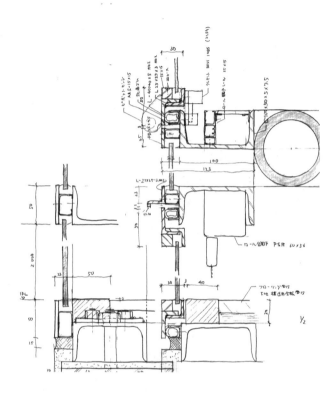

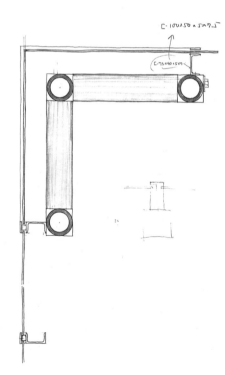

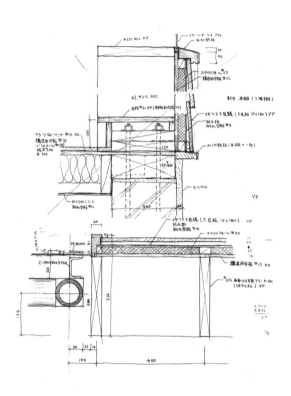

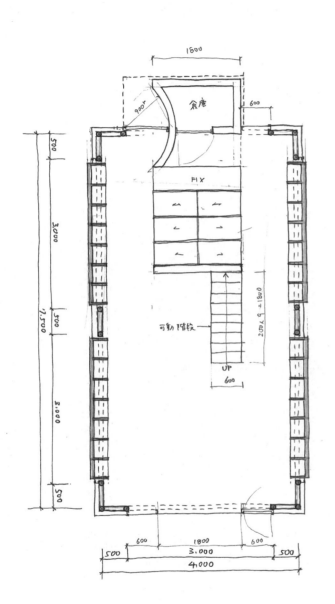
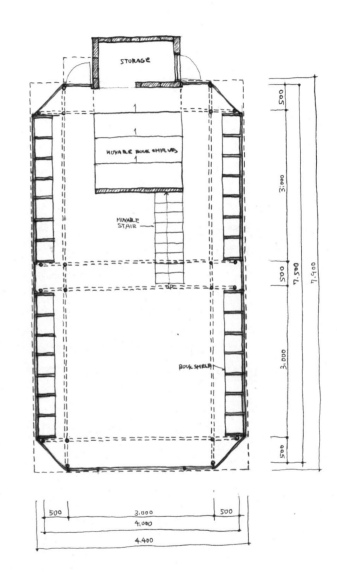

Villa Kuru
ヴィラ　クル

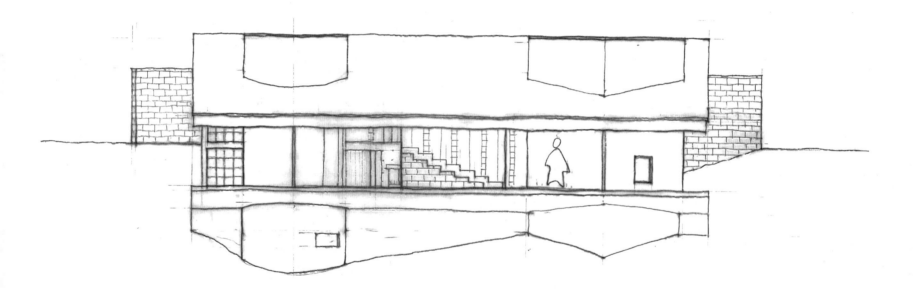

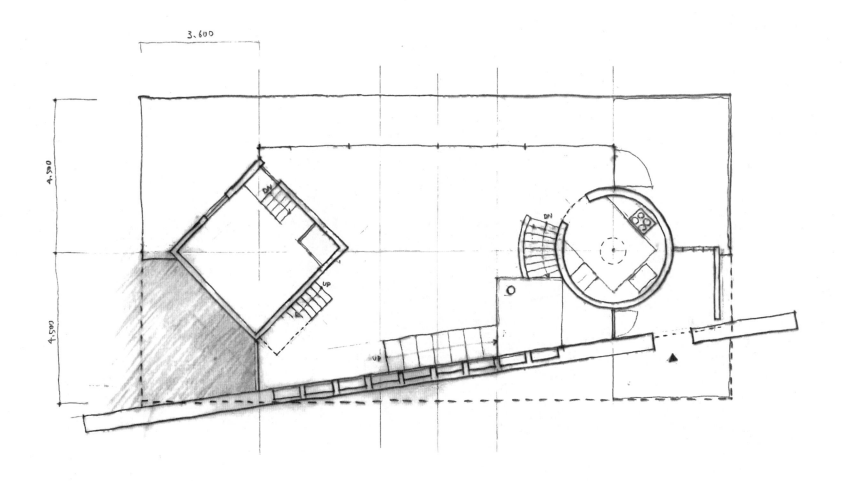

1FL

Villa Kuru
ヴィラ　クル

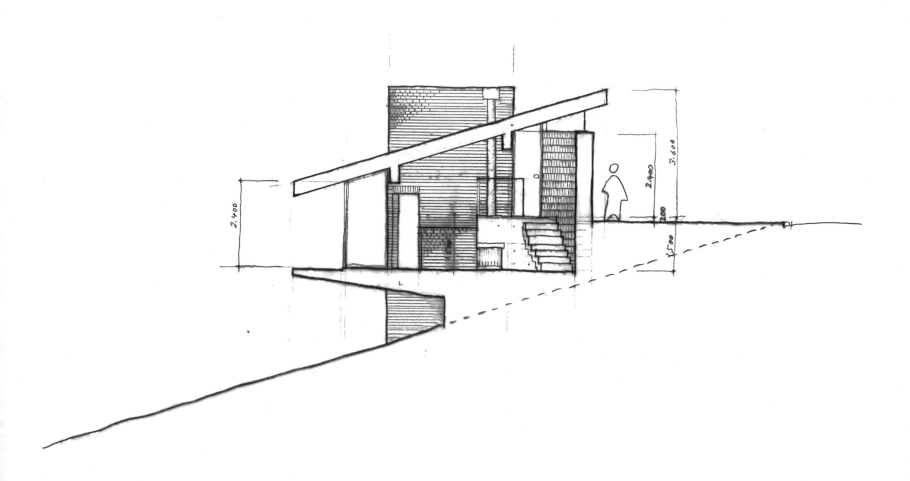

MDS Gallery
紙のギャラリー

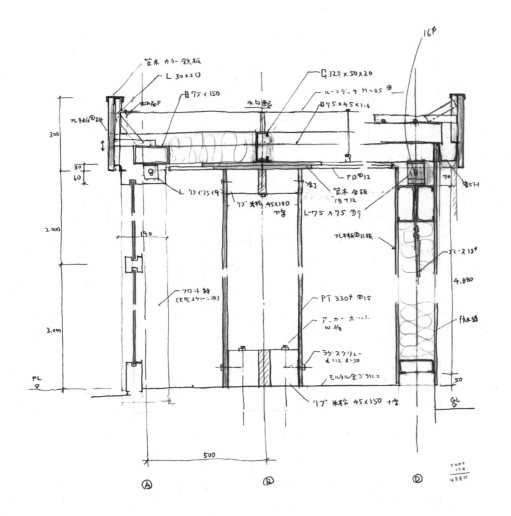
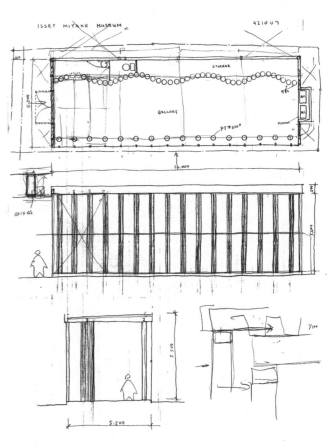

SHIGERU BAN, ARCHITECT

Paper House
紙の家

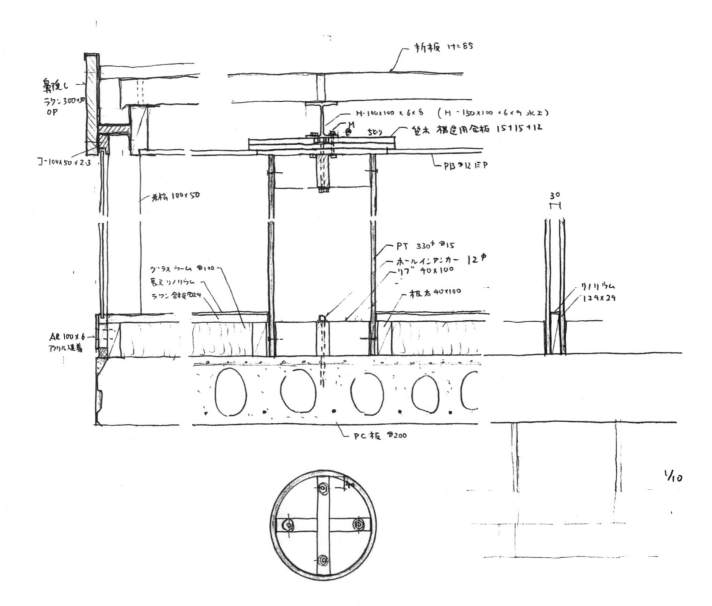

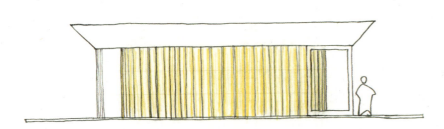
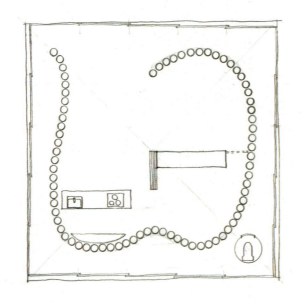
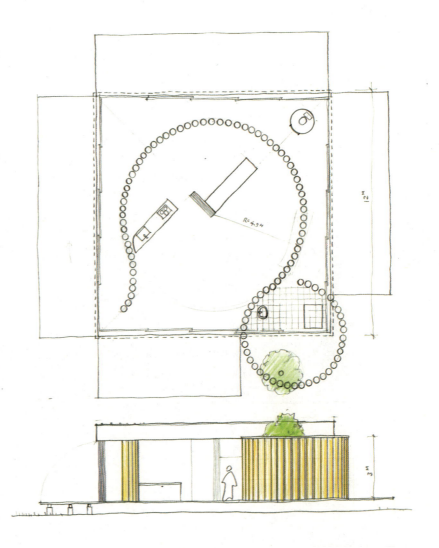

17

Dengyosha Factory at Hamura
羽村の工場　電業社

Studio for Vocalists
声楽家の家

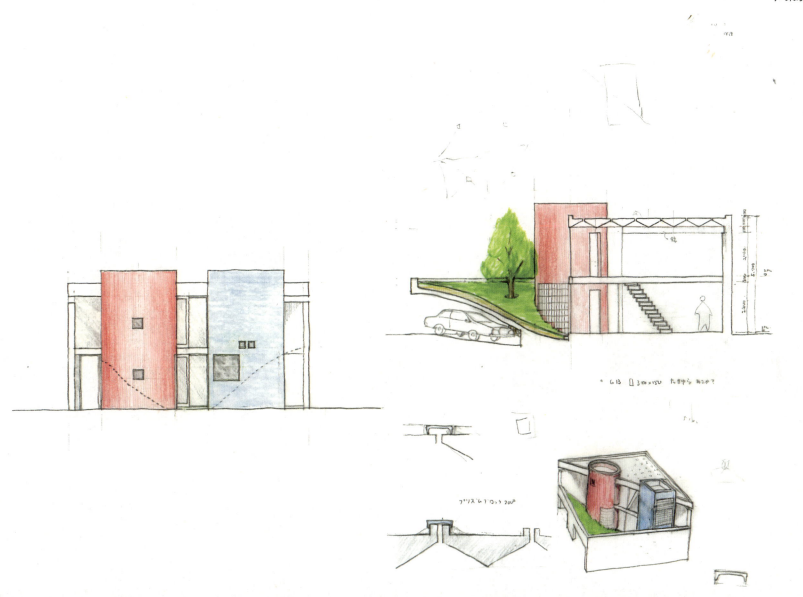

Studio for Vocalists
声楽家の家

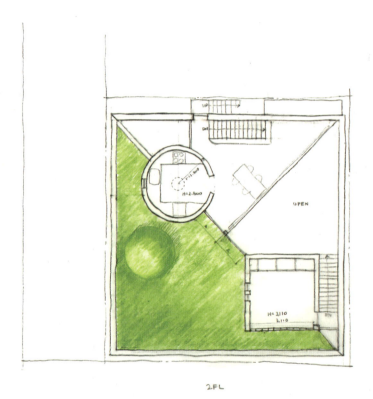

2FL

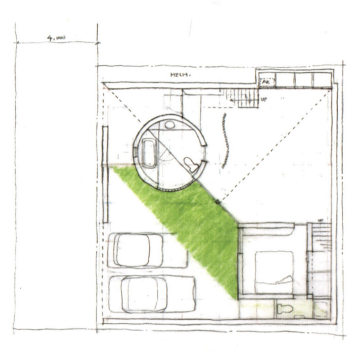

1FL

House of Double-Roof
ダブル・ルーフの家

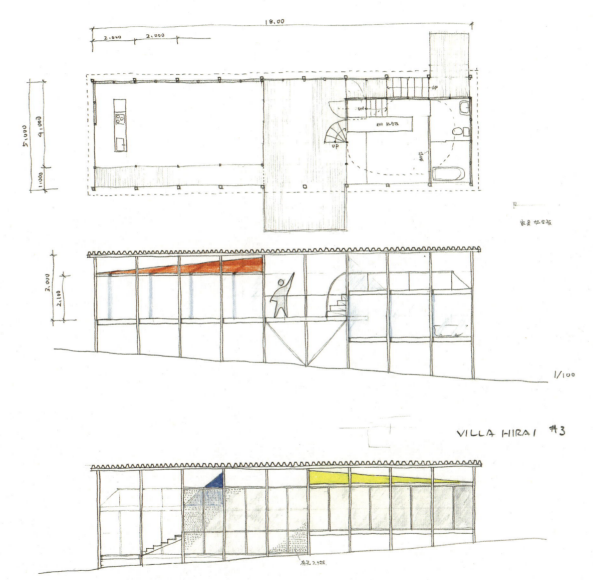

House for a Dentist
デンティストの家

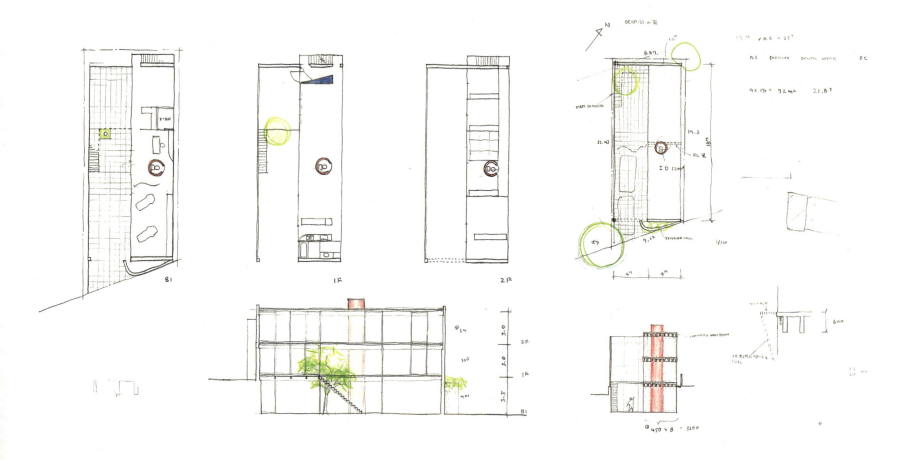

Paper Temporary Studio
紙の仮設スタジオ

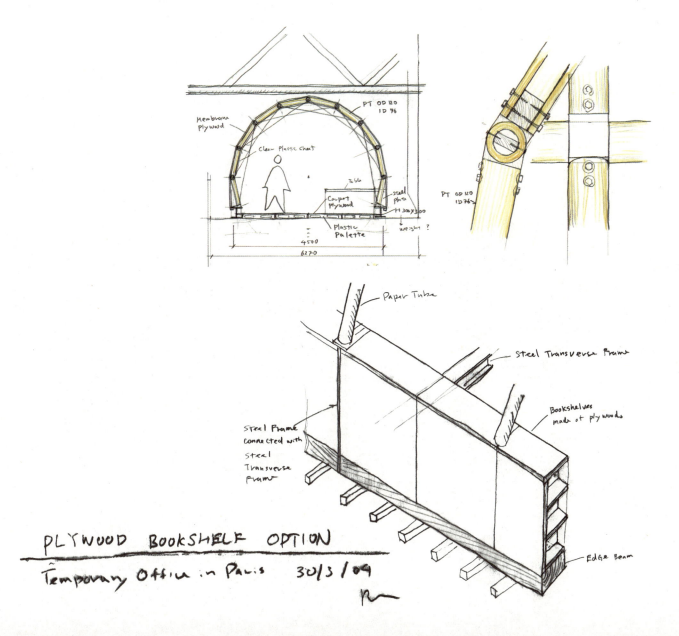

23

Maison E
メゾン E

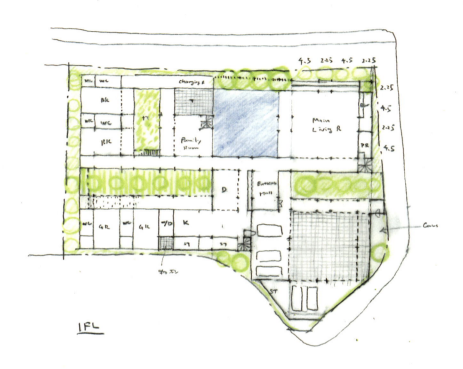
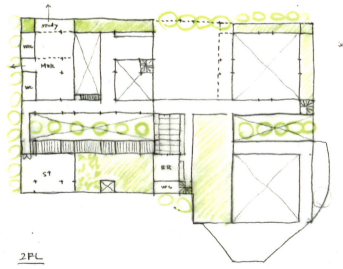

Papertainer Museum
ペーパーテイナー美術館

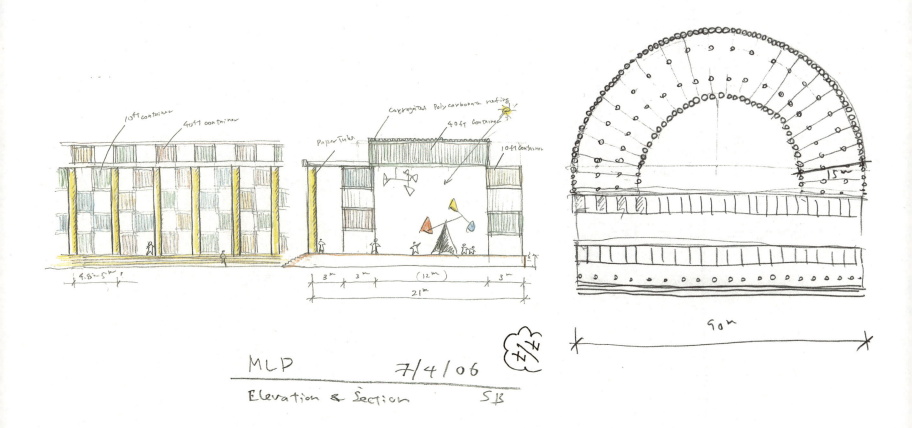

25

Sagaponac House
サガポナック・ハウス

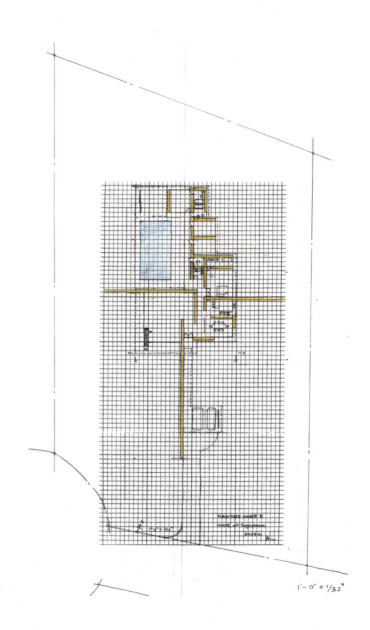

Kennedys Bush House
ケネディーズ・ブッシュ・ハウス

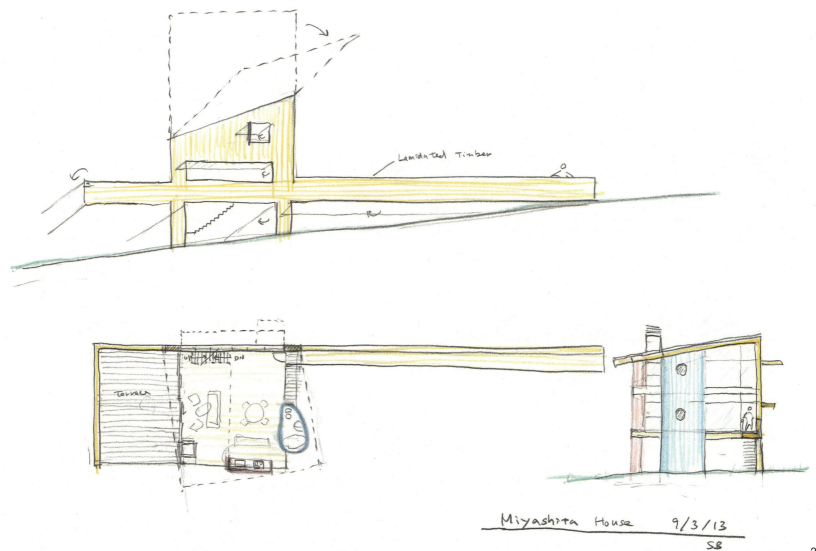

Miyashita House 9/3/13
SB

House at Hanegi Park - Vista
羽根木公園の家 - 景色の道

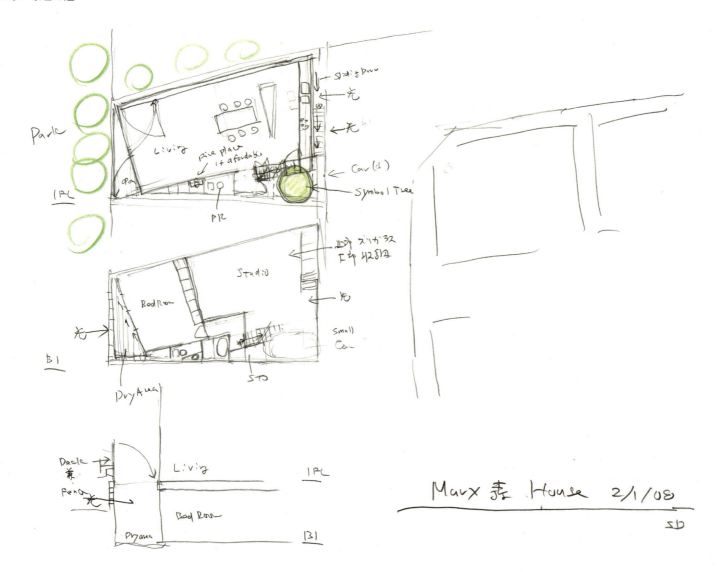

28

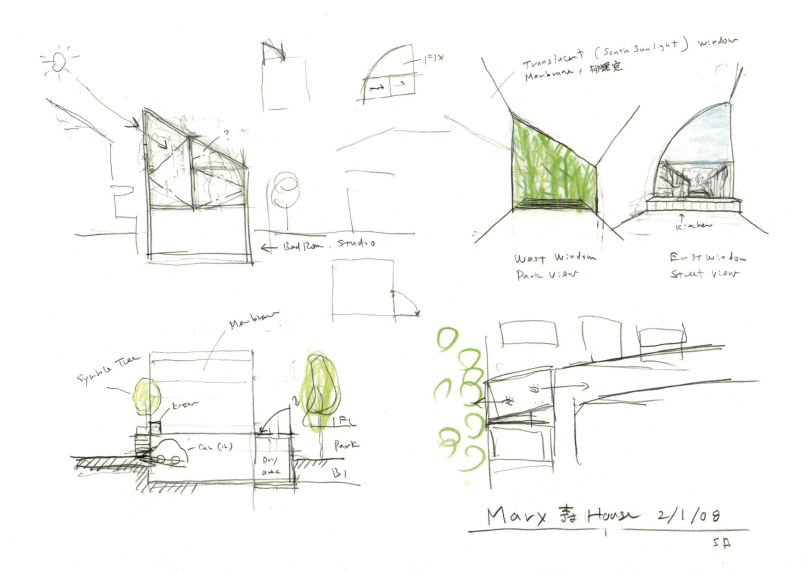

Chenjia Town Clubhouse, Chongming Island
崇明島陳家クラブハウス

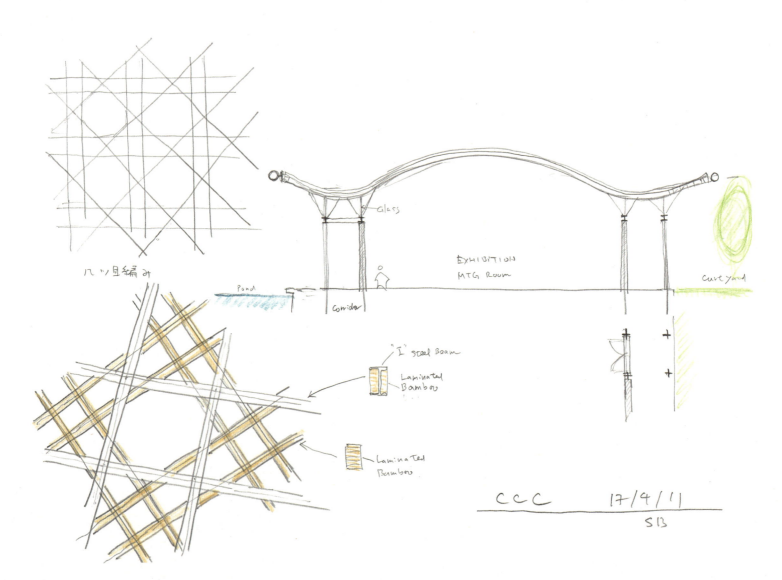

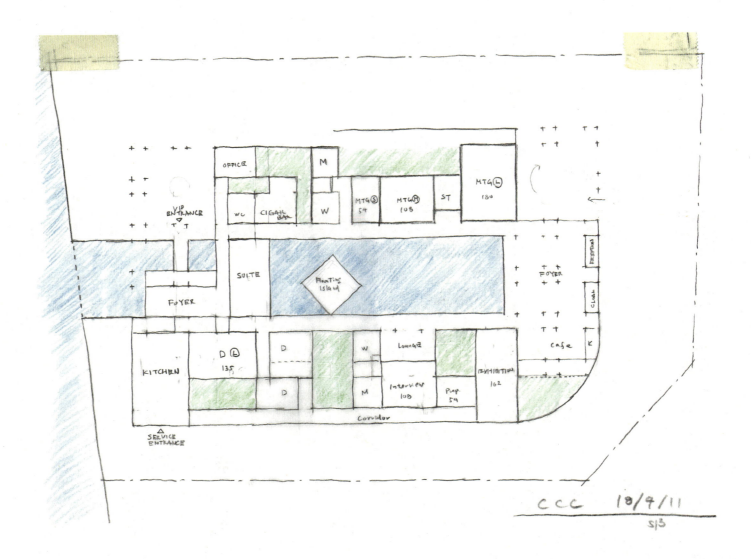

Japan Pavilion Hannover EXPO 2000
ハノーバー国際博覧会 2000　日本館

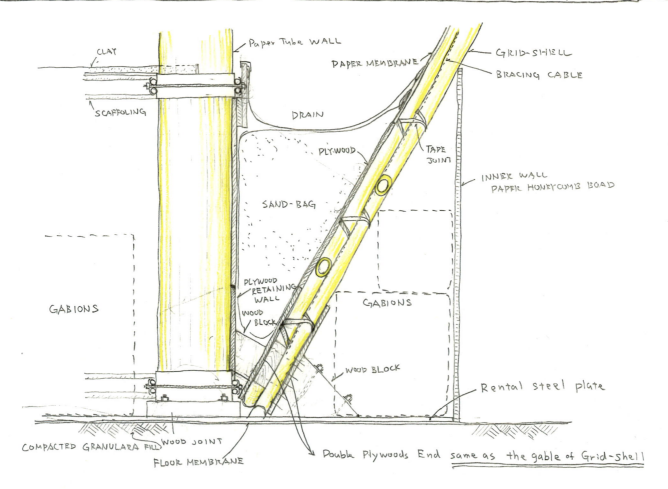

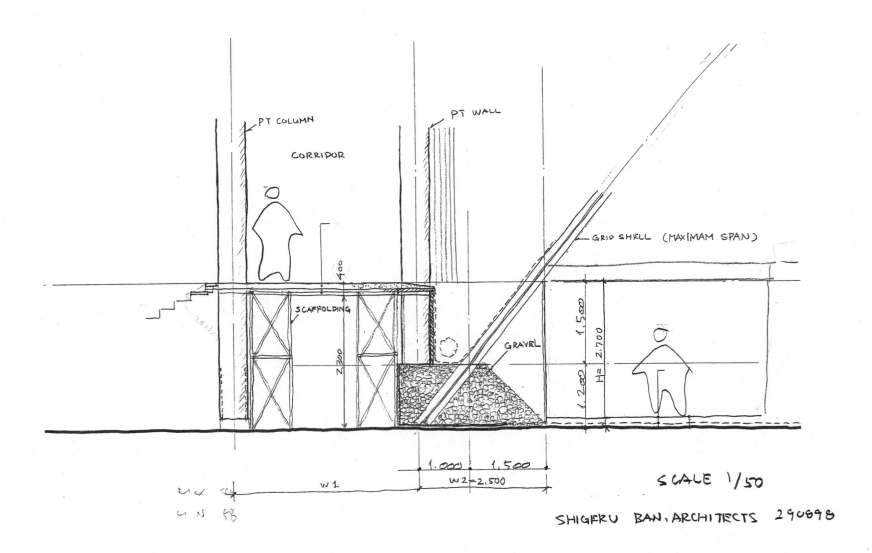

Japan Pavilion Hannover EXPO 2000
ハノーバー国際博覧会 2000　日本館

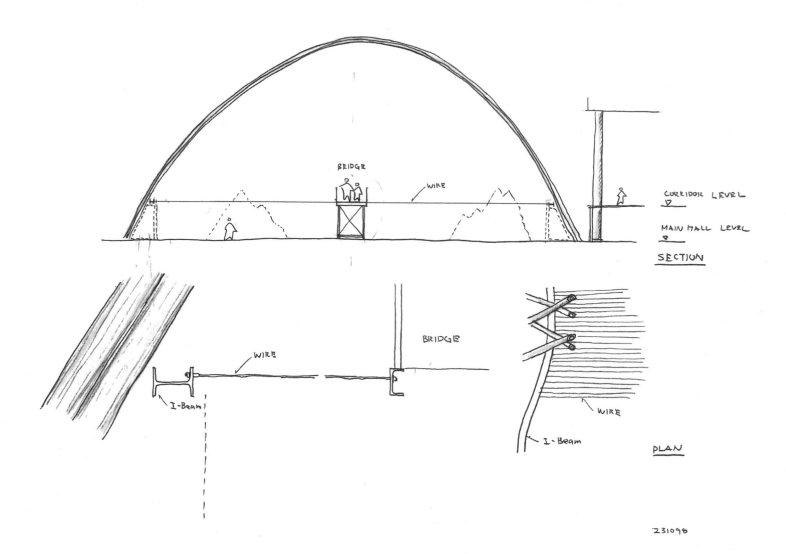

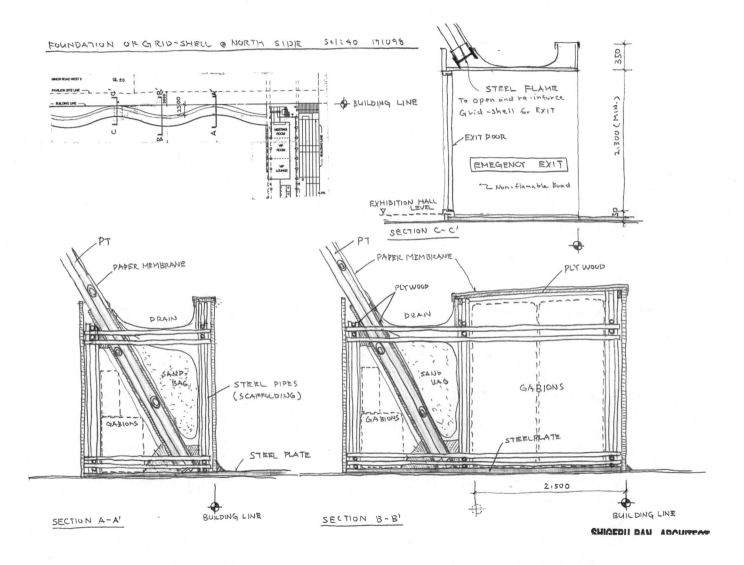

Japan Pavilion Hannover EXPO 2000
ハノーバー国際博覧会 2000　日本館

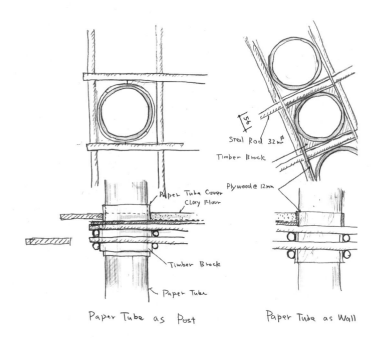

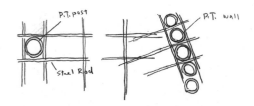

Details 1

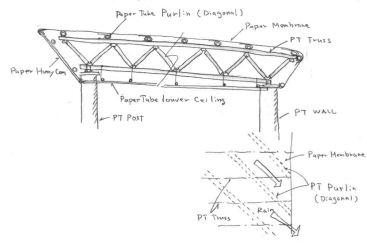

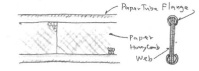

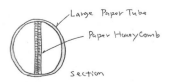

Details 2

WOOD PILE for FOUNDATION OF GRID SHELL   201098

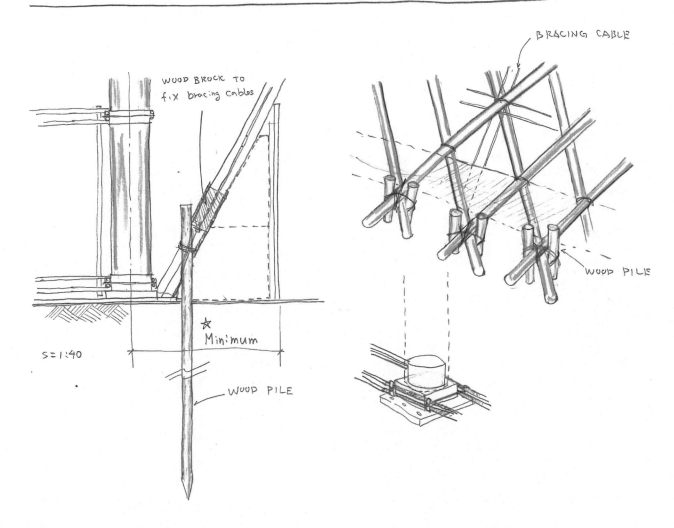

Paper Log House - Kobe
紙のログハウス - 神戸

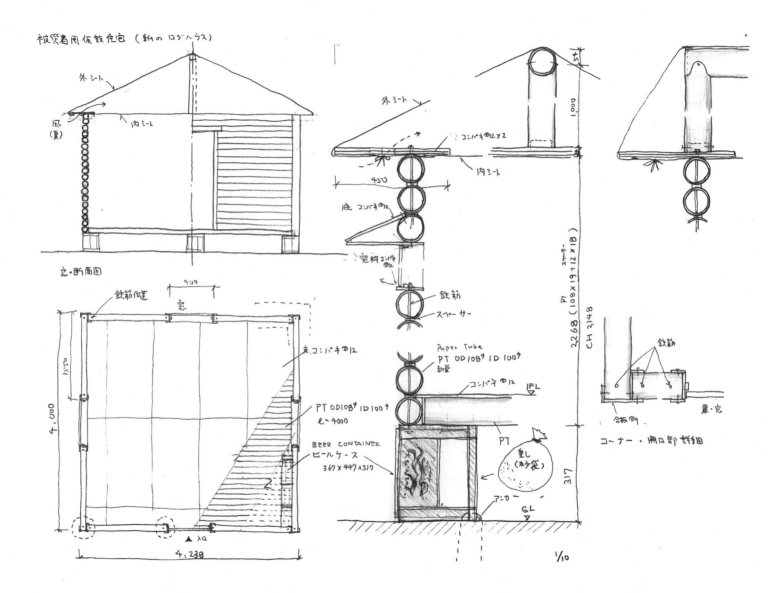

作業手順 1/3

① ビールケースの配置

ビールケースの位置は床パネルで調整するのでラフでよい。

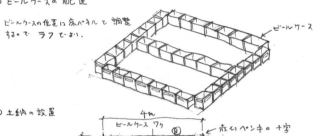

② 土納の設置

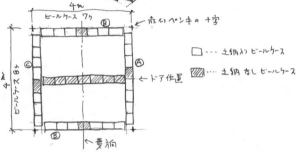

③ 床パネルの設置及びジョイント

ジョイント用木材で内側を固定し上をベニアで床面をふたをする。

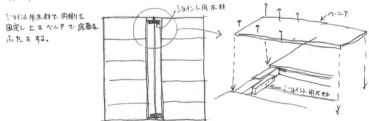

④ 床パネルとビールケースをインシュロックで結ぶ

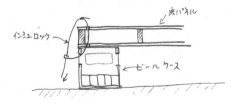

⑤ 壁面パネルの建込 2/3

Ⓐ→Ⓑ→Ⓒ→Ⓓ の順

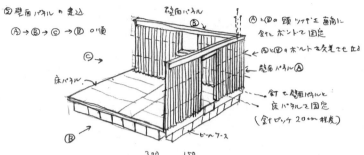

⑥ 笠木の取付

⑦ 笠木軒下にLアングルをビスで取付
(ビスのピッチ 30cm程度)

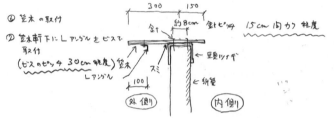

⑧ 屋根用 大梁の組立 (地上で) 及 笠木の上に仮止めする

⑨ 傾材の取付

棟木の次に両脇 ②③
最後に釘で固定

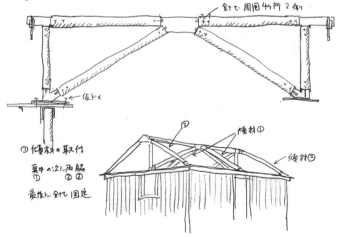

39

Paper Church
紙の教会

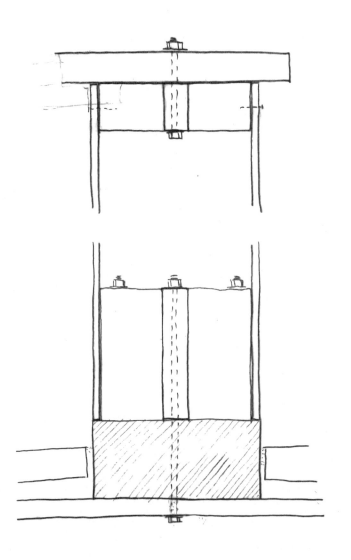
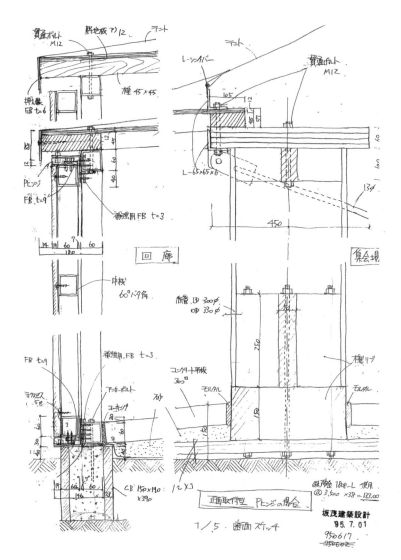

2/5 House
2/5 ハウス

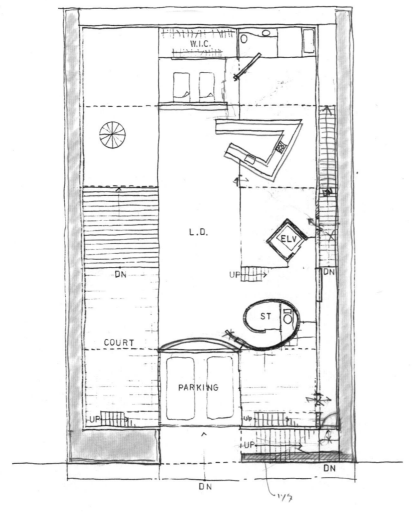

1 F

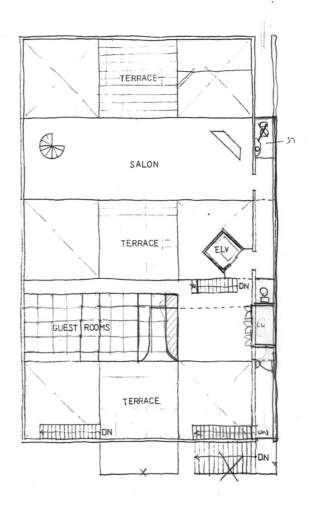

2 F

Tazawako Station
JR 田沢湖駅／田沢湖観光情報センター

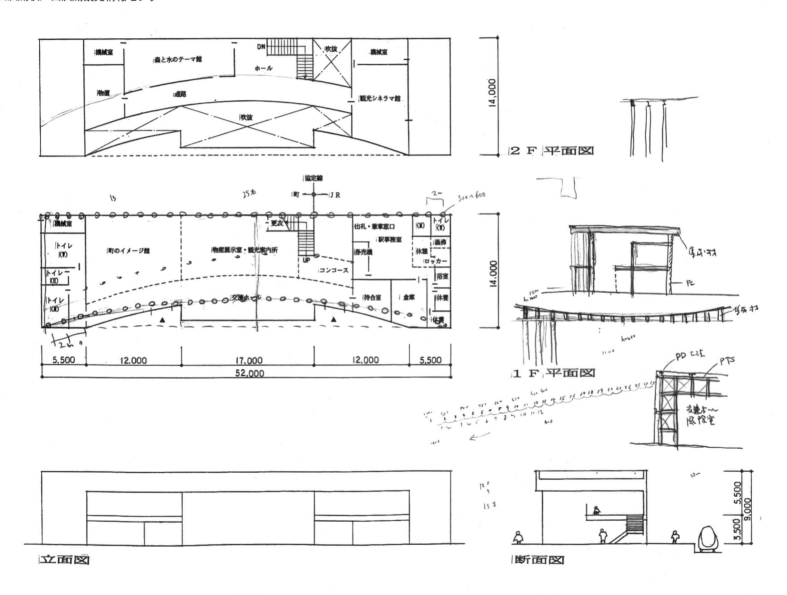

Hanegi Forest
羽根木の森

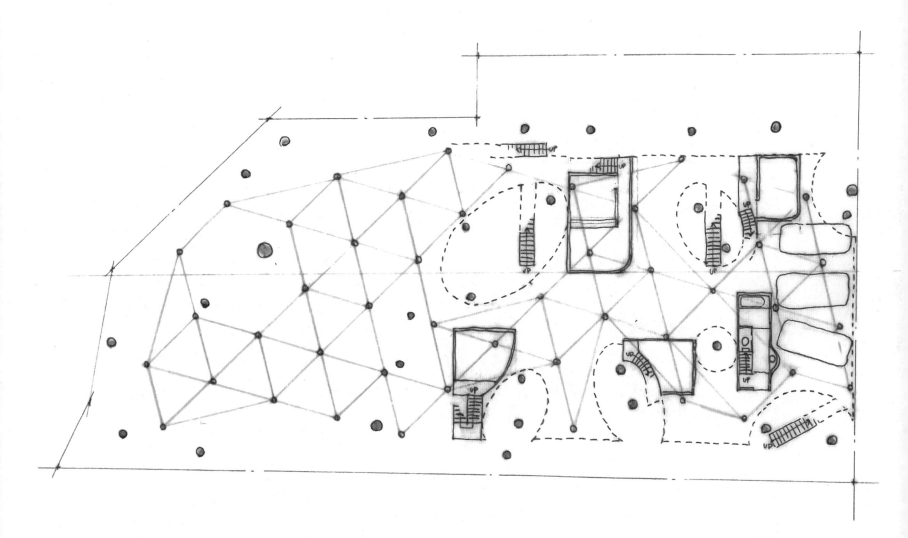

Hanegi Forest
羽根木の森

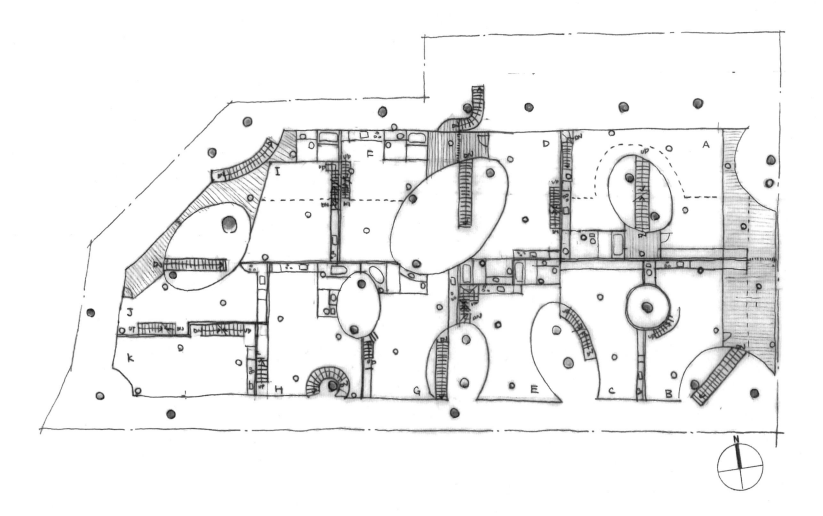

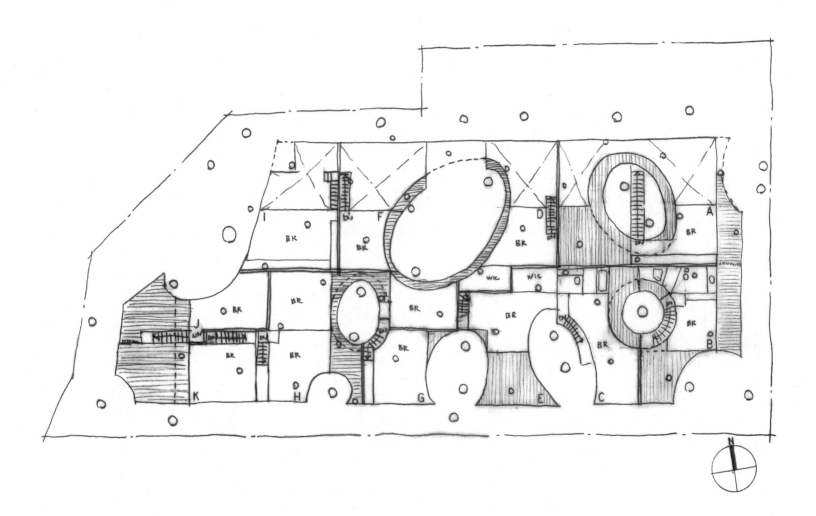

Paper Dome
紙のドーム

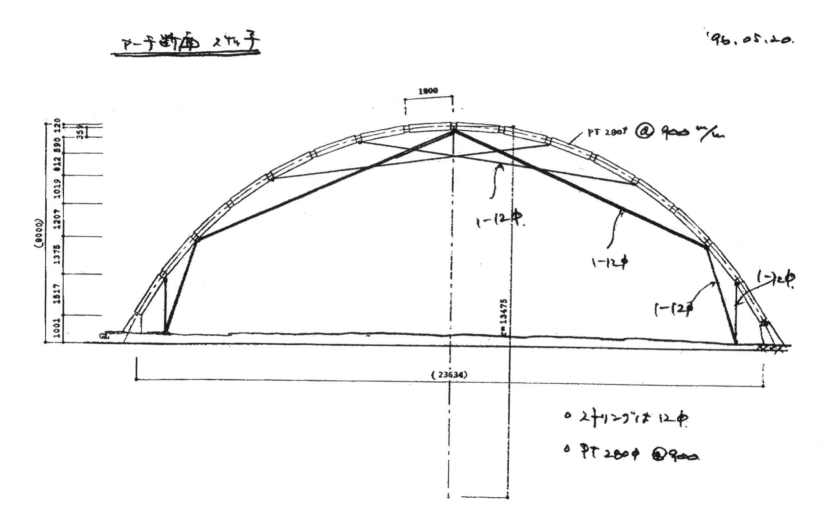

Ivy Structure 1
アイビー・ストラクチャー１

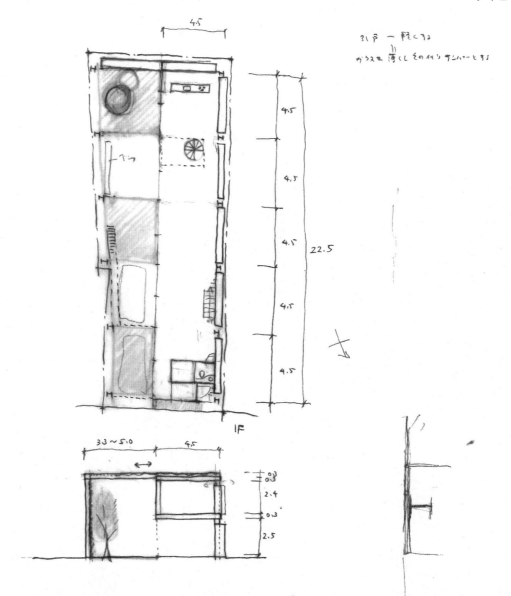

Paper Emergency Shelter for UNHCR
国民難民高等弁務官事務所用の紙のシェルター

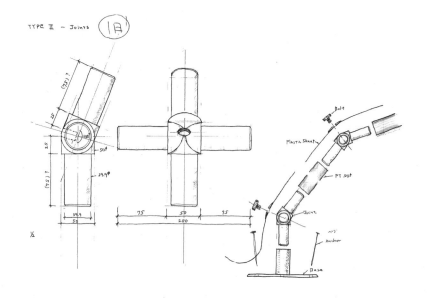

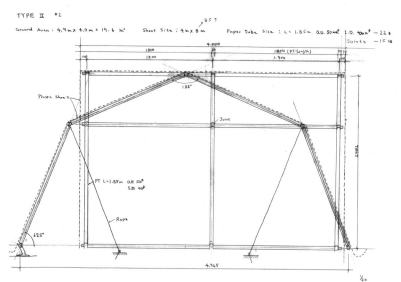

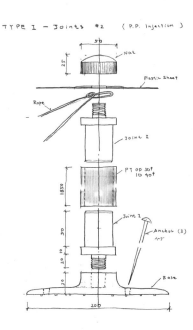

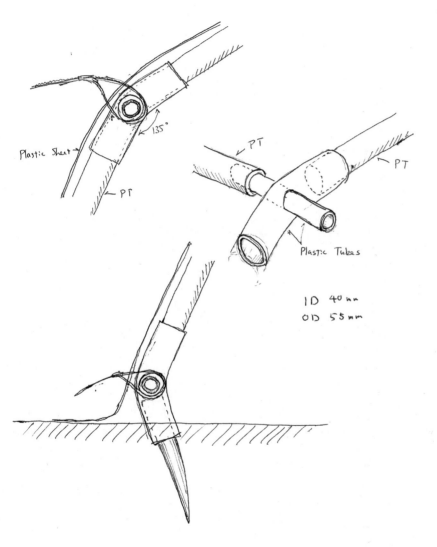

Paper Tube Refugee Shelter for UNHCR

Nemunoki Children's Art Museum
ねむの木こども美術館

ペーパーハニカム スペースフレーム (PHSF) ジョイント

030798
Ban

1、6角形とボルトを一体にできるか

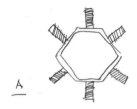

A

2、アルミとスチール、どちらがよいか？
3、板厚が違うもの (ex ベニア) に対応できるジョイント
・ハニカムを2枚で挟み、ボルトを使わず、スパイクと接着のみにできるか？ (ベニアの場合は木ルト使う。)

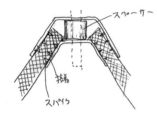

4、上記のジョイントを 小三角形ジョイントにも使う。

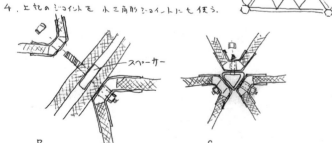

B C

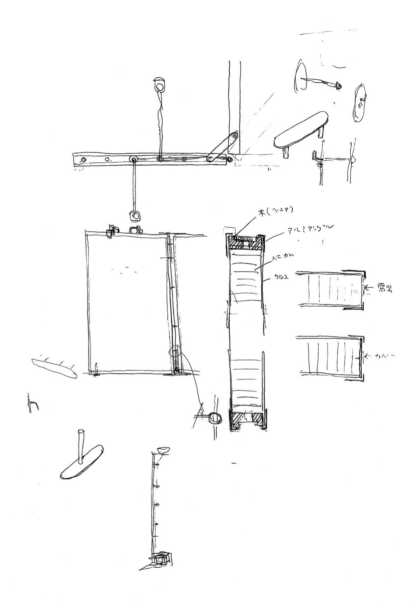

GC Osaka Building
GC 大阪営業所ビル

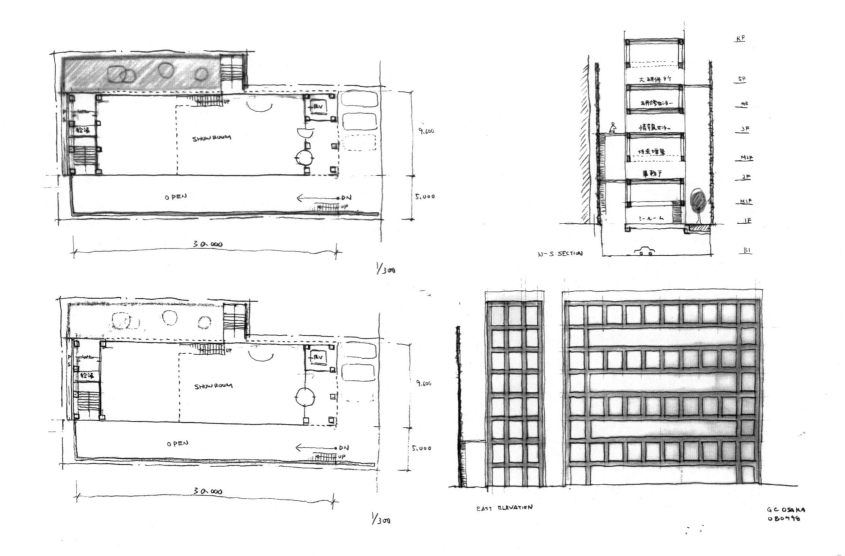

Imai Hospital Daycare Center
今井病院付属託児所

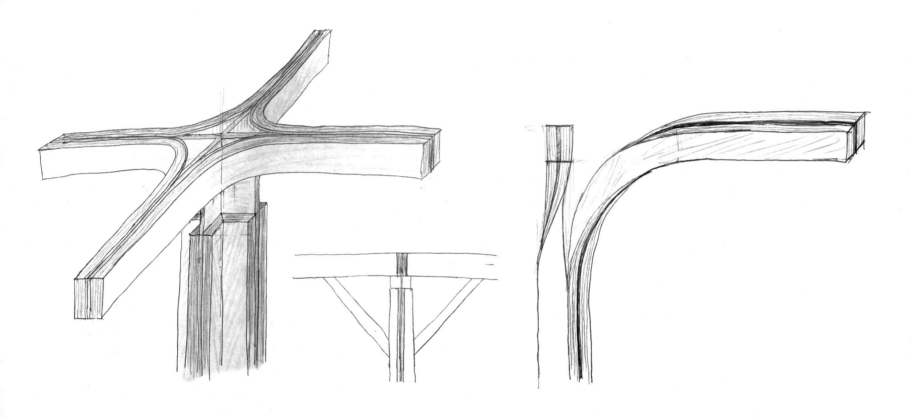

Shutter House for a Photographer
写真家のシャッター・ハウス

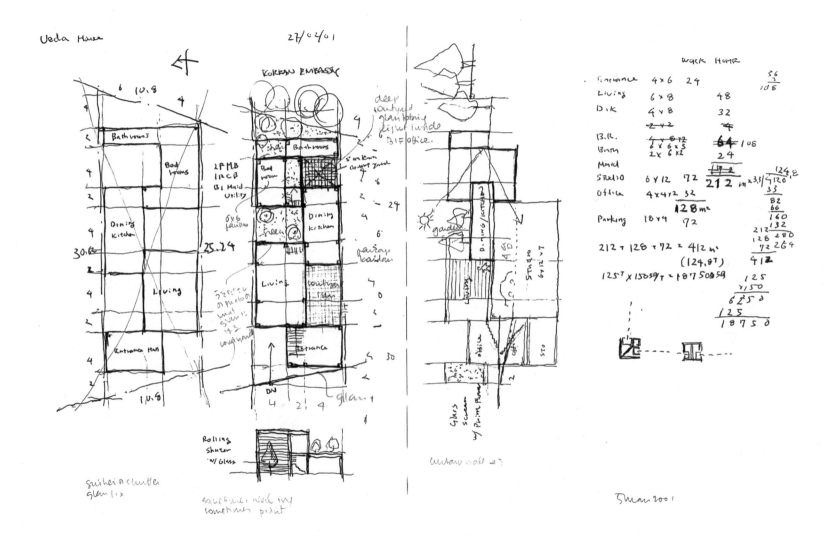

Picture Window House
ピクチャー・ウィンドウの家

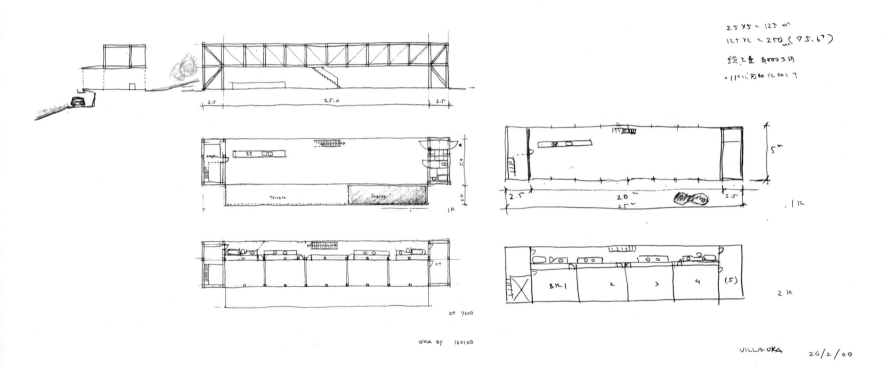

Bamboo Furniture House
竹の家具の家

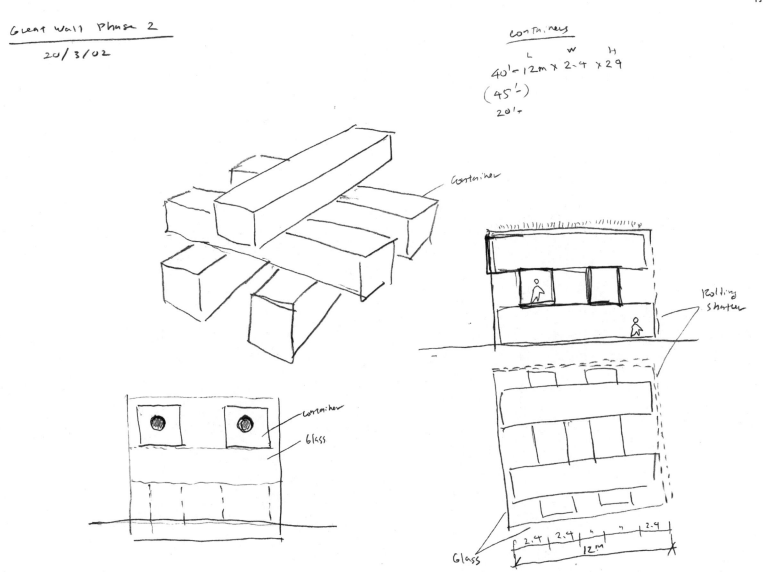

Sugar Muddler
砂糖のマドラー

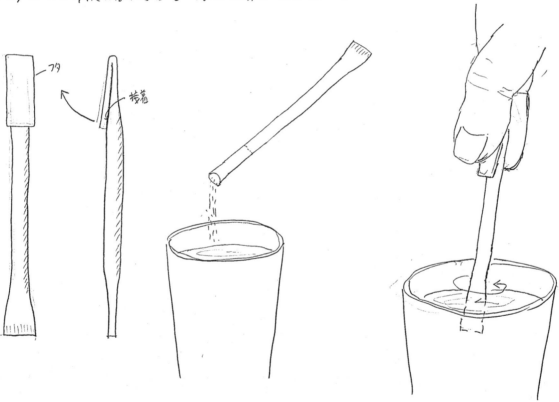

Atsushi Imai Memorial Gymnasium
今井篤記念体育館

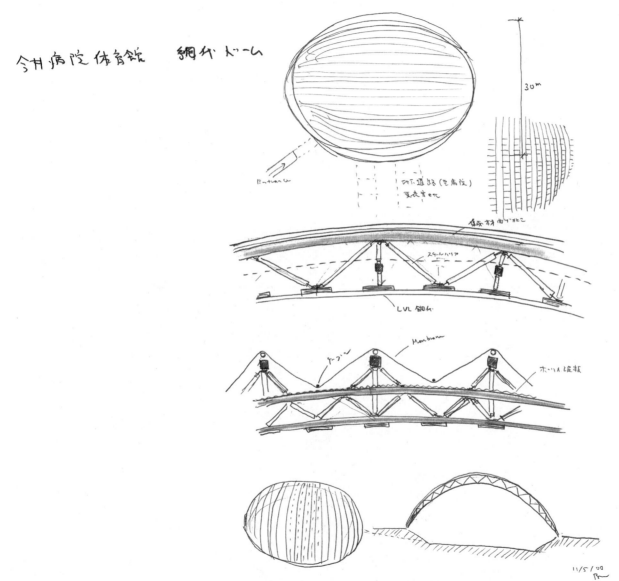

Takatori Catholic Church
膜の教会　カトリックたかとり教会

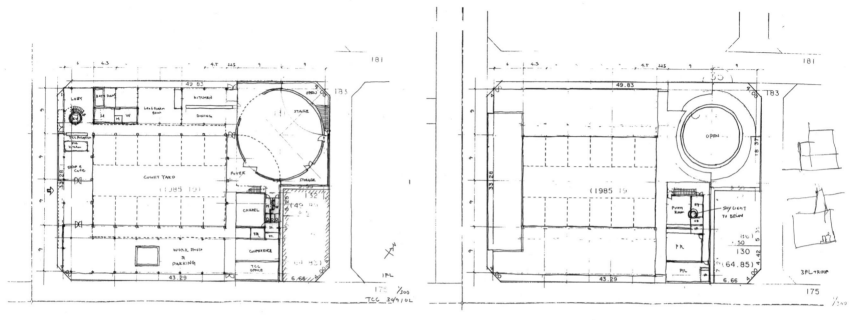

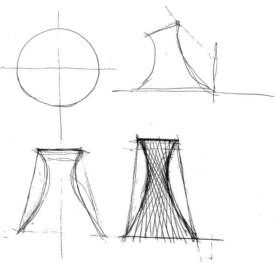

Nicolas G. Hayek Center
ニコラス・G・ハイエック・センター

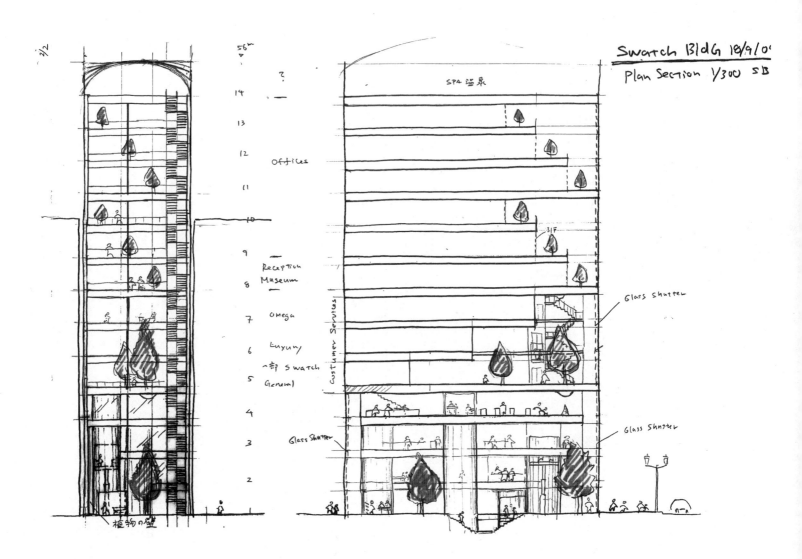

Nicolas G. Hayek Center
ニコラス・G・ハイエック・センター

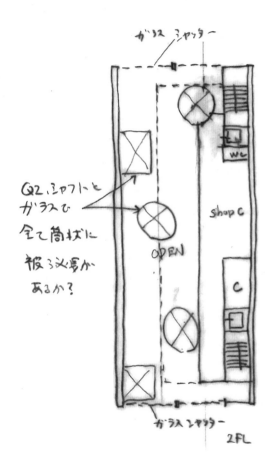
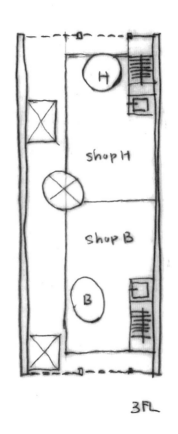
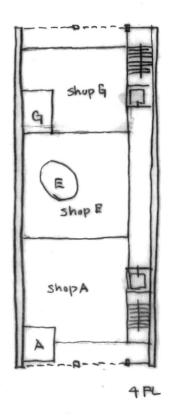

Dormitory H
社員寮 H

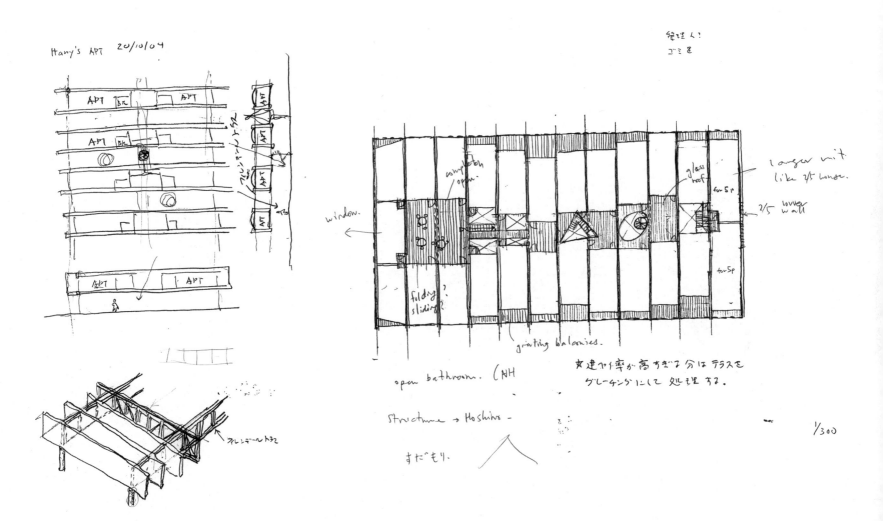

Kirinda House – Tsunami Reconstruction Project
津波後のキリンダ村復興プロジェクト

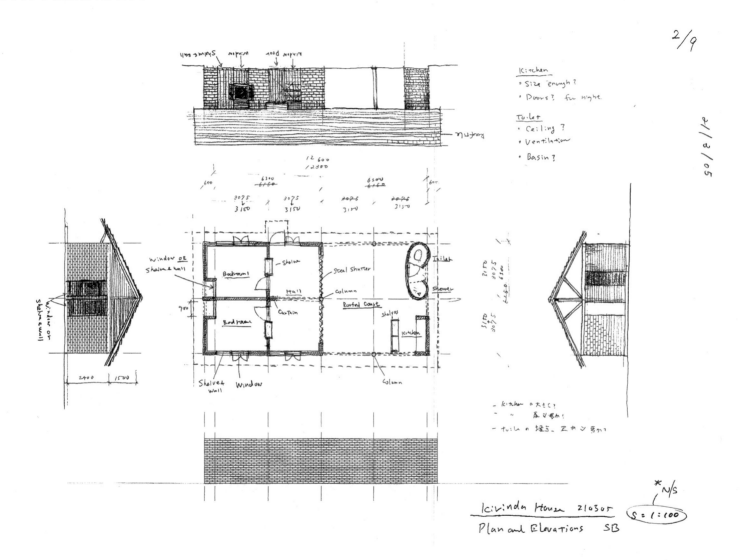

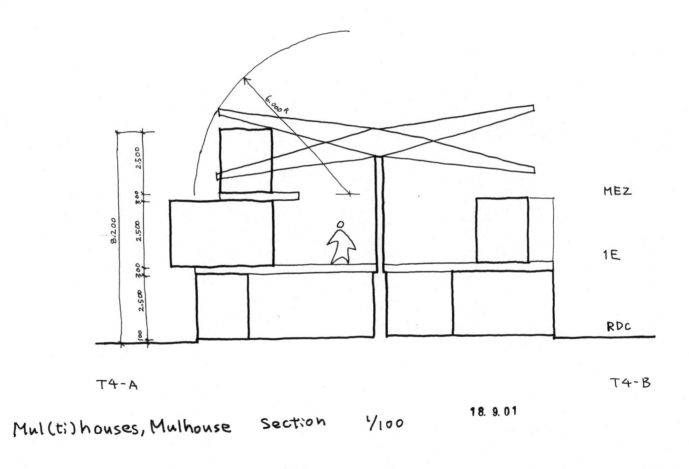

Mul(ti)houses
マルチ・ハウス

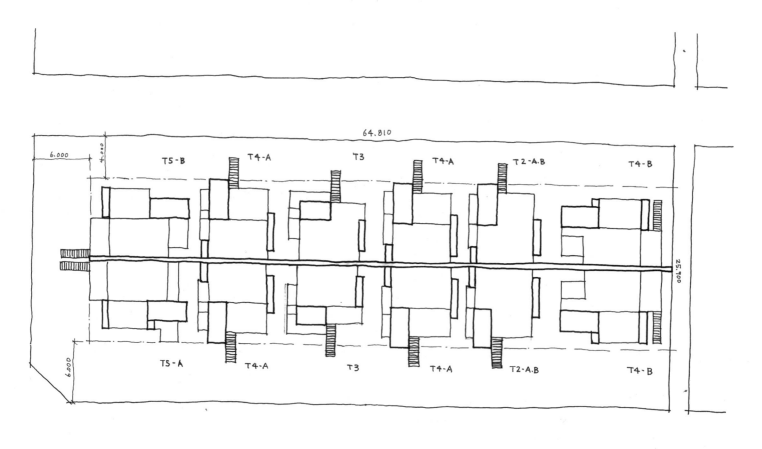

Mul(ti)houses, Mulhouse   Site Plan   1/200

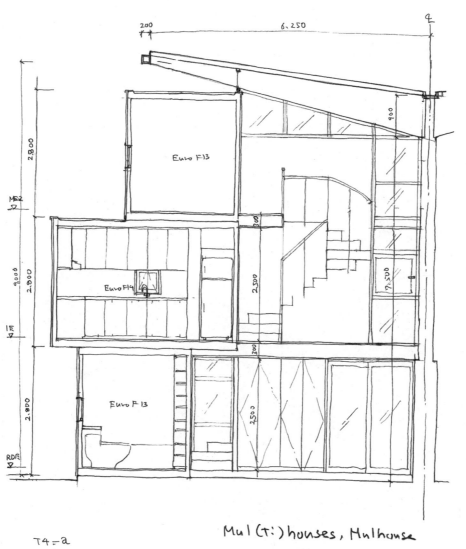

T4-2 Mul(t:)houses, Mulhouse
SECTION 1/50

Nomadic Museum New York
ノマディック美術館　ニューヨーク

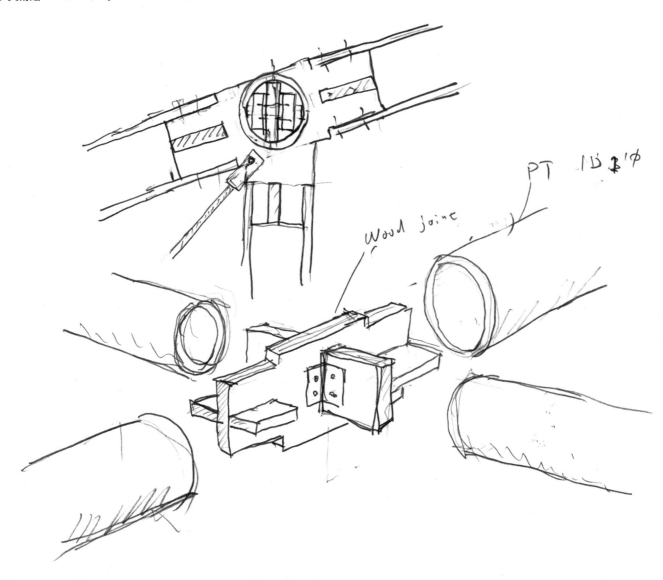

JM — Paper Tube Truss Joints
10803 58

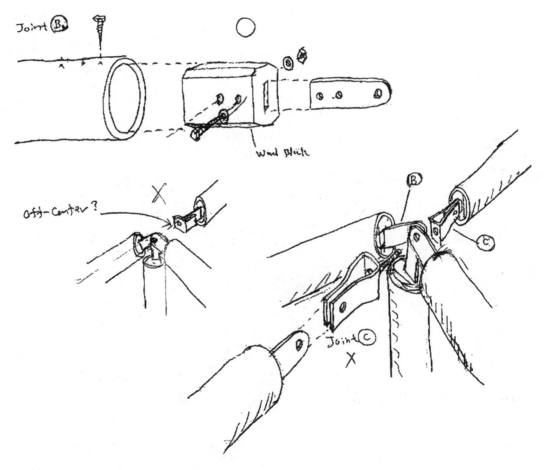

Joint B

Wood Block

Off-Center?

Joint C

②

Nomadic Museum New York
ノマディック美術館　ニューヨーク

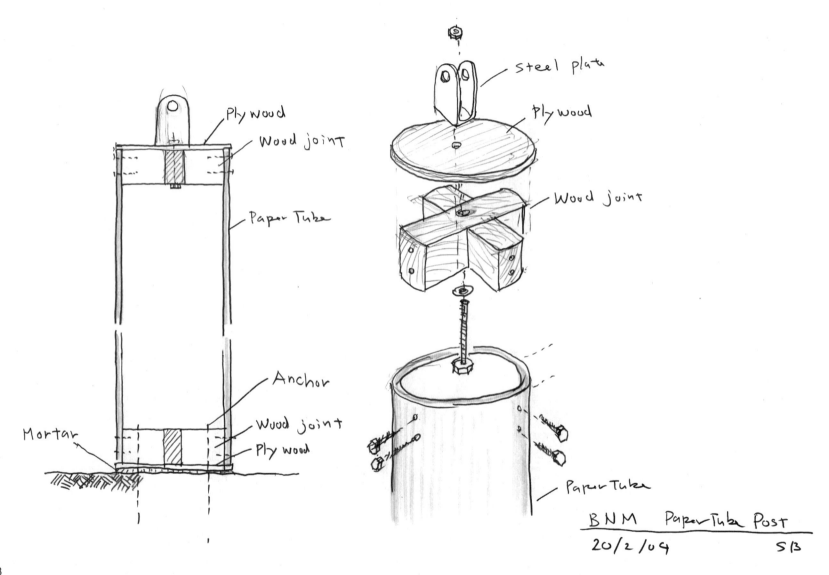

68

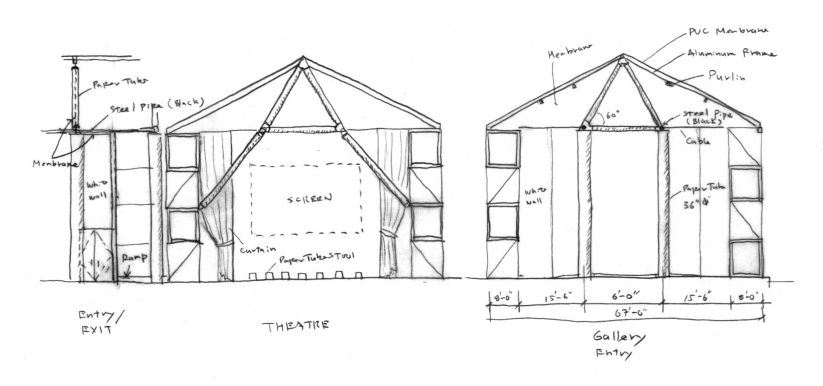

Nomadic Museum New York
ノマディック美術館　ニューヨーク

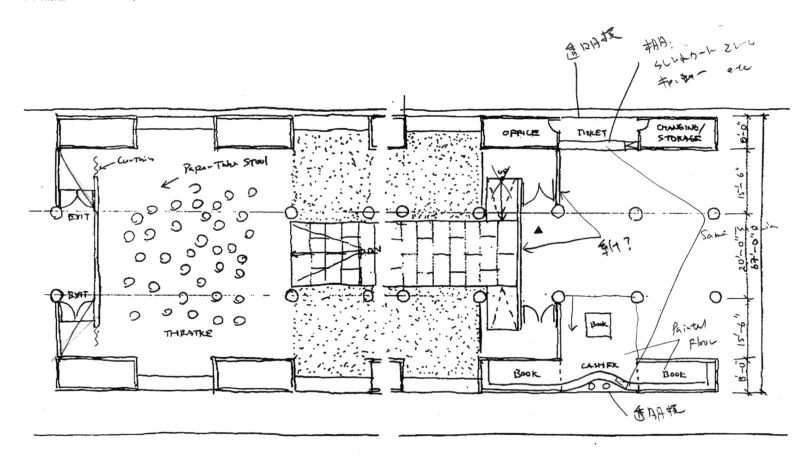

Atelier for a Glass Artist
ガラス作家のアトリエ

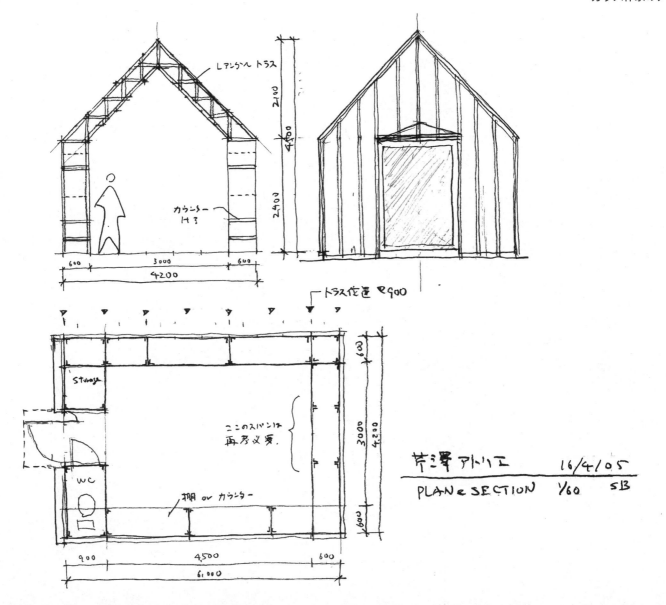

Atelier for a Glass Artist
ガラス作家のアトリエ

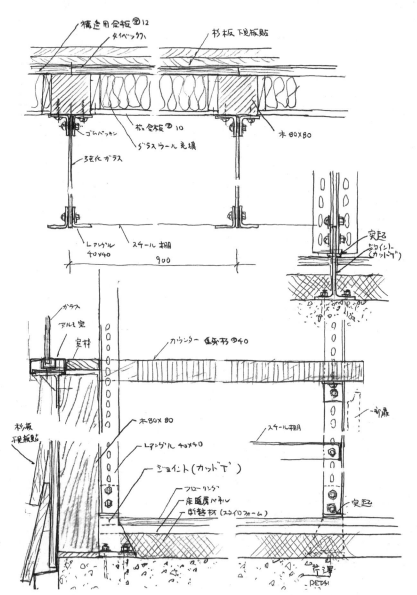

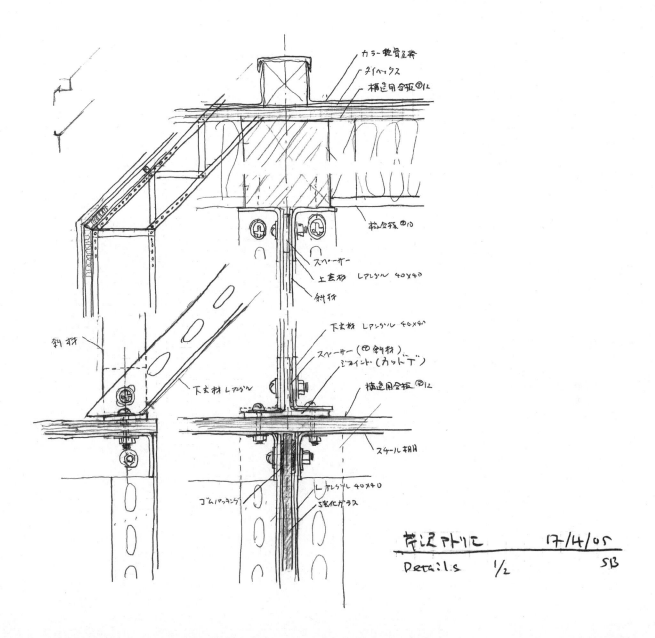

Seikei Library
成蹊大学情報図書館

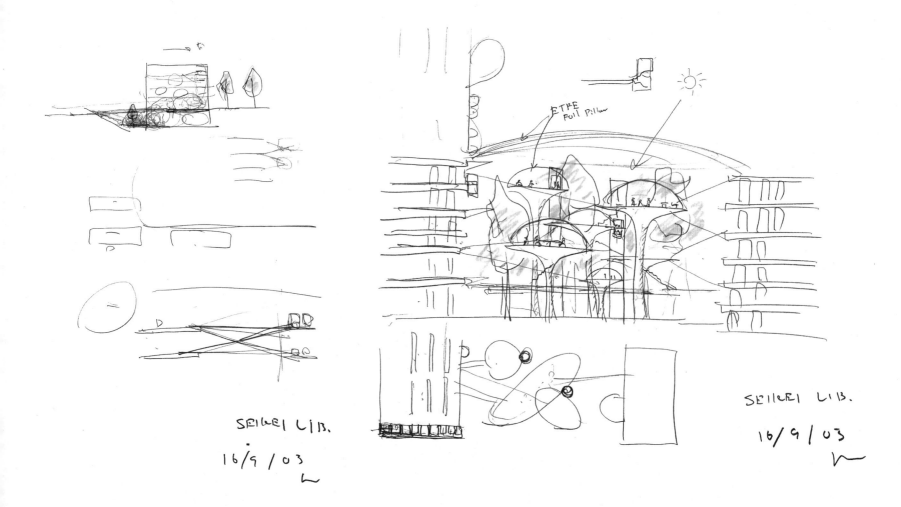

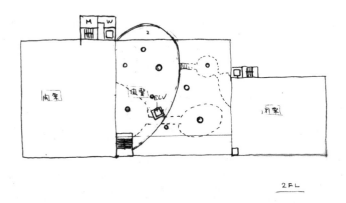

2FL

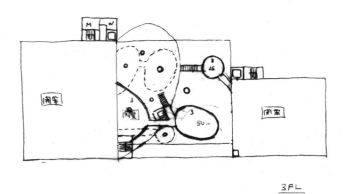

3FL

SEIKEI LIB PLANS
12/10/03   1/500 S.B.

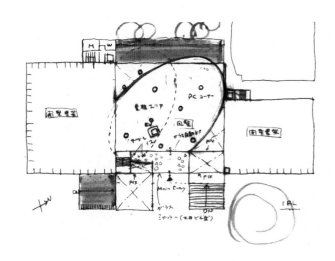

1FL

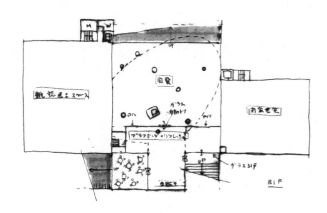

B1F

SEIKEI LIB. PLANS
12/10/03   1/500 S.B.

Haesley Nine Bridges Golf Clubhouse
ヘスリー・ナインブリッジズ・ゴルフ・クラブハウス

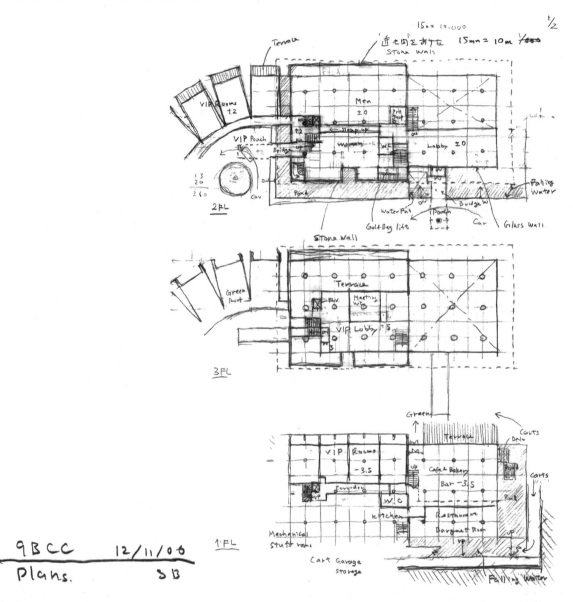

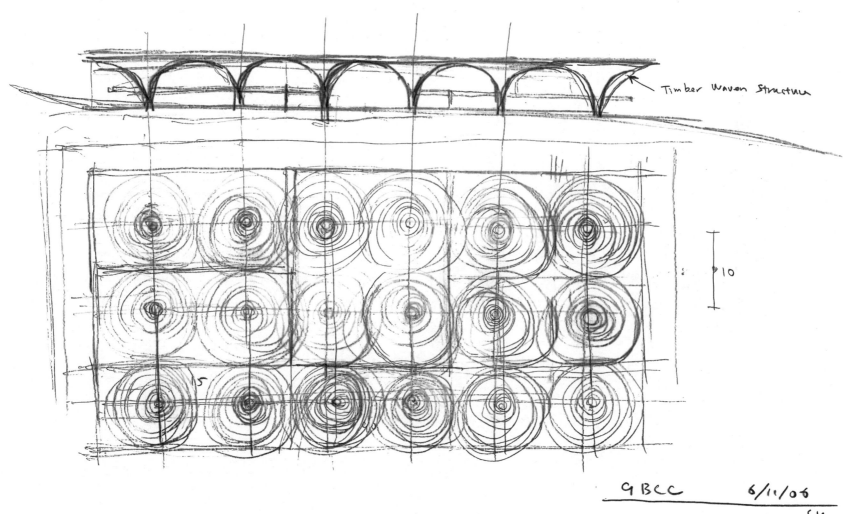

Haesley Nine Bridges Golf Clubhouse
ヘスリー・ナインブリッジズ・ゴルフ・クラブハウス

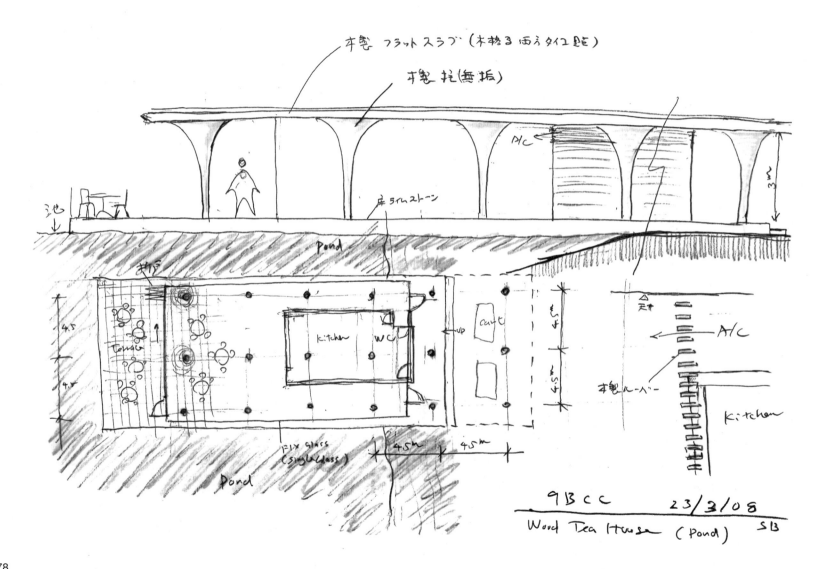

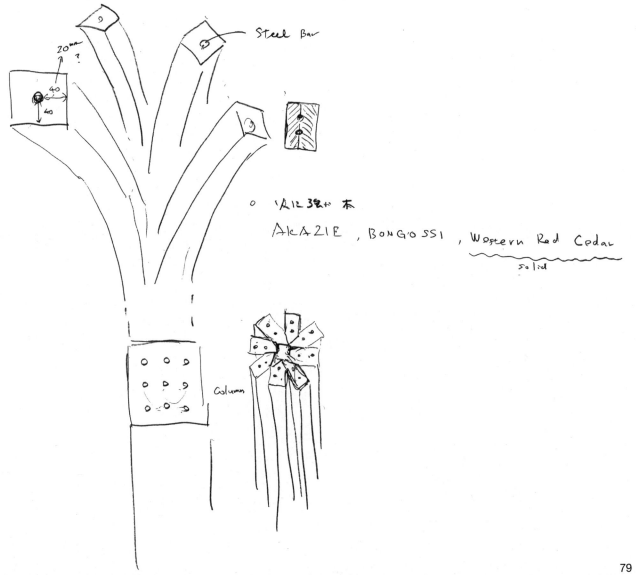

Haesley Nine Bridges Golf Clubhouse
ヘスリー・ナインブリッジズ・ゴルフ・クラブハウス

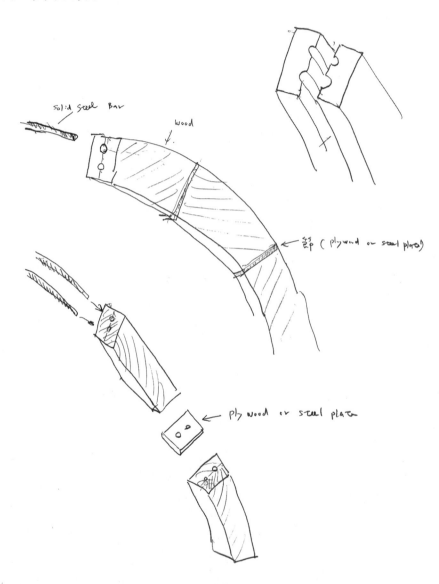

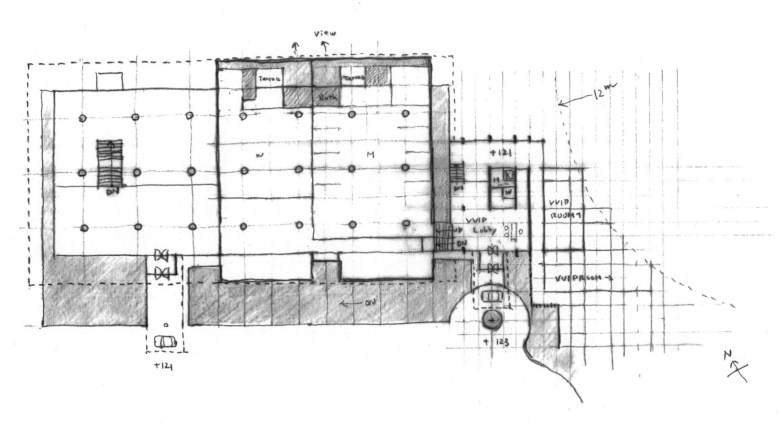

Haesley Nine Bridges Golf Clubhouse
ヘスリー・ナインブリッジズ・ゴルフ・クラブハウス

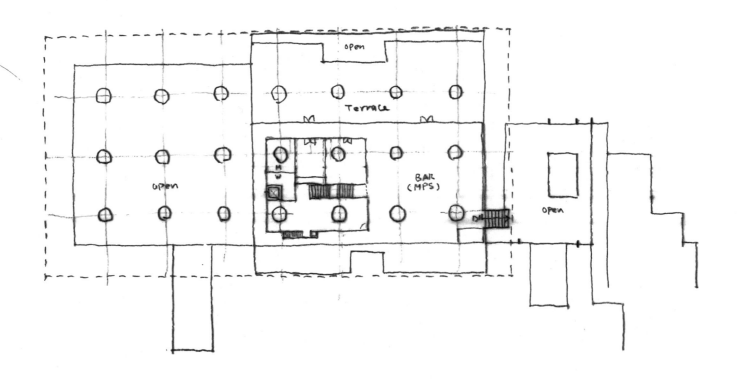

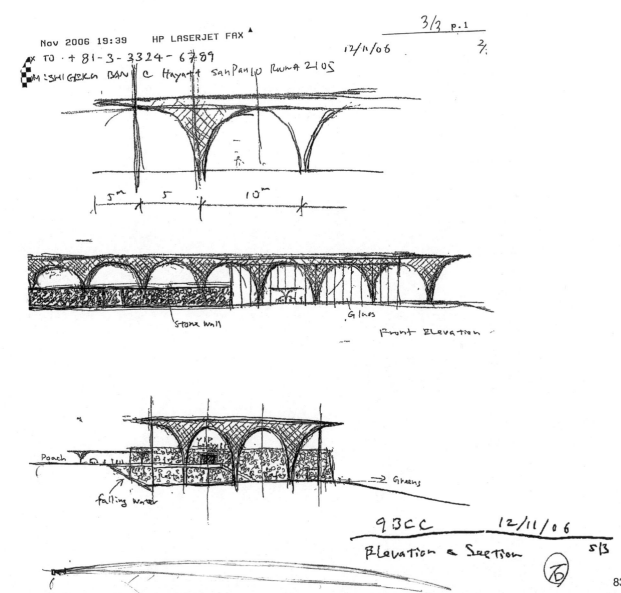

Paper Bridge, Remoulin
紙の橋

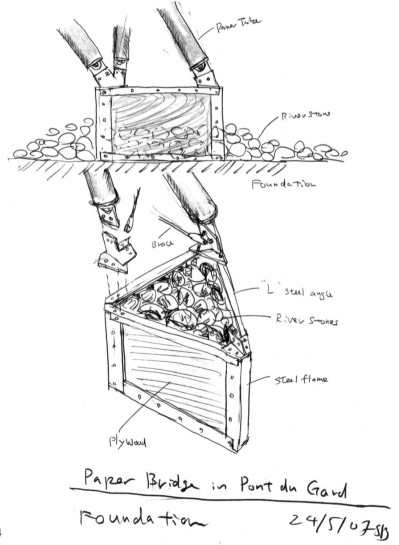
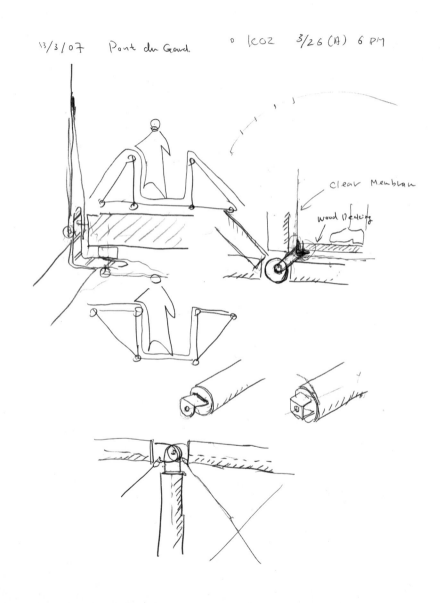

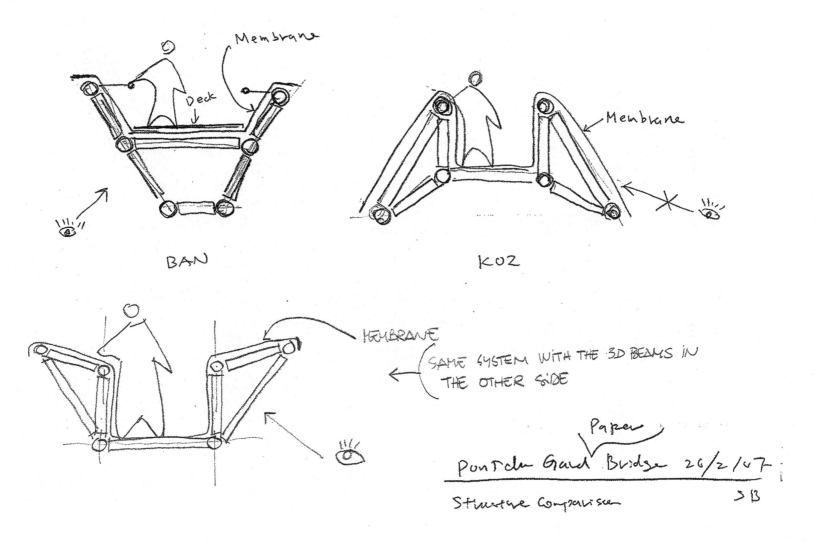

Sheikh Zayed National Museum
シェイク・ザイード国立博物館

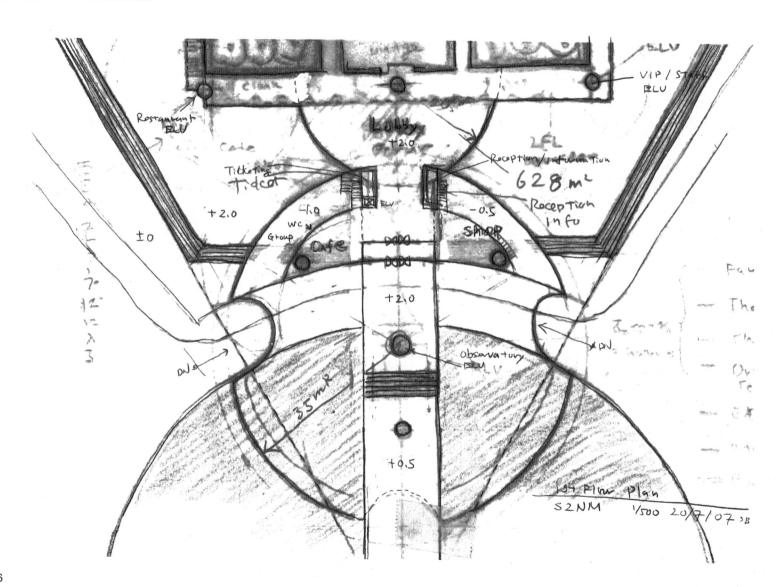

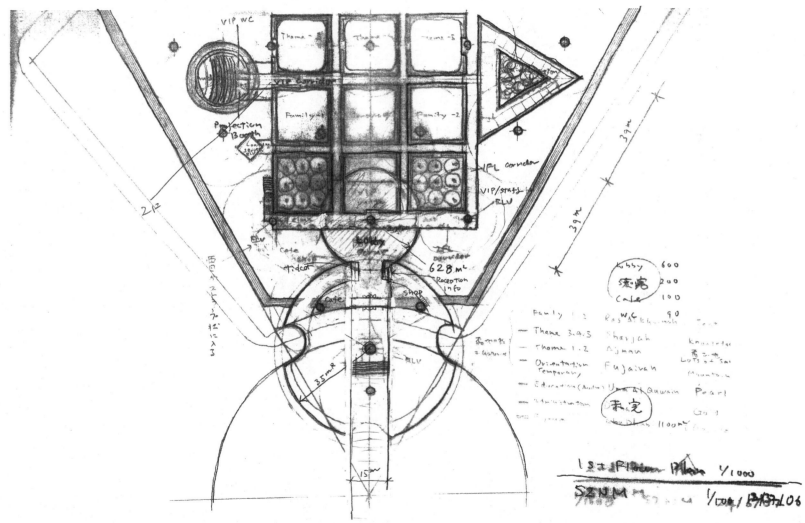

Sheikh Zayed National Museum
シェイク・ザイード国立博物館

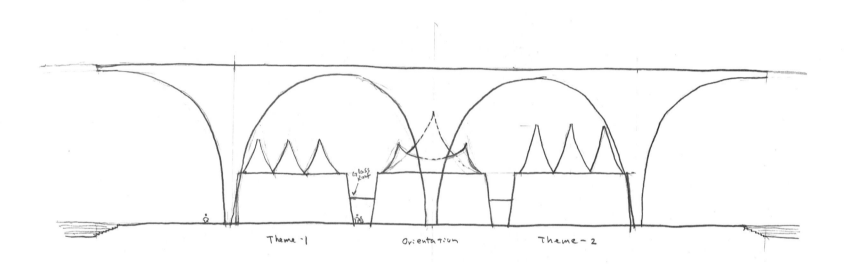

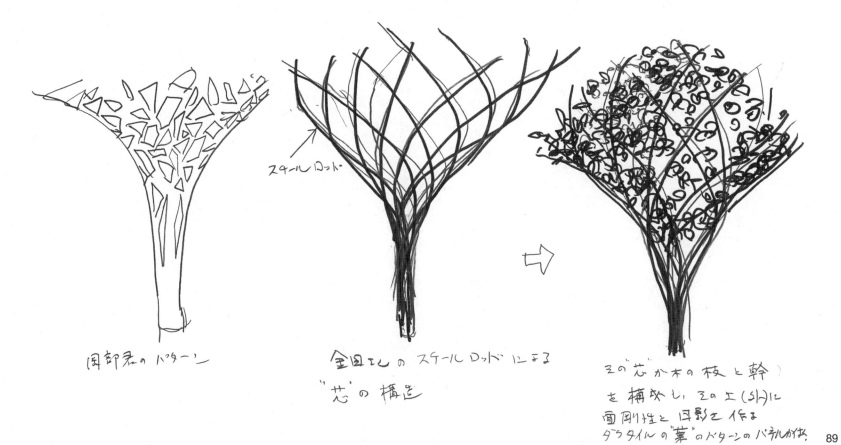

Sheikh Zayed National Museum
シェイク・ザイード国立博物館

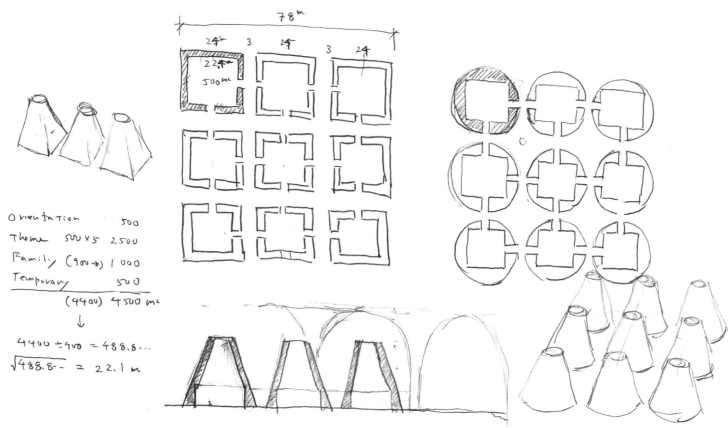

Galleries

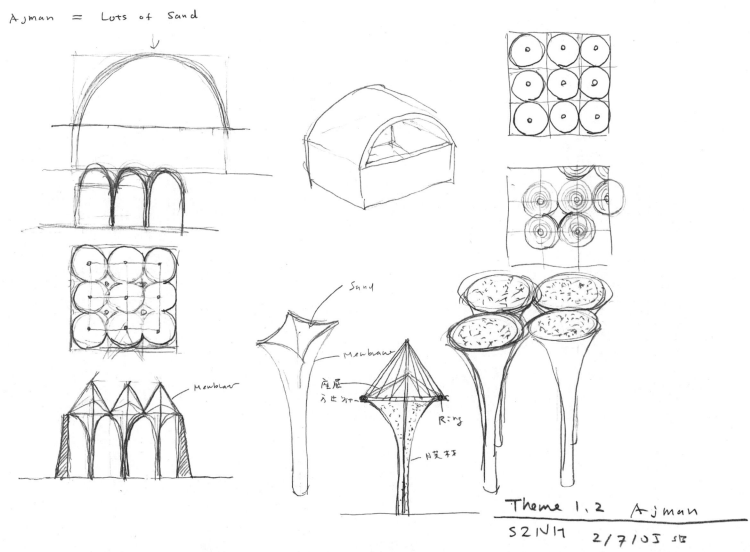

Sheikh Zayed National Museum
シェイク・ザイード国立博物館

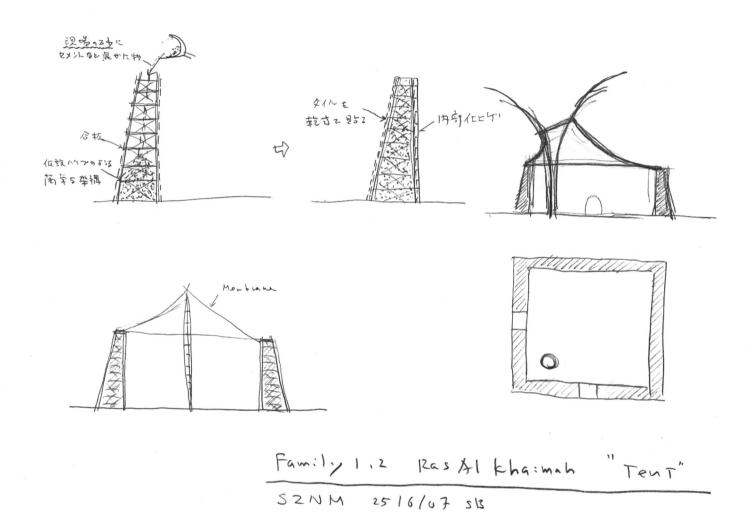

Family 1.2   Ras Al Khaimah   "Tent"
SZNM   25/6/07 sb

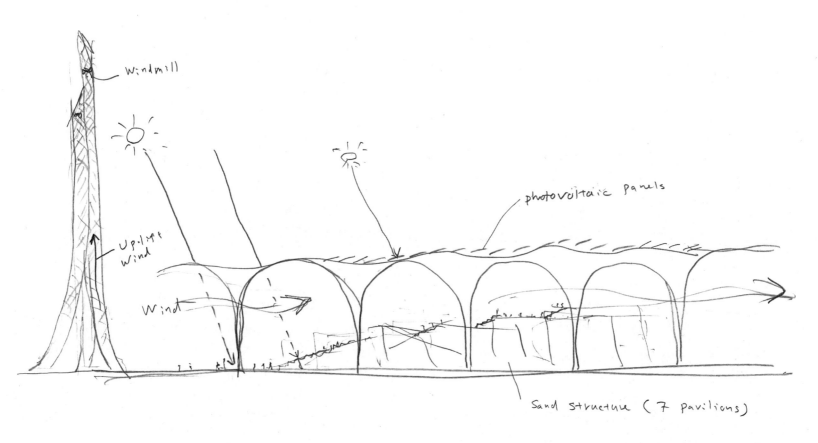
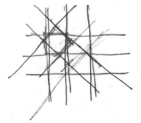

Sheikh Zayed National Museum
シェイク・ザイード国立博物館

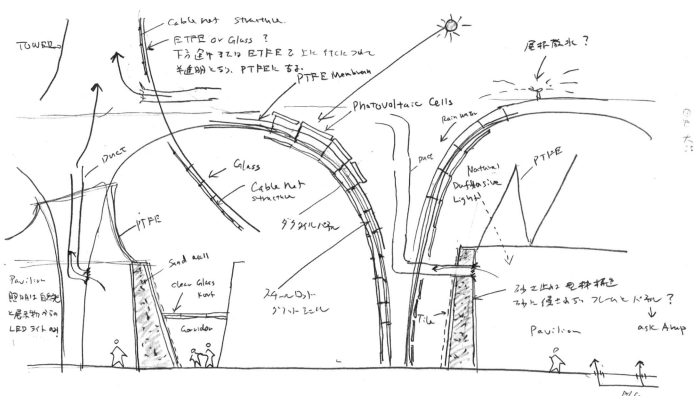

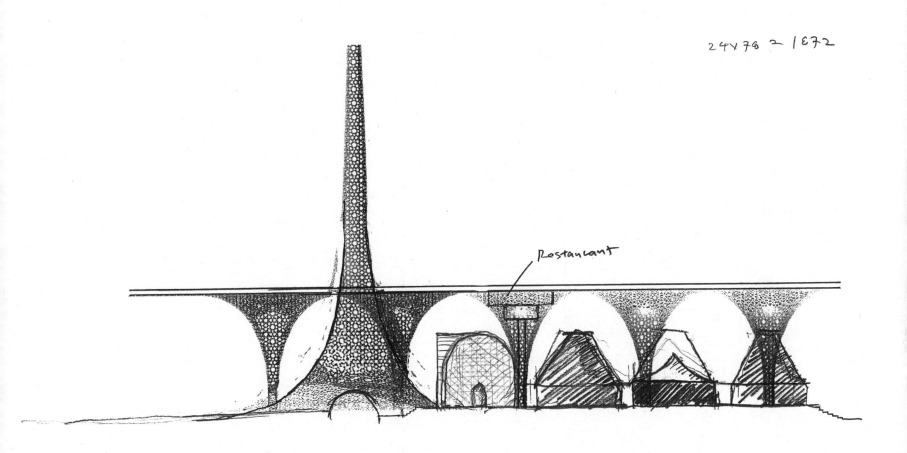

Aspen Art Museum
アスペン美術館

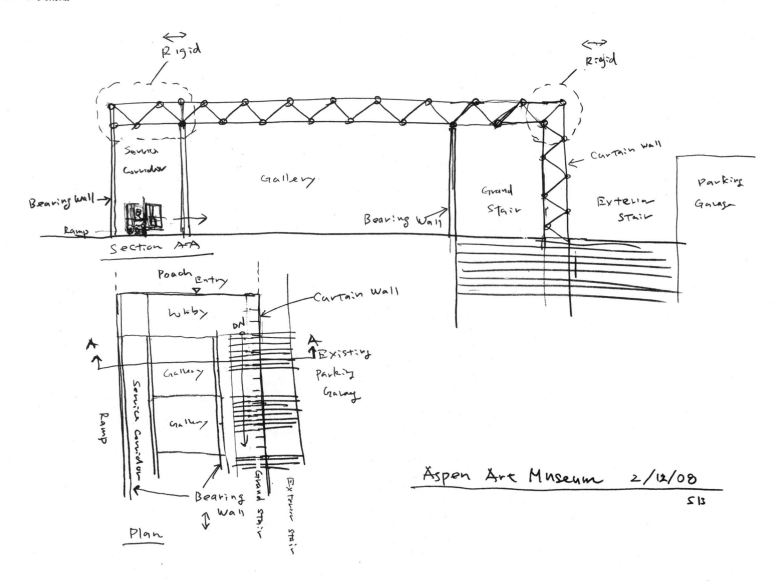

Aspen Art Museum
アスペン美術館

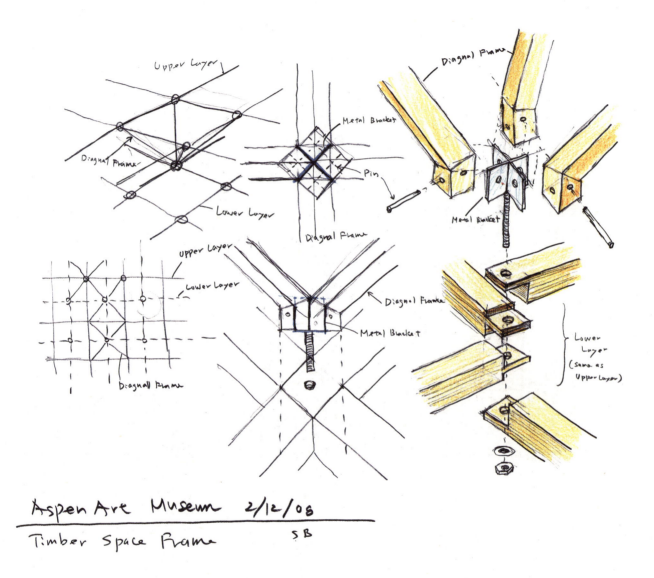

98

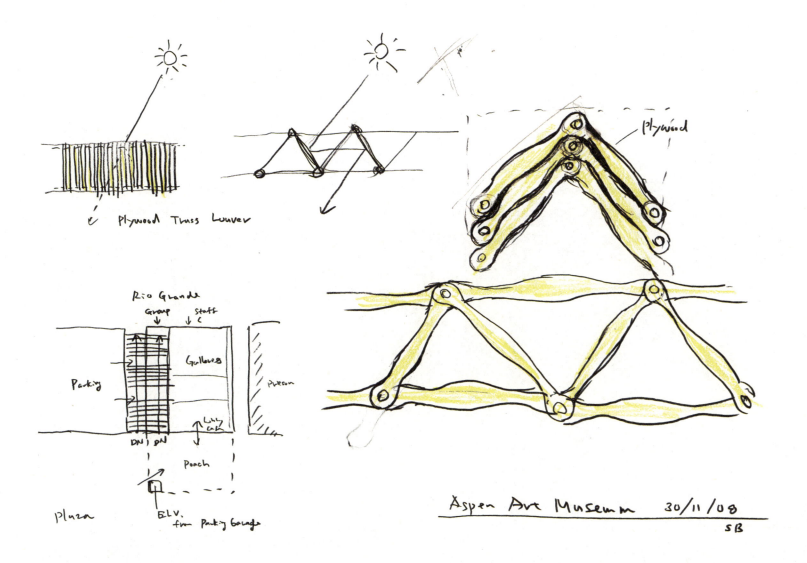

Aspen Art Museum
アスペン美術館

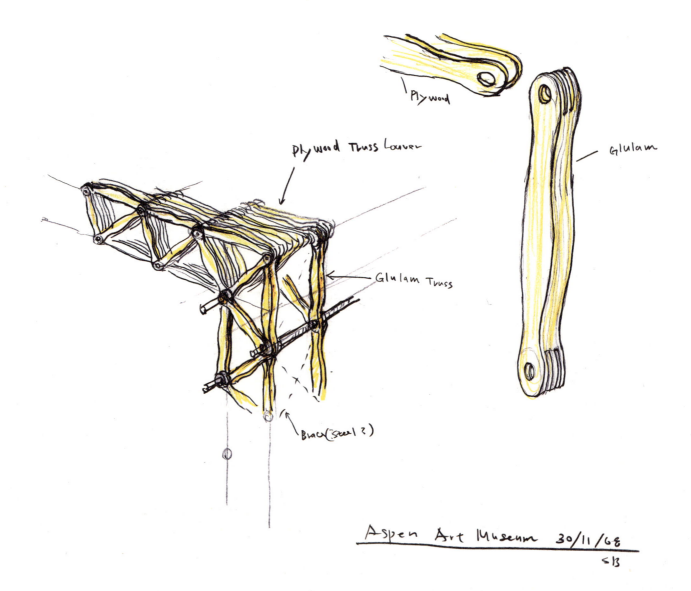

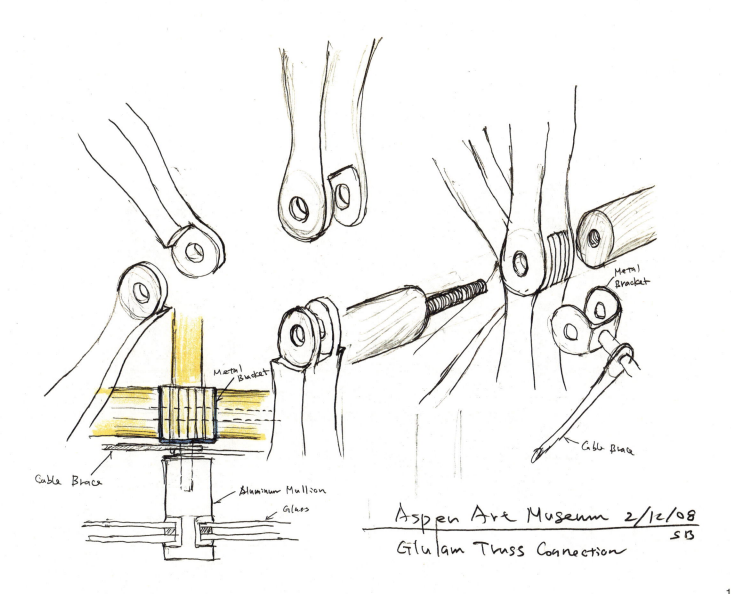

Aspen Art Museum
アスペン美術館

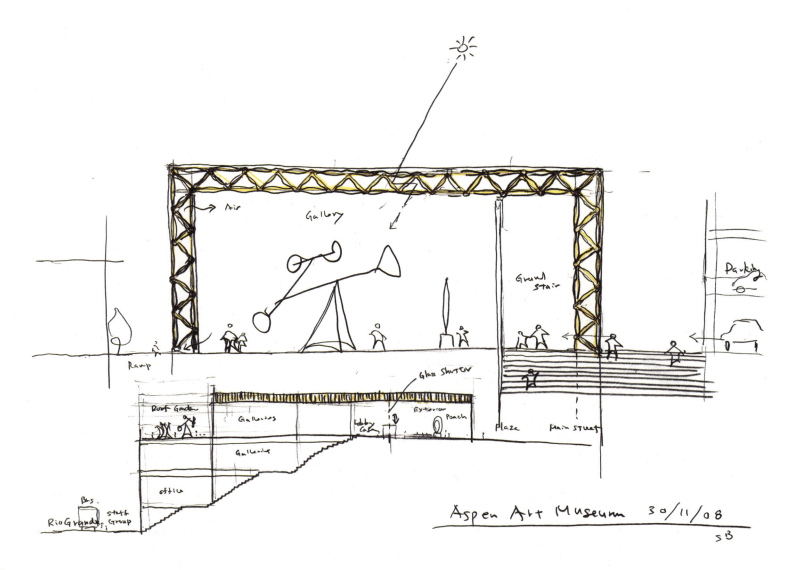

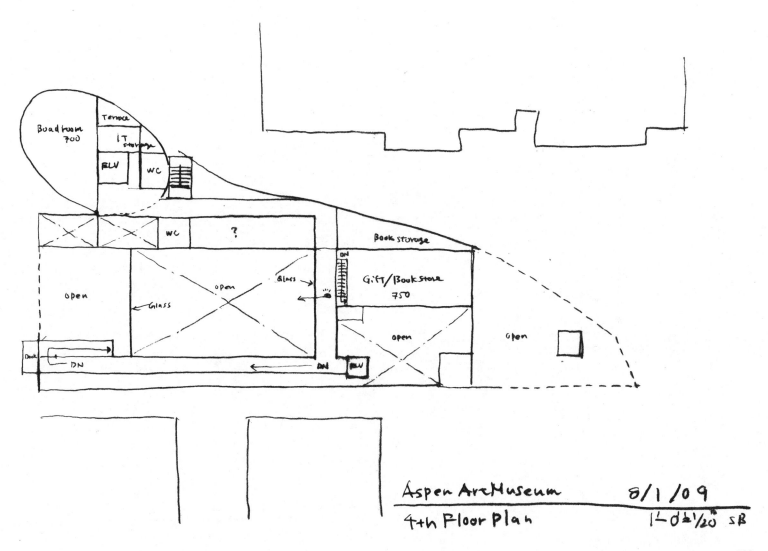

Aspen Art Museum
アスペン美術館

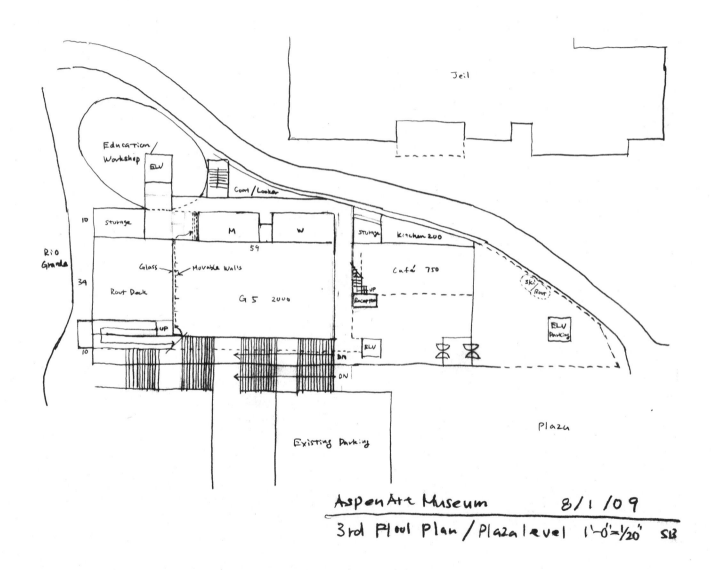

Tamedia New Office Building
タメディア新本社

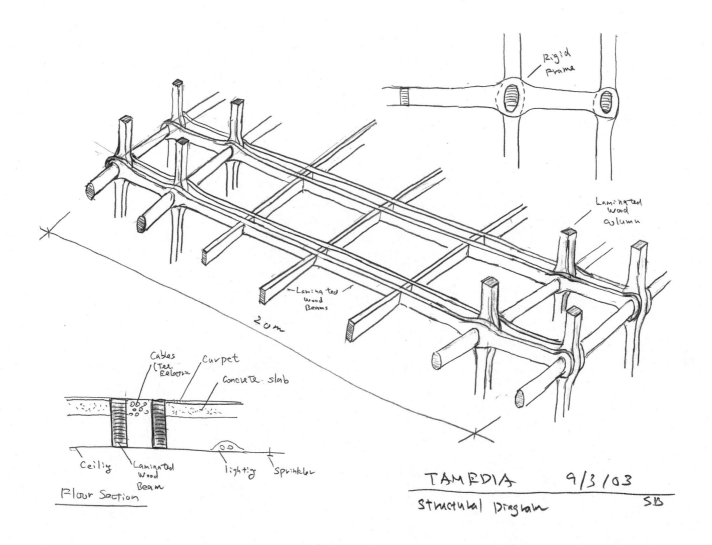

Paper Temporary School - Chengdu Hualin Elementary School
成都市華林小学校　紙管仮設校舎

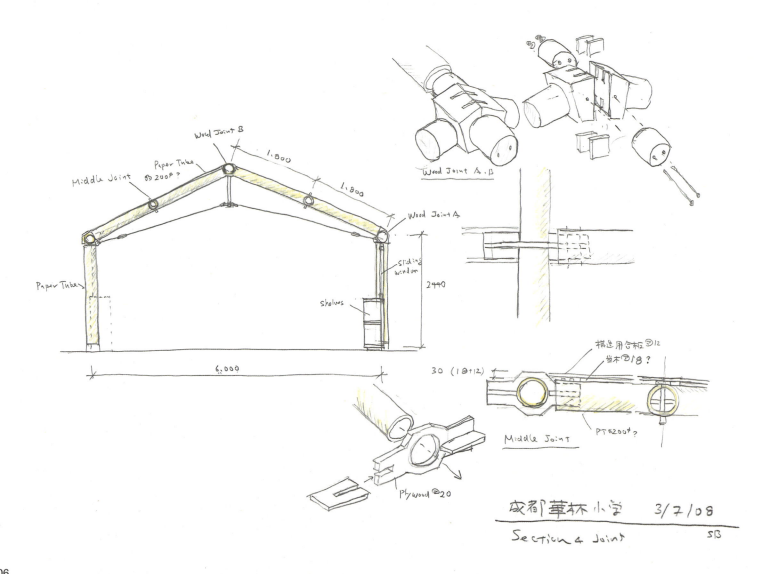

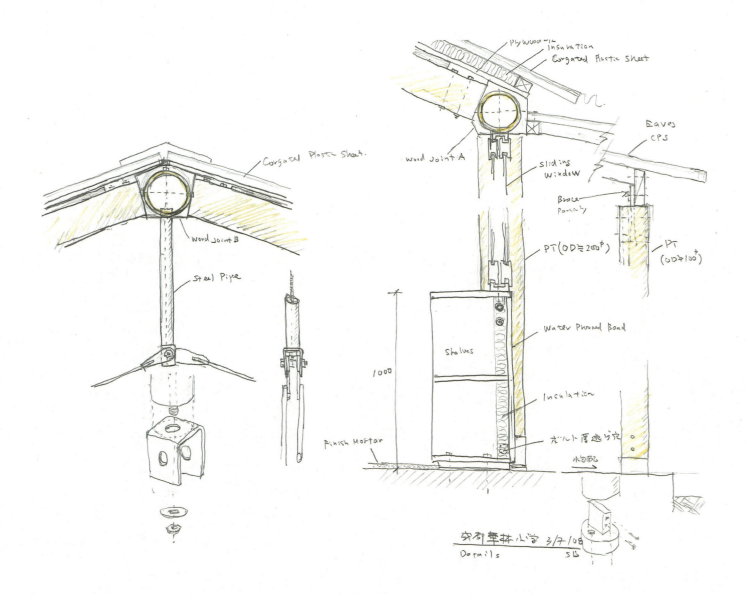

Centre Pompidou-Metz
ポンピドー・センター メス

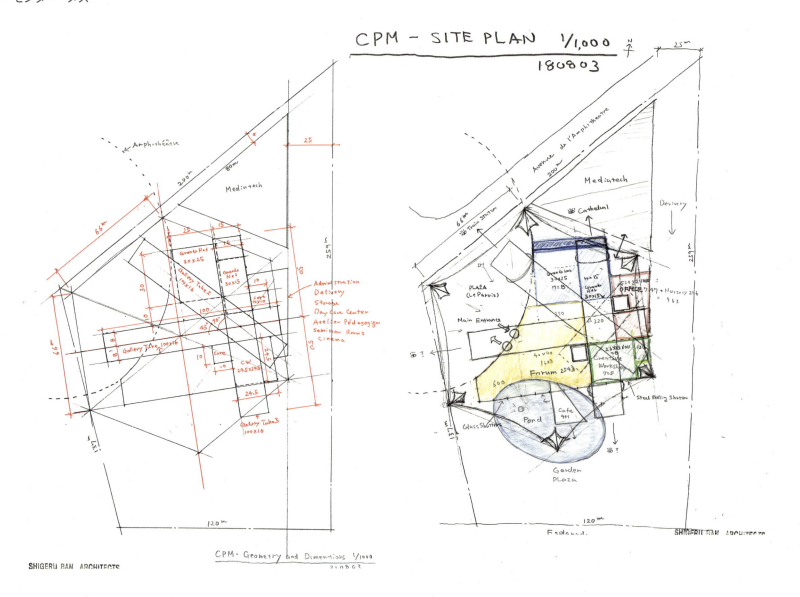

Centre Pompidou-Metz
ポンピドー・センター　メス

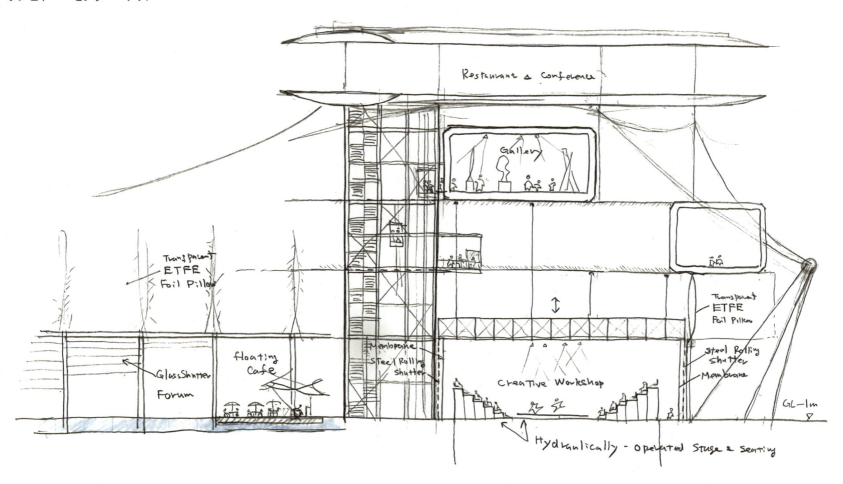

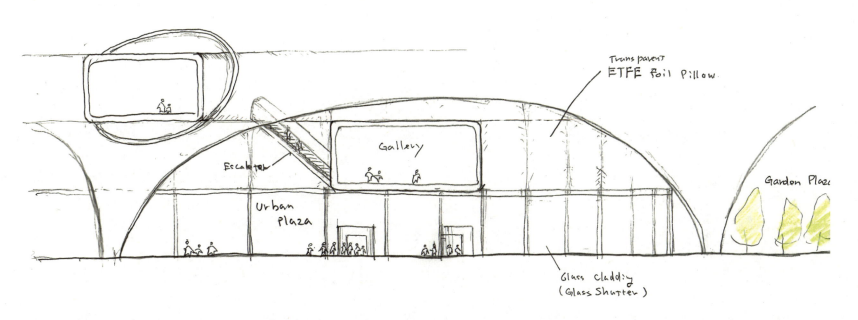

CPM - Urban Plaza Entrance 1/300
180803

Centre Pompidou-Metz
ポンピドー・センター　メス

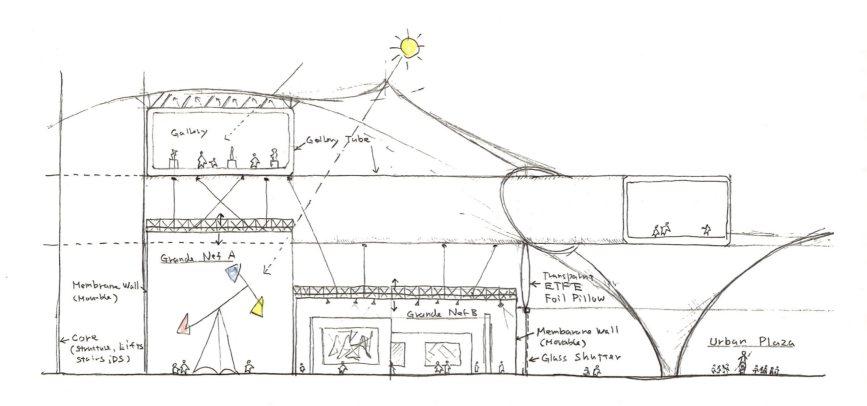

CPM- Scheme NO 2   South Elevation   1/1000

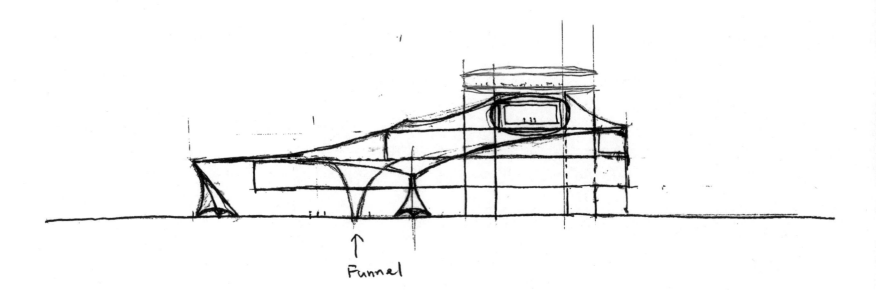

Funnel

Centre Pompidou-Metz
ポンピドー・センター　メス

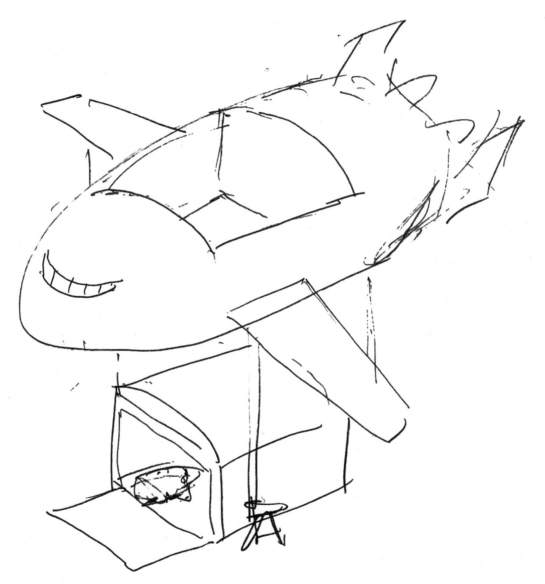

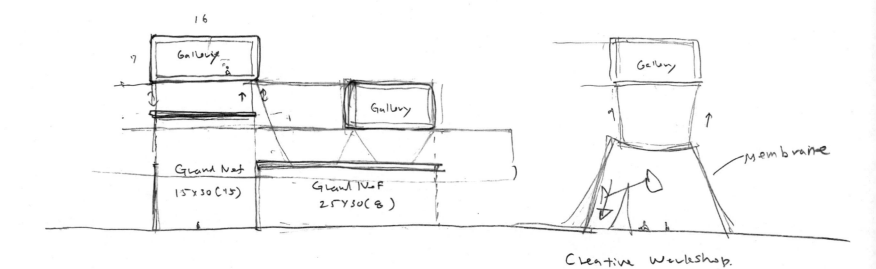

Creative Workshop.

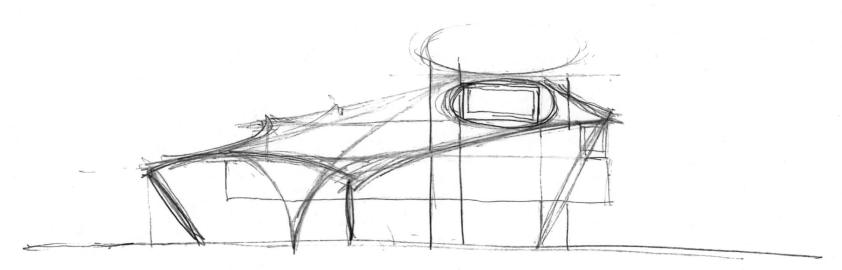

Centre Pompidou-Metz
ポンピドー・センター メス

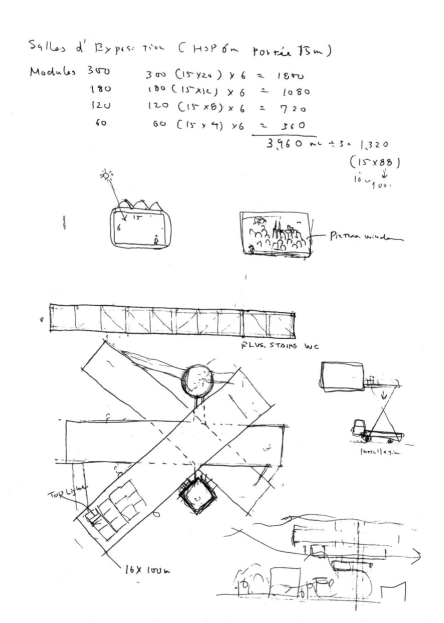

Centre Pompidou-Metz
ポンピドー・センター　メス

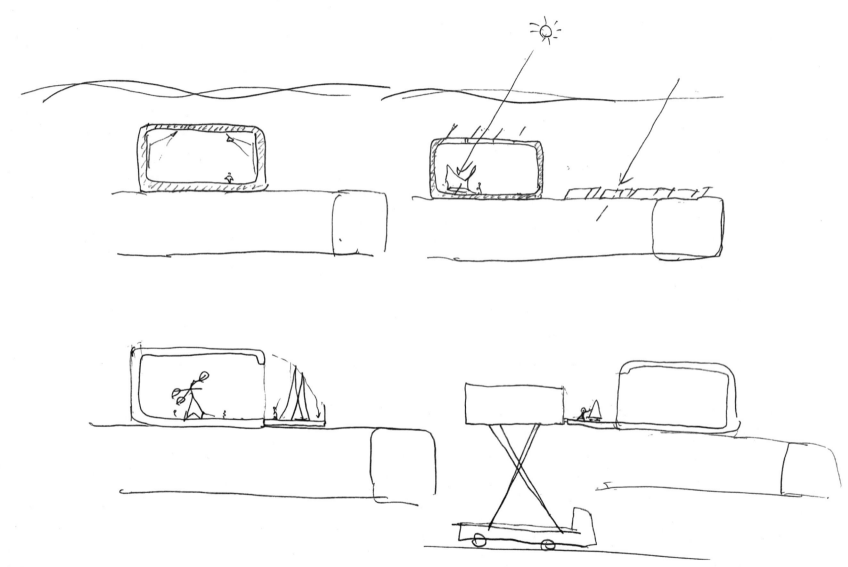

8/5/03 @ CDG   Special automobiles for airport

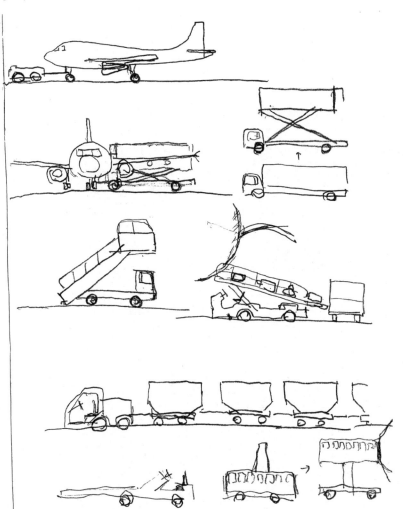

Centre Pompidou-Metz
ポンピドー・センター　メス

展示準備品（Loadingのこと）に移動できる。

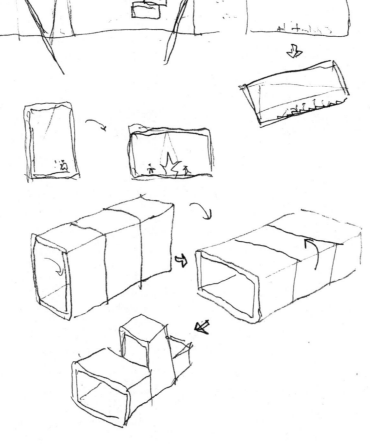

Centre Pompidou-Metz
ポンピドー・センター　メス

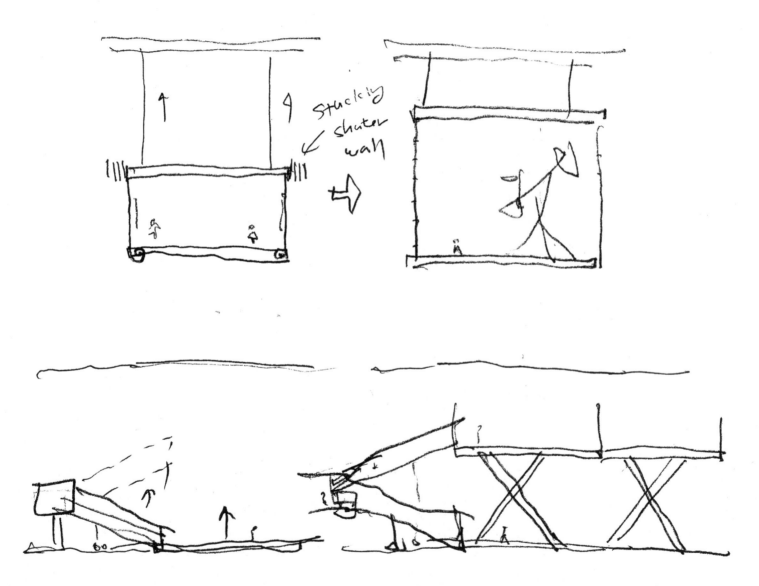

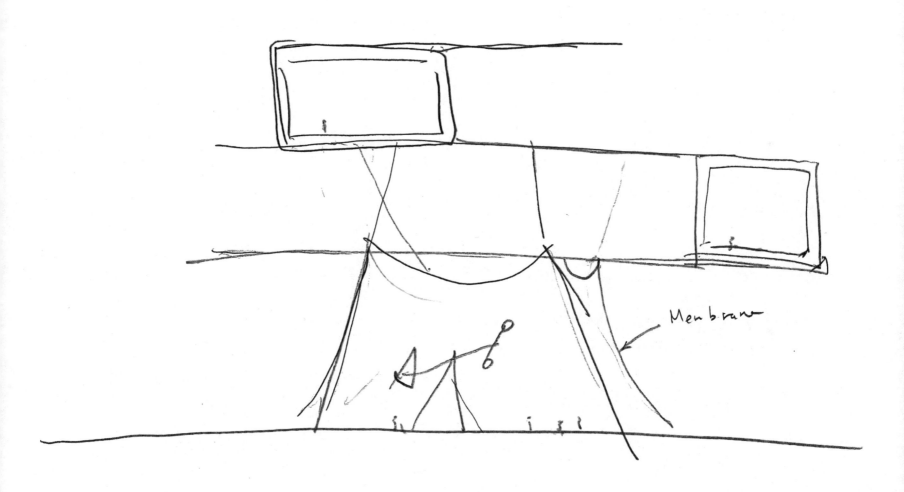

Centre Pompidou-Metz
ポンピドー・センター メス

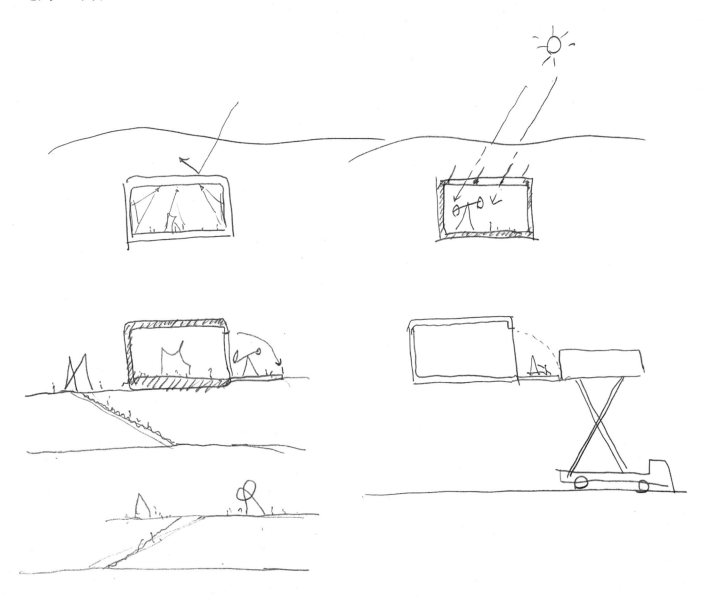

124

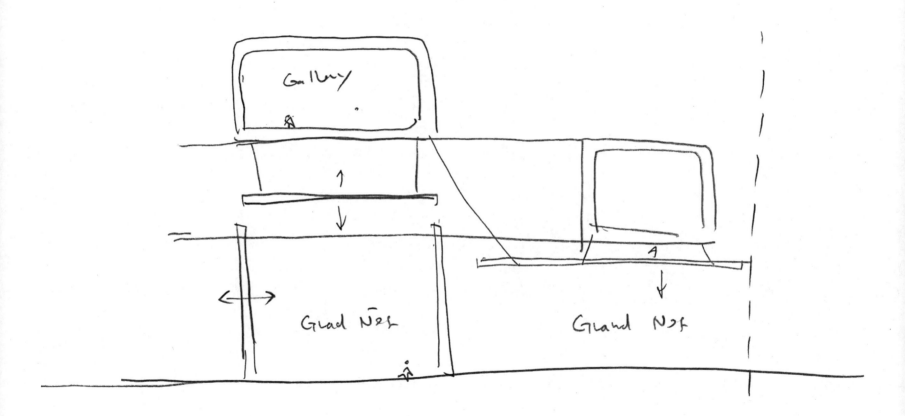

Centre Pompidou-Metz
ポンピドー・センター　メス

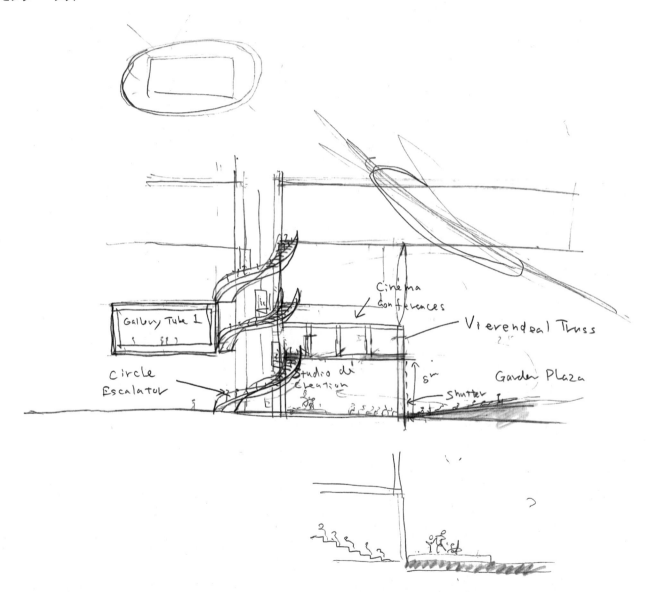

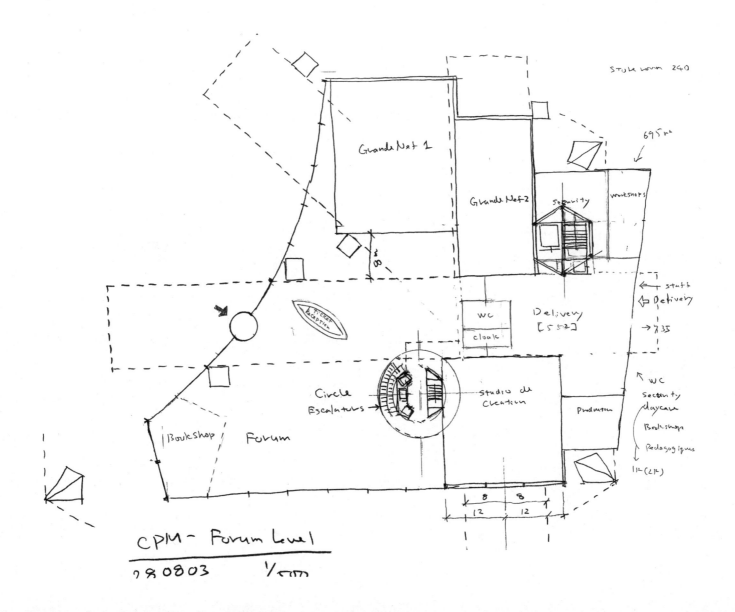

Centre Pompidou-Metz
ポンピドー・センター　メス

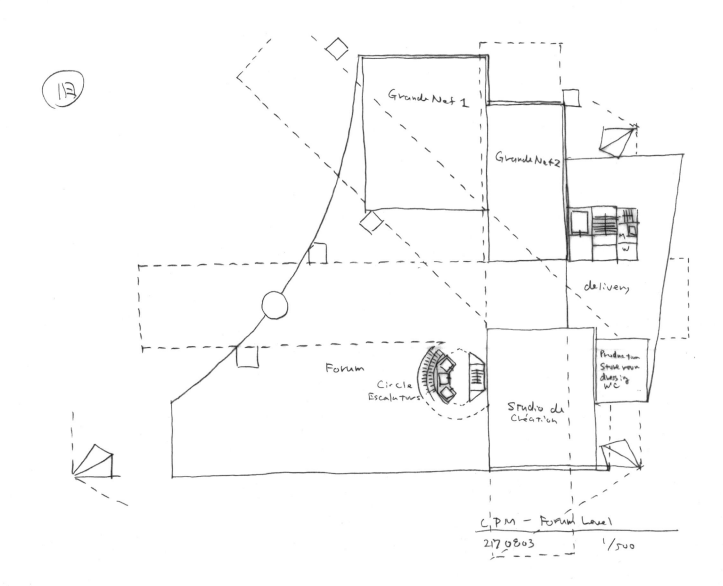

TO: Arup
ATTN: Martin Self
FROM: SHIGERU BAN @ PGA
RE: CPM
CC: Cormac Deavy

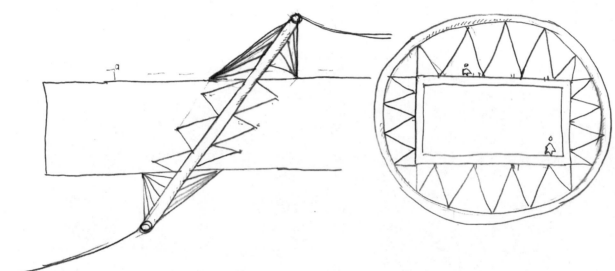

14/10/03

Dear Martin.
Thank you for your sketch of the "bicycle wheel".
How many steel rod shall we put?
I know that the less steel rod we put, the bigger the size of steel ring become.
What could be the appropriate number?
I hope to see you tomorrow.
Thanks.   SHIGERU Ban

Centre Pompidou-Metz
ポンピドー・センター　メス

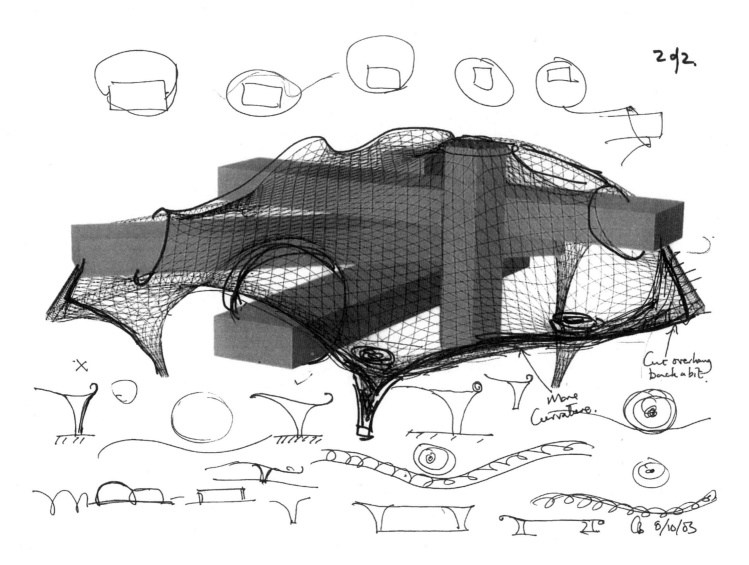

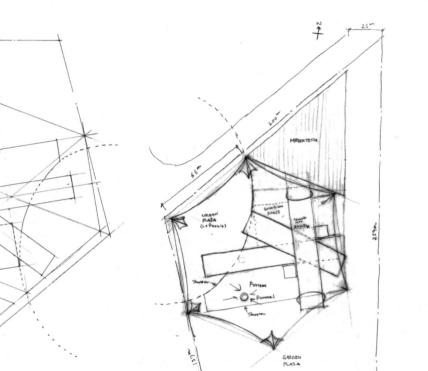

CPM - Scheme NO.2 PLAN 1/1000

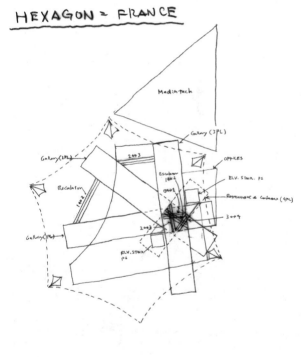

CPM - Vertical Circulation 1/3000

180803

HEXAGON = FRANCE

SHIGERU BAN ARCHITECTS

Centre Pompidou-Metz
ポンピドー・センター　メス

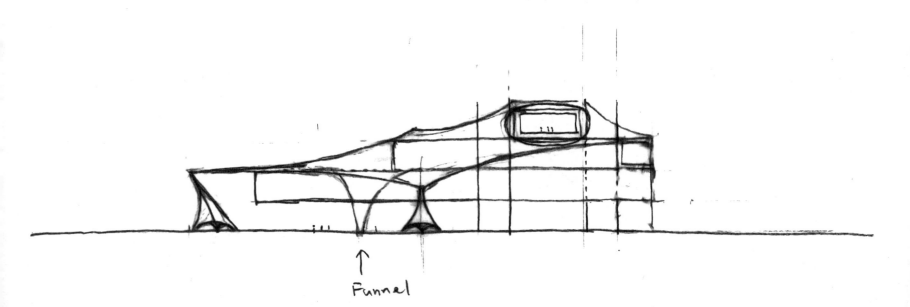

CPM – Scheme No.3 1/1000

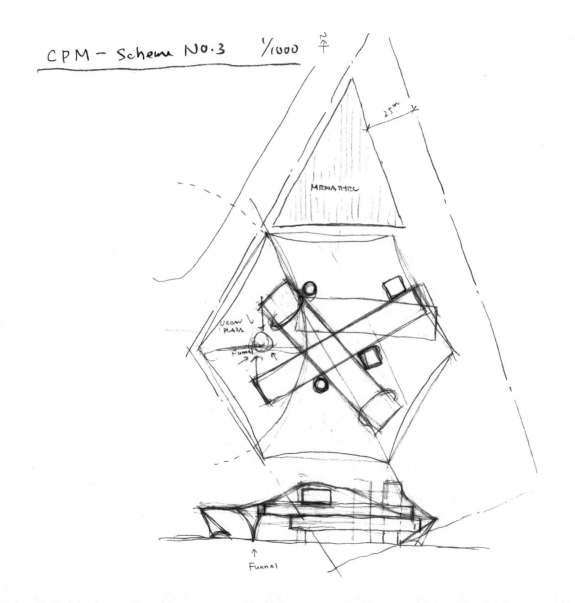

Centre Pompidou-Metz
ポンピドー・センター メス

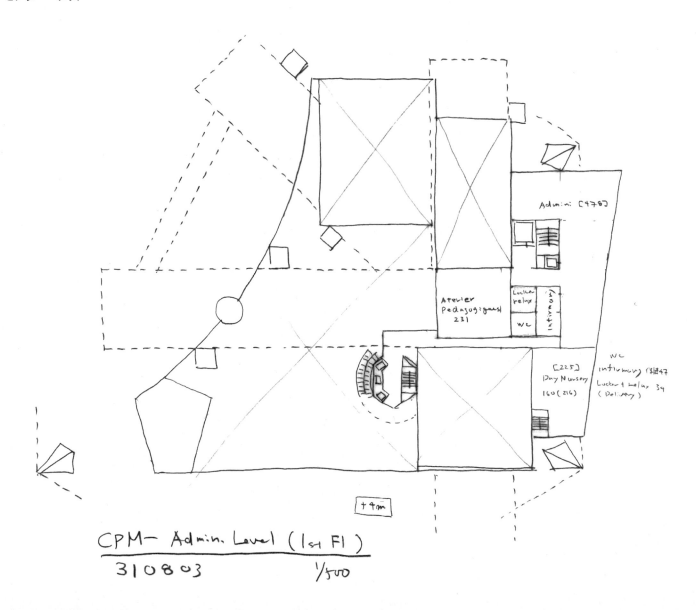

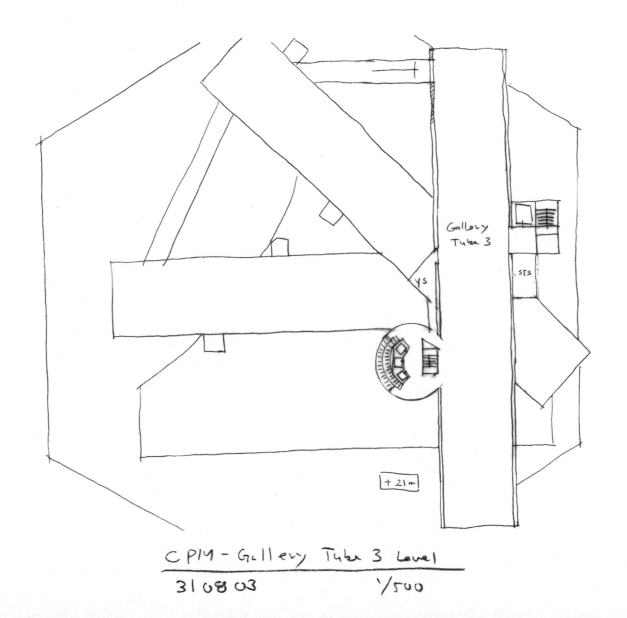

CPM - Gallery Tube 3 Level
310803 1/500

Centre Pompidou-Metz
ポンピドー・センター メス

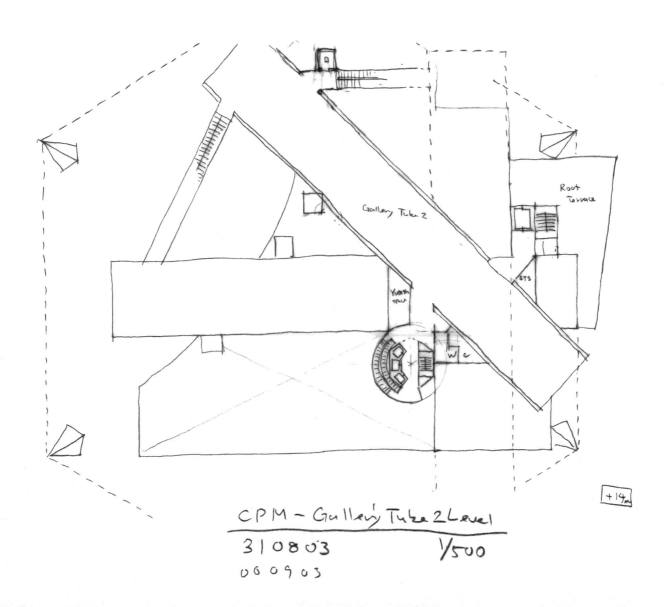

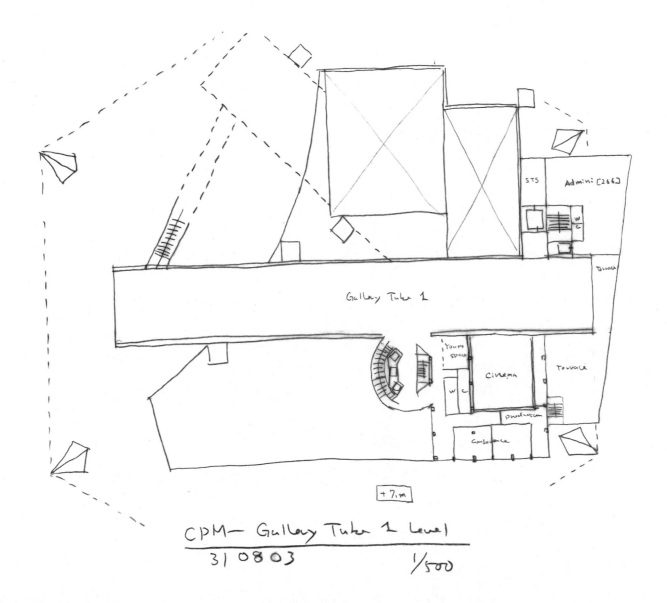

Centre Pompidou-Metz
ポンピドー・センター メス

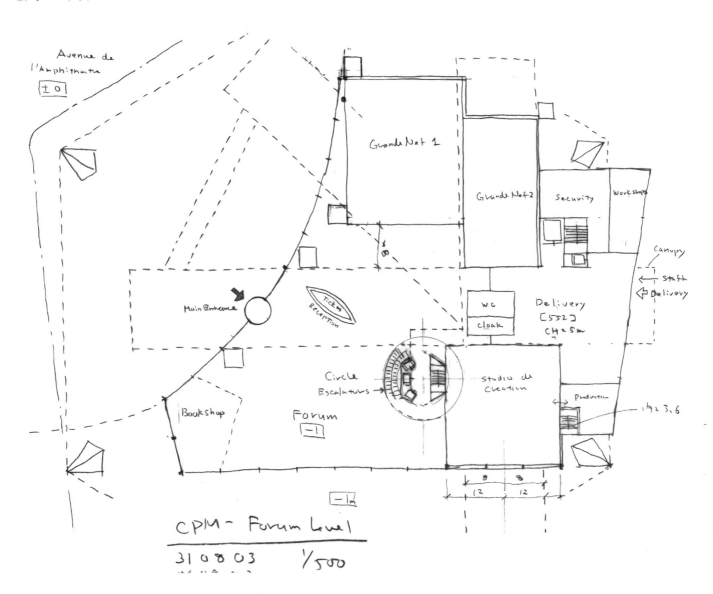

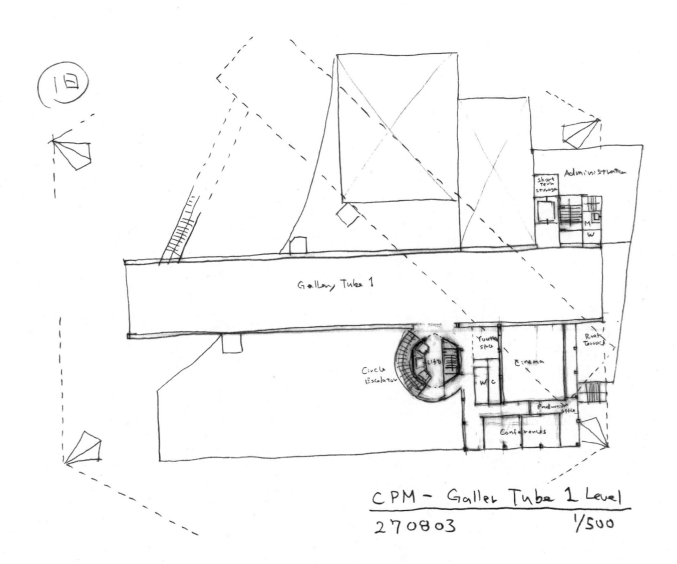

Centre Pompidou-Metz
ポンピドー・センター メス

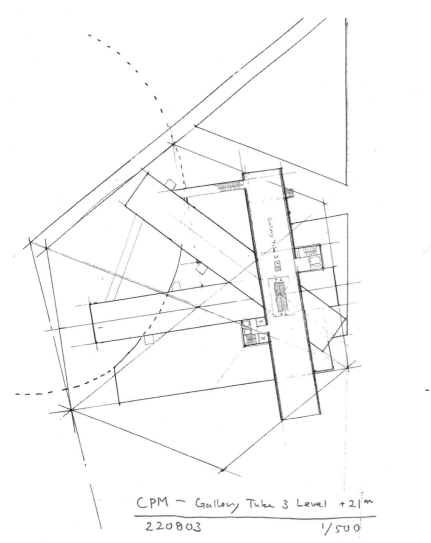

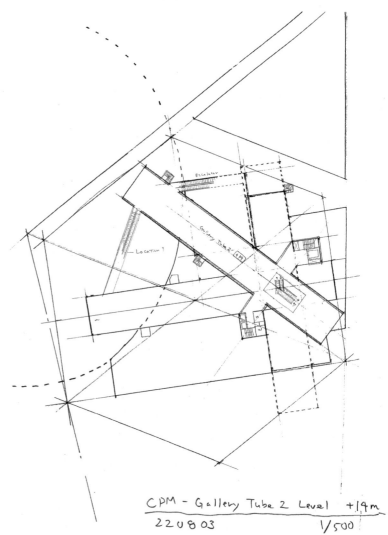

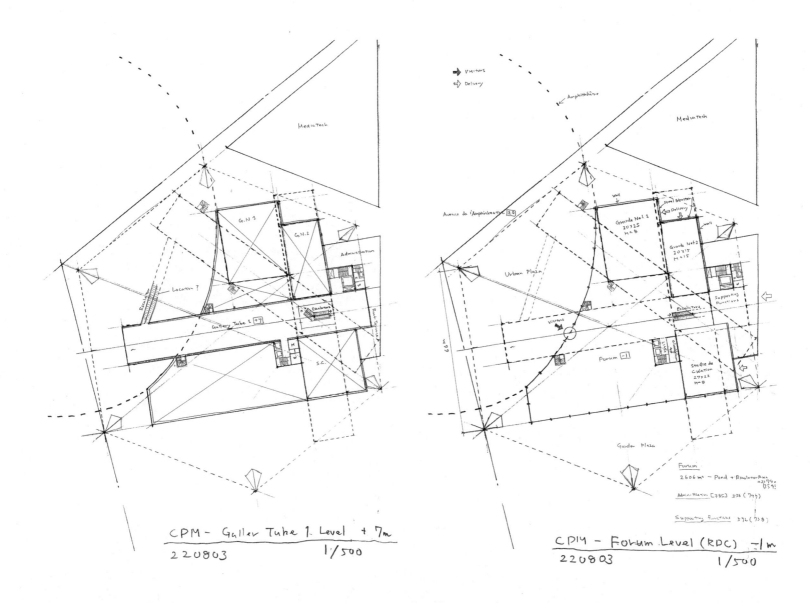

Centre Pompidou-Metz
ポンピドー・センター　メス

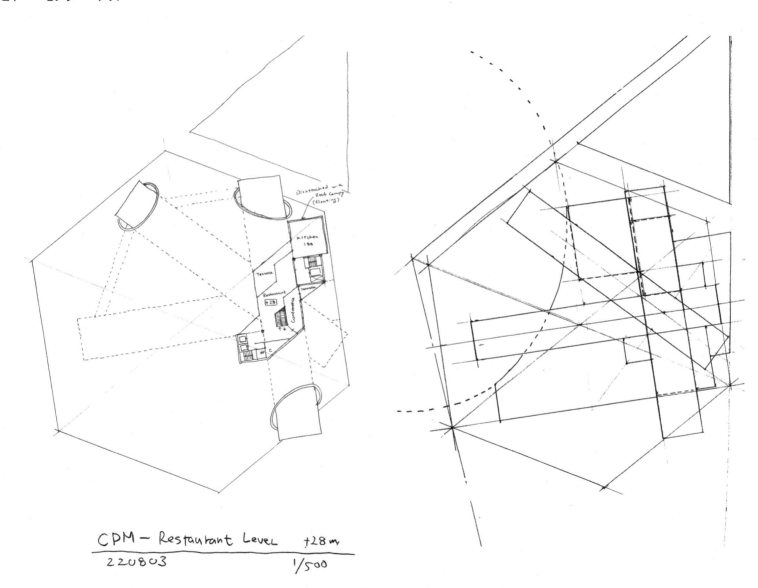

CPM — Restaurant Level +28m
220803   1/500

EXPO 2012 Yoesu Thematic Pavilion
麗水国際博覧会 2012 テーマ館

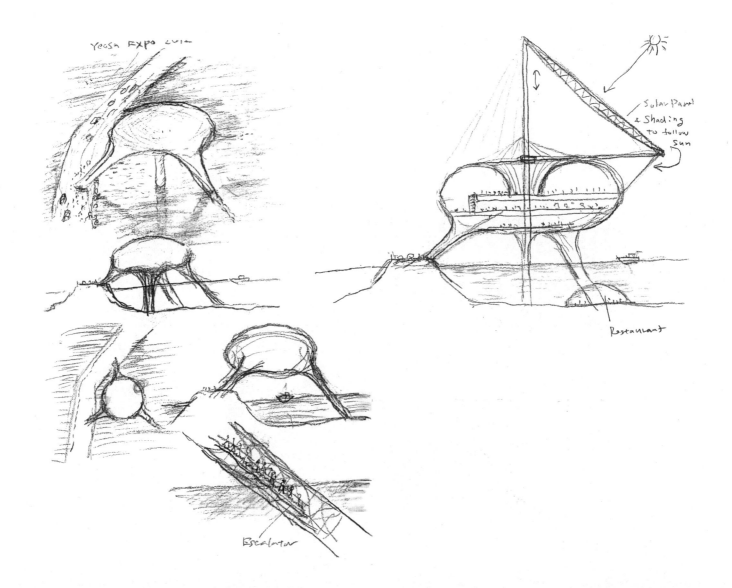

EXPO 2012 Yoesu Thematic Pavilion
麗水国際博覧会 2012 テーマ館

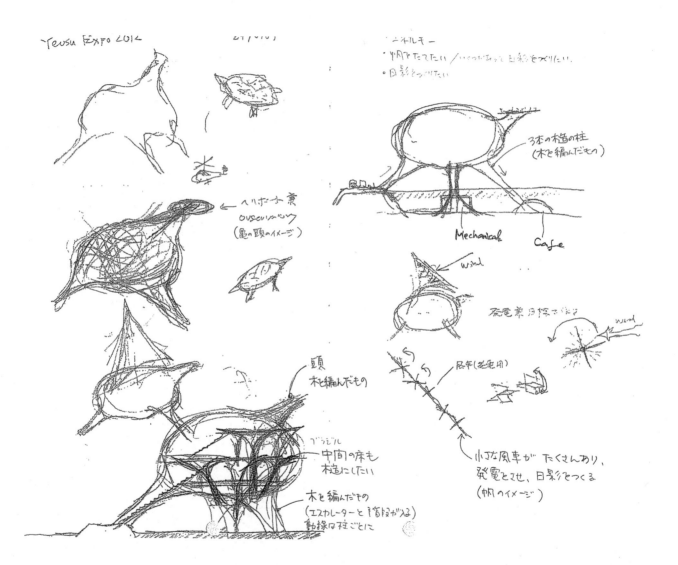

Hong Kong- Shenzhen Bi-City Biennale Pavilion
香港深圳ビエンナーレ パビリオン

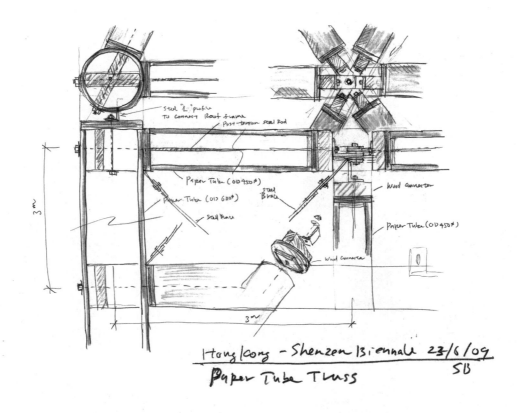

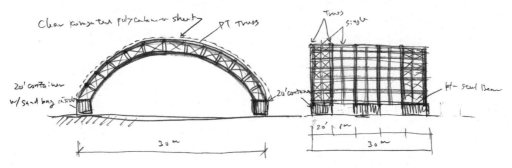

L'Aquila Temporary Concert Hall
ラクイラ仮設音楽ホール

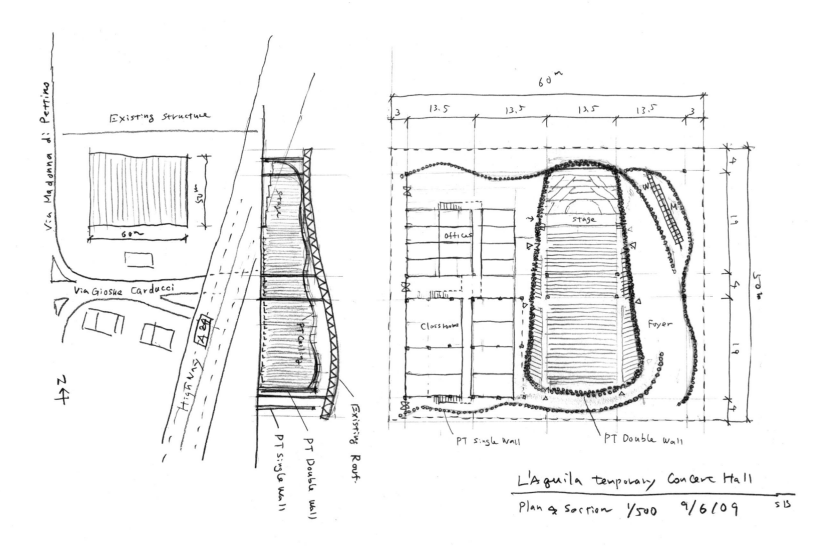

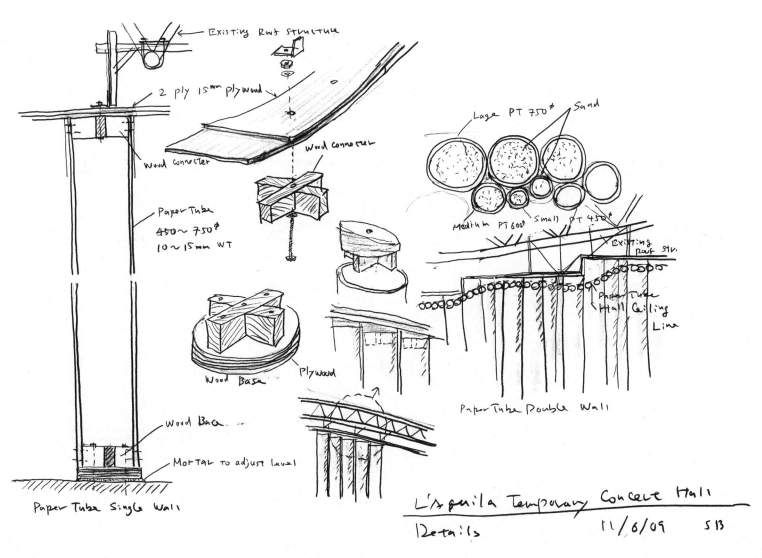

Kazakhstan Drama Theater
カザフスタン国立劇場

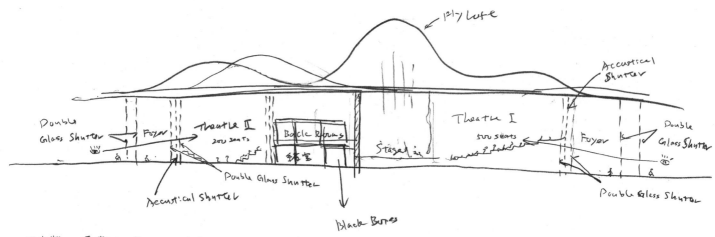

- 中間期と夏期はFoyerのガラスシャッターを全て開き冷房をしない。
- 客席の回りのガラスのシャッターの内外に、遮音用カーテン、シャッター等を使い状況に合わせて遮音する。
- 演目により、客席の回りを開き、外部からもパーフォーマンスが見えるようにする。

Kazakh Drama Theatre 19/12/09
Elevation & Section
S13

Paper Emergency Shelters – Haiti
ハイチ緊急シェルター

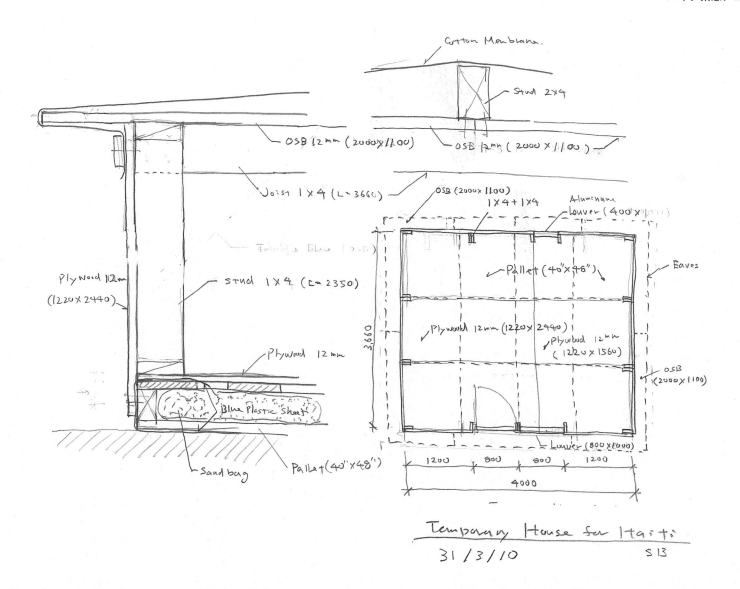

Kaohsiung Port and Cruise Service Center
高雄　港クルーズ・サービスセンター

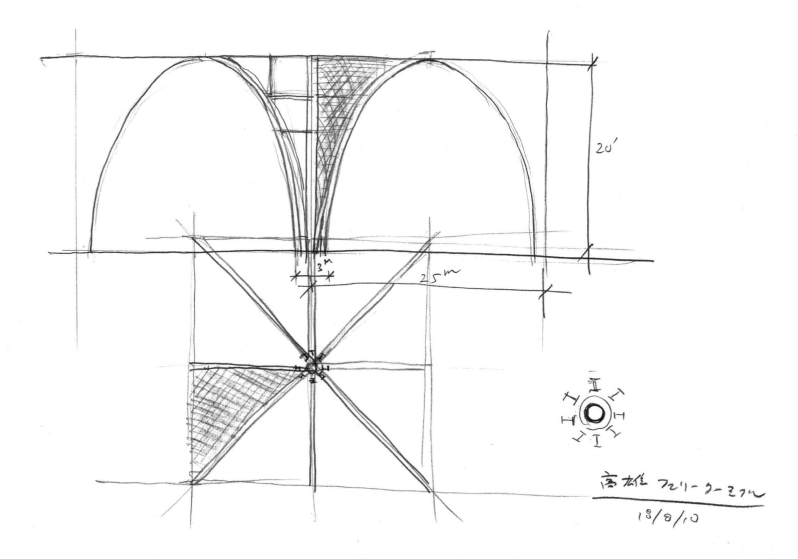

Haesley Condominium
ヘスリー・コンドミニアム

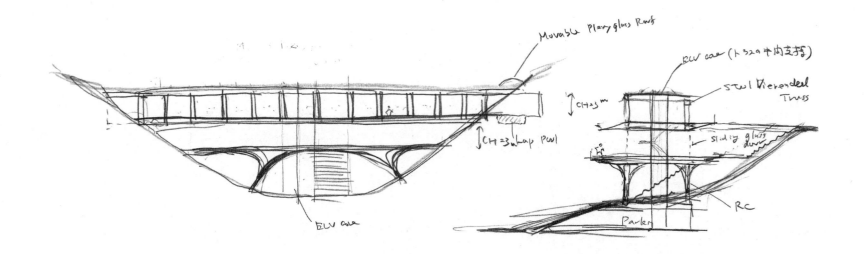

Hangzhou Golf Clubhouse
杭州市 ゴルフ・クラブハウス

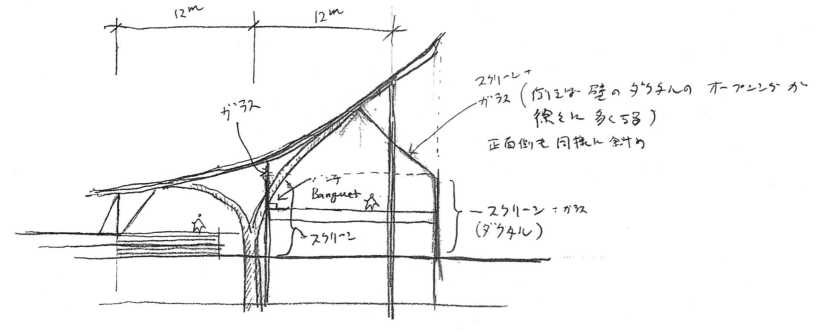

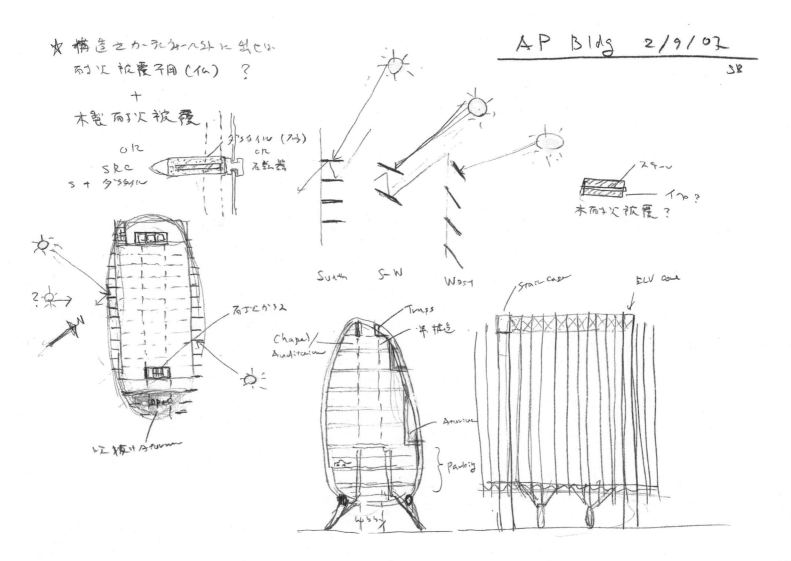

Cardboard Cathedral
紙のカテドラル

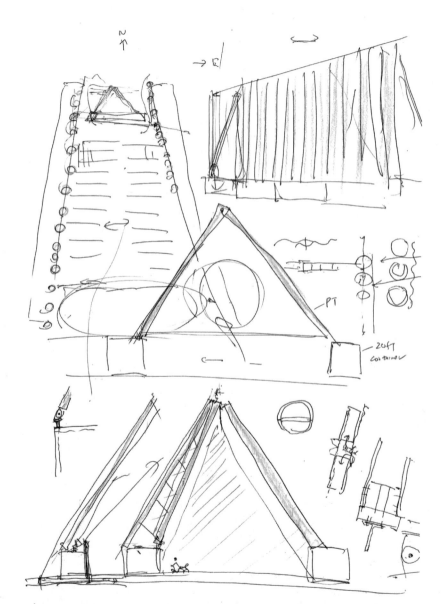

154

Skolkovo Golf Clubhouse
スコルコボ・ゴルフ・クラブハウス

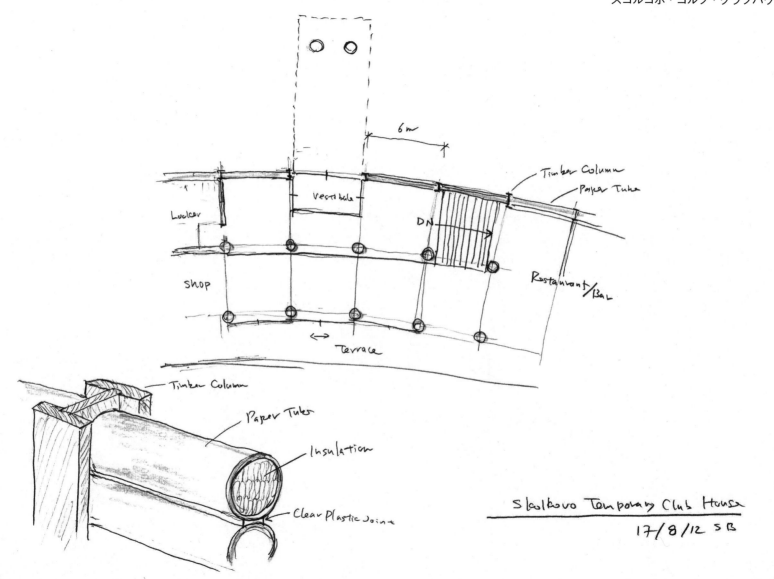

Skolkovo Golf Clubhouse
スコルコボ・ゴルフ・クラブハウス

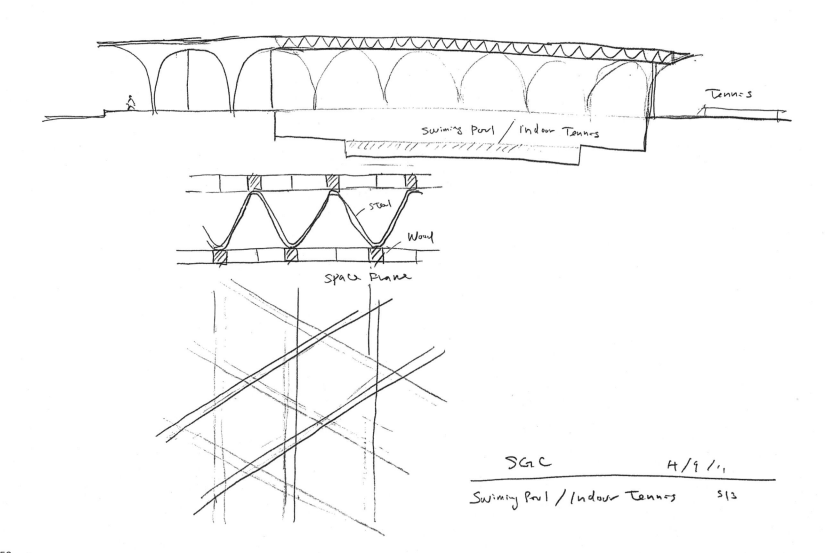

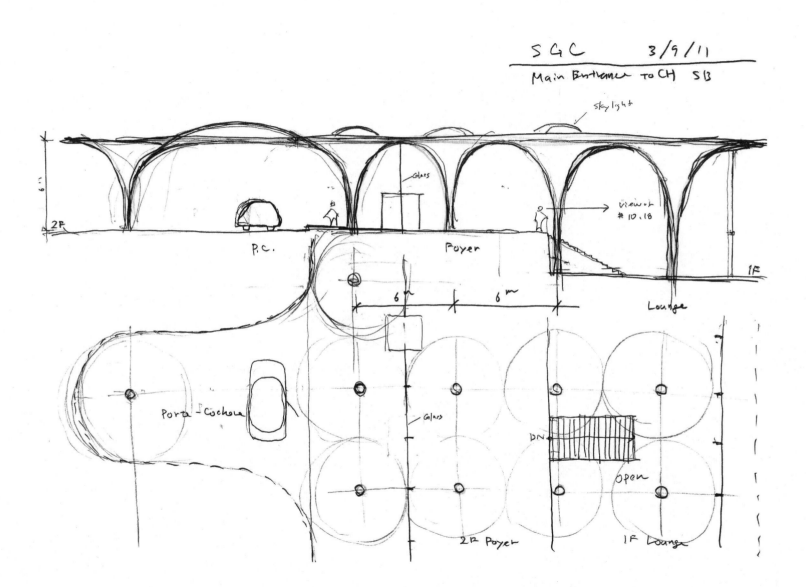

Skolkovo Golf Clubhouse
スコルコボ・ゴルフ・クラブハウス

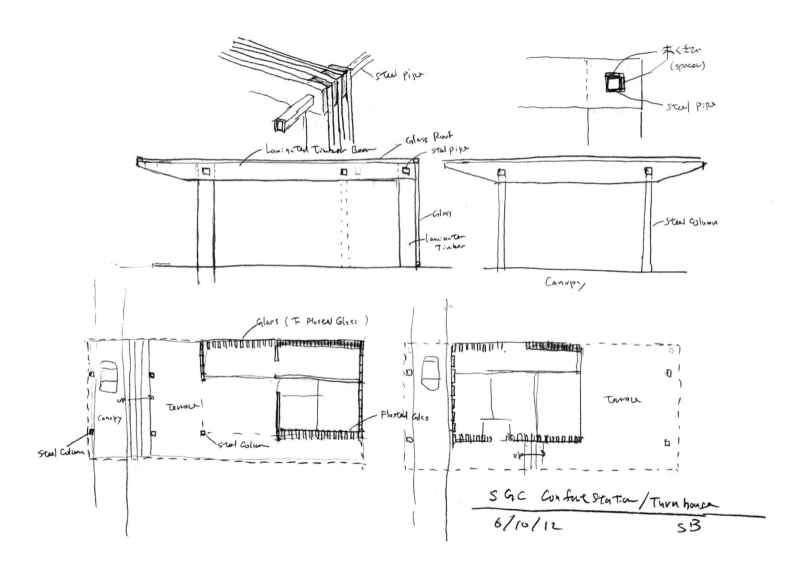

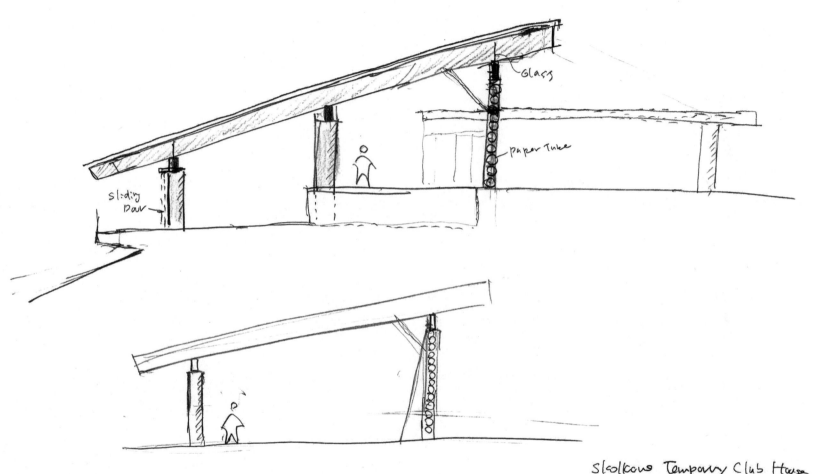

Skolkovo Temporary Club House
17/8/12 SB

Villa at Sengokubara
仙石原の住宅

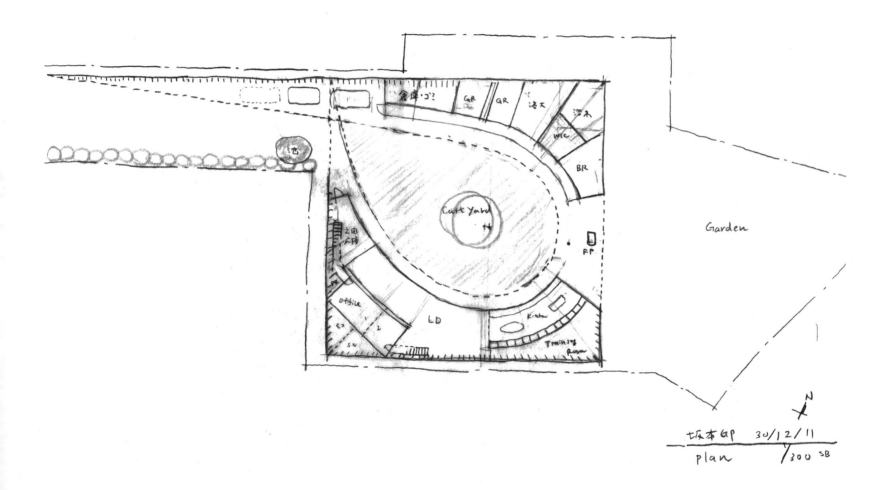

Ristia Resort, Bali
リスティア・リゾート

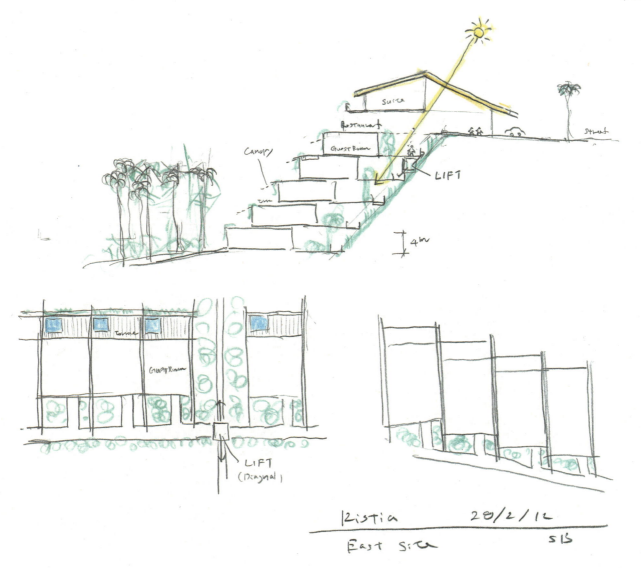

Ristia Resort, Bali
リスティア・リゾート

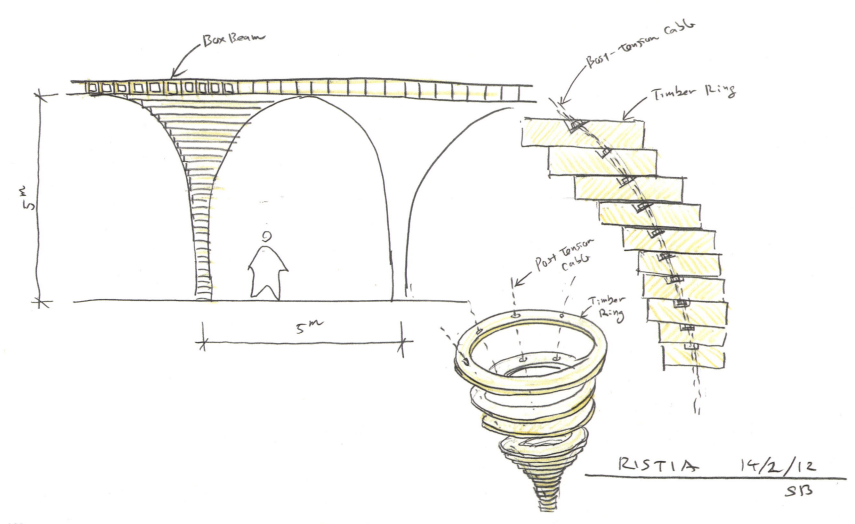

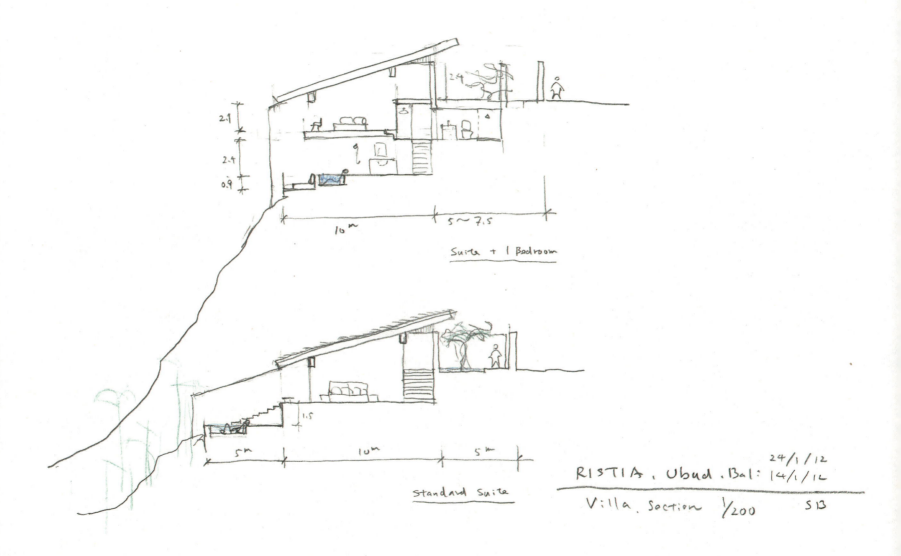

Ristia Resort, Bali
リスティア・リゾート

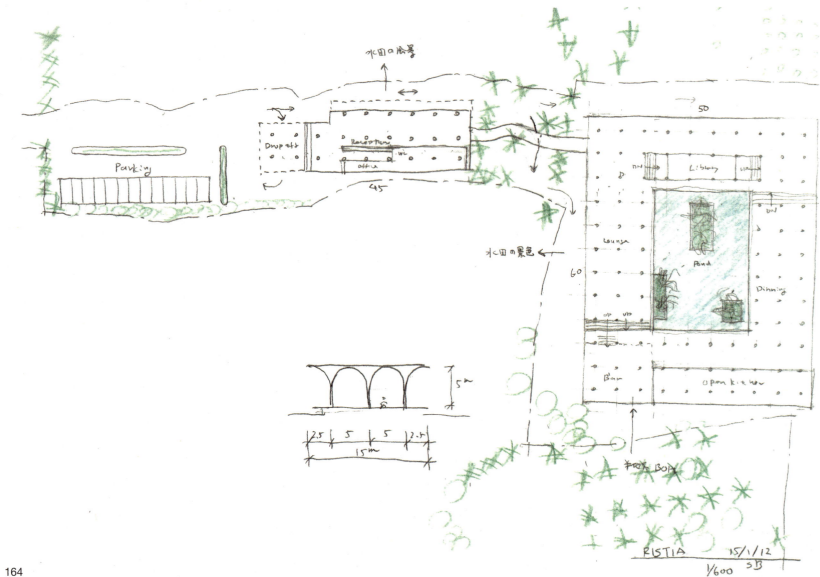

Module H
モジュラー・アッシュ

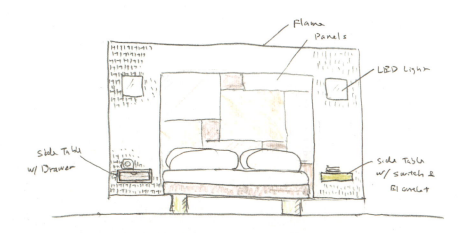

Bed board w/ Table & Lighting

Bathroom

Wall Storage

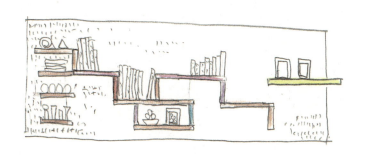

Shelves

Module H 14/9/12
SB

Module H
モジュラー・アッシュ

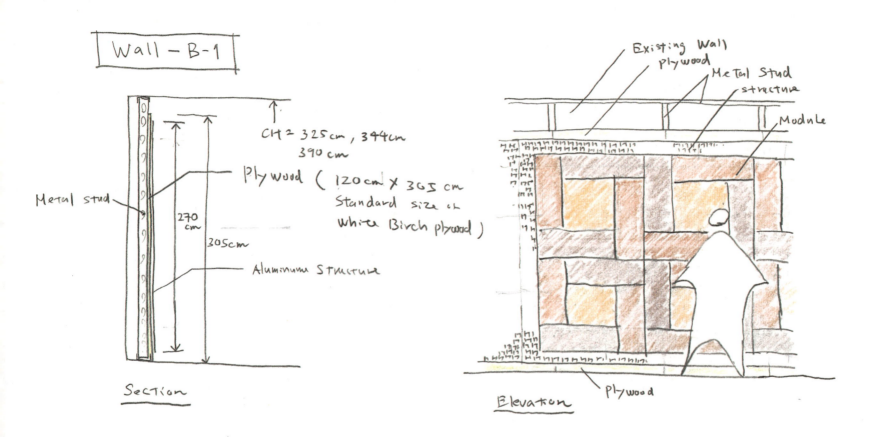

166

National Library of Israel
イスラエル国立図書館

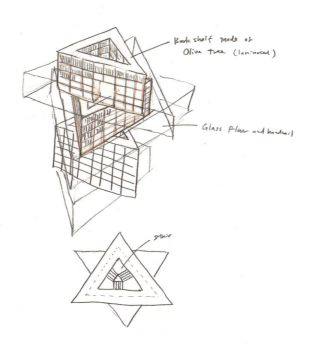

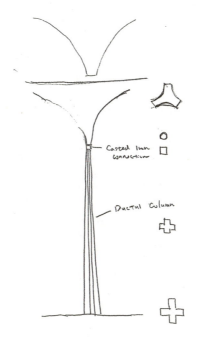

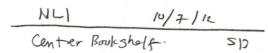

NLI   22/7/12
Ductal Column   SD

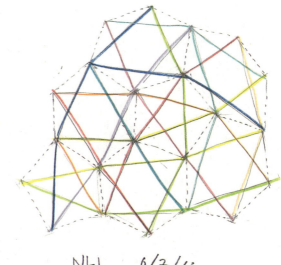

NLI   6/7/12
            SD

Ginza Façade Project
銀座ファサードプロジェクト

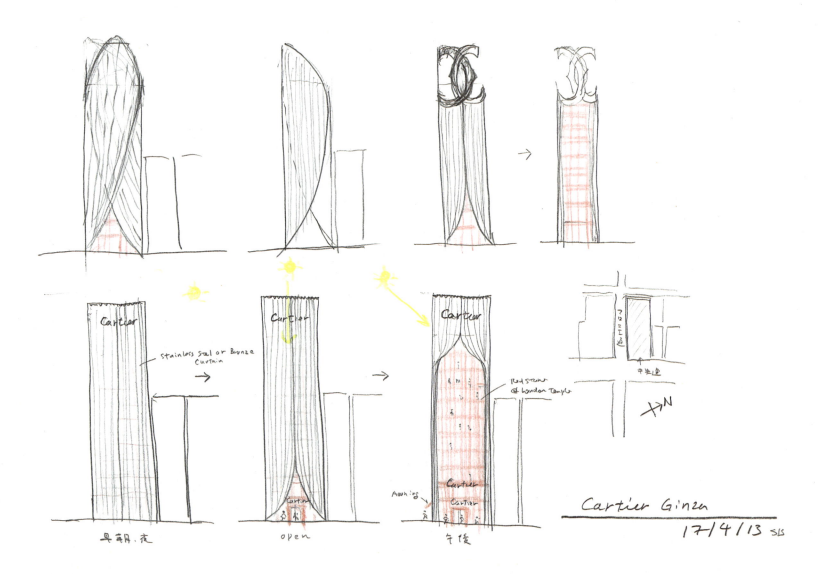

New Museum of Modern Art Toyama
新富山県立近代美術館

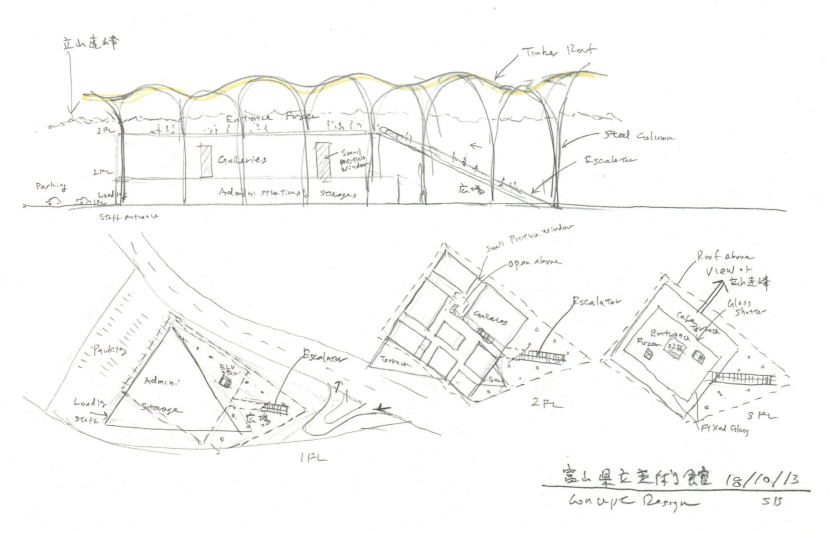

New Museum of Modern Art Toyama
新富山県立近代美術館

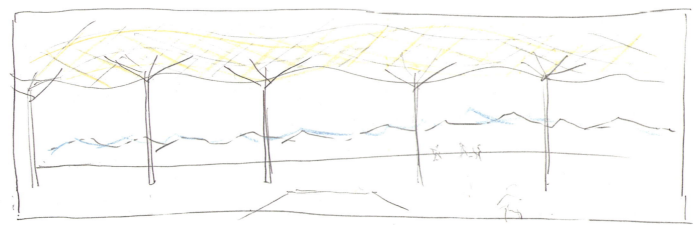

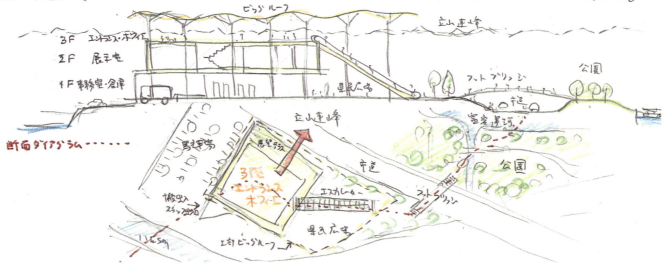

La Seine Musicale
ラ・セーヌ・ミュジカル

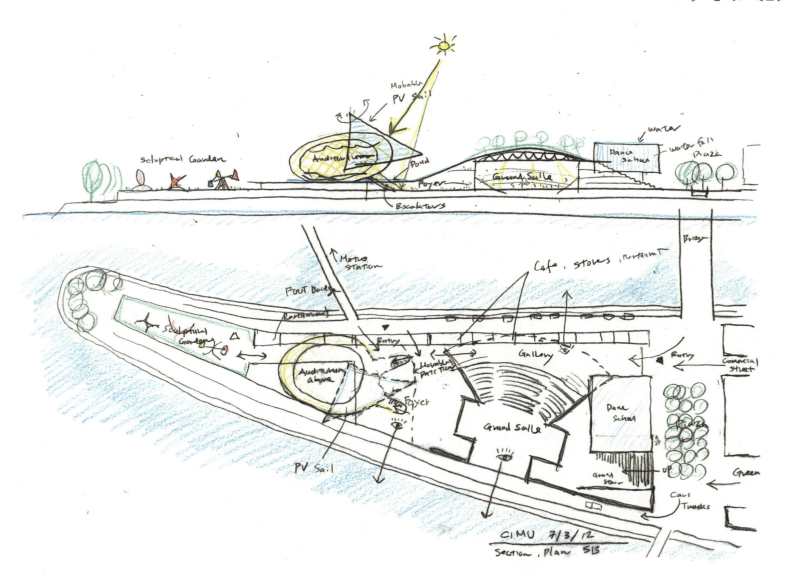

La Seine Musicale
ラ・セーヌ・ミュジカル

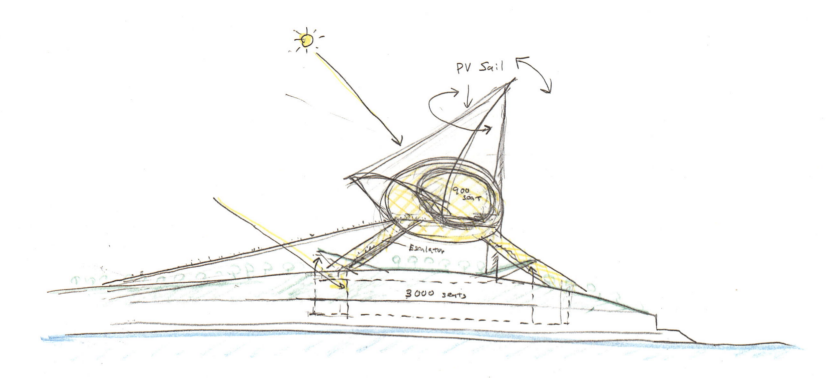

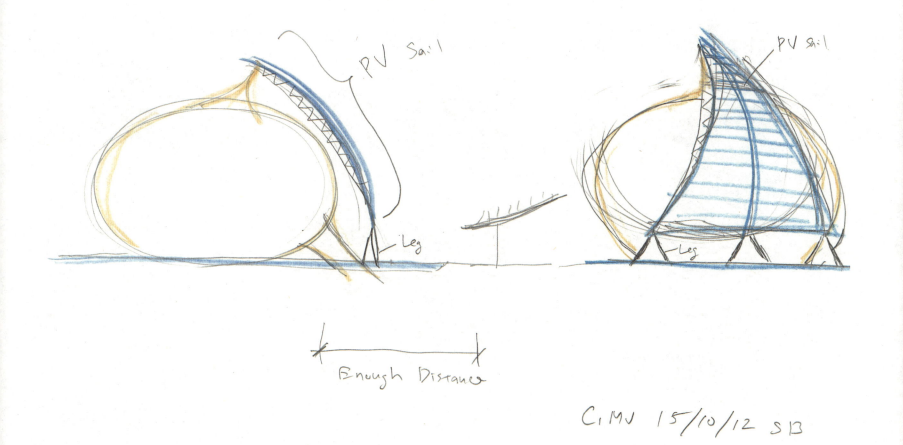

La Seine Musicale
ラ・セーヌ・ミュジカル

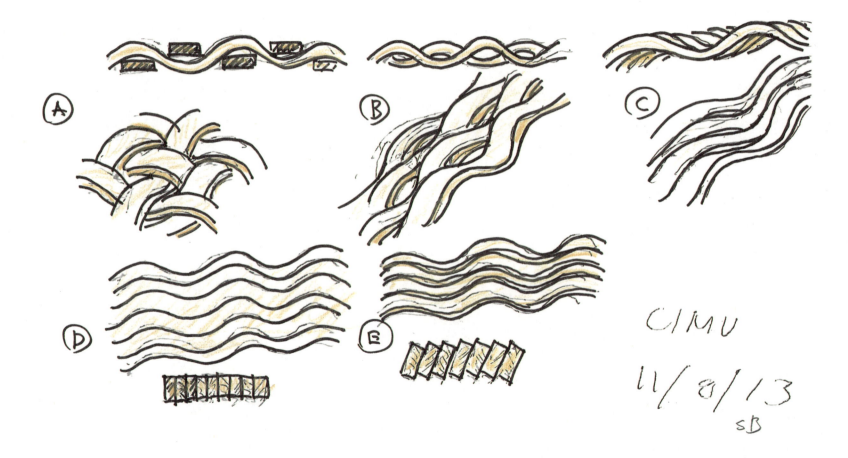

Oita Prefectural Art Museum
大分県立美術館

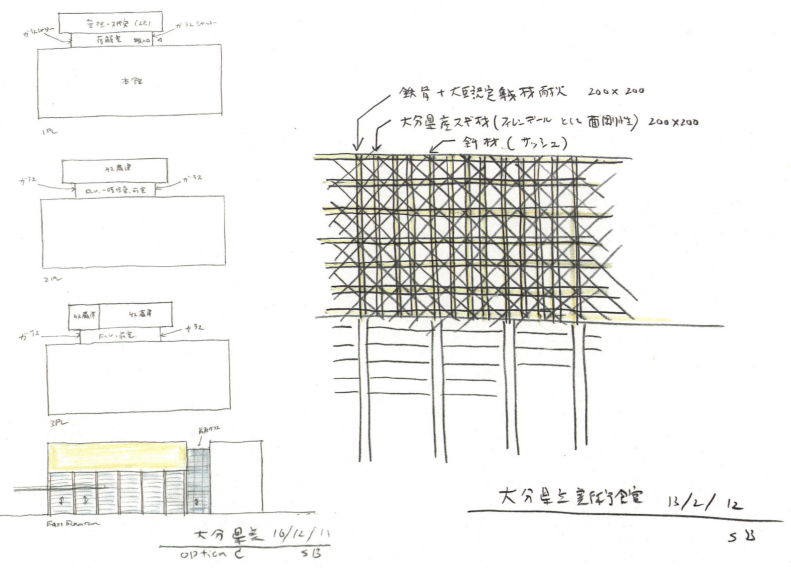

New National Stadium Japan
新国立競技場コンペ

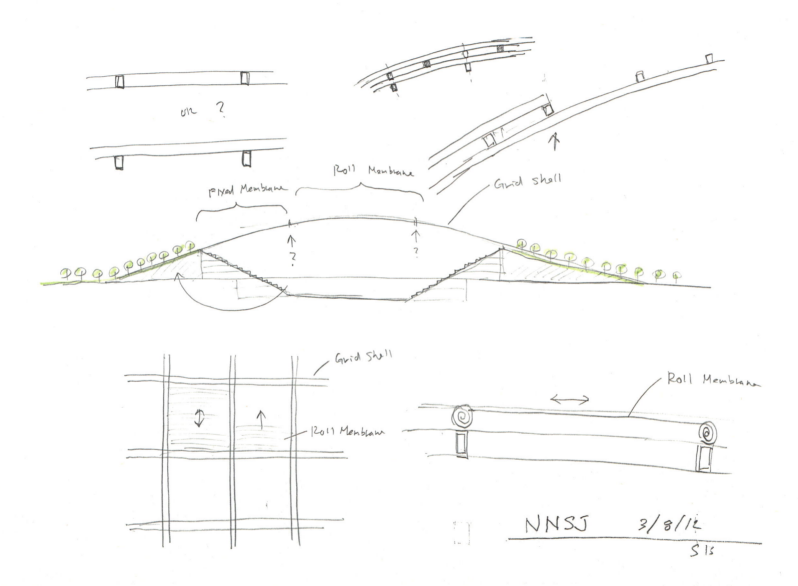

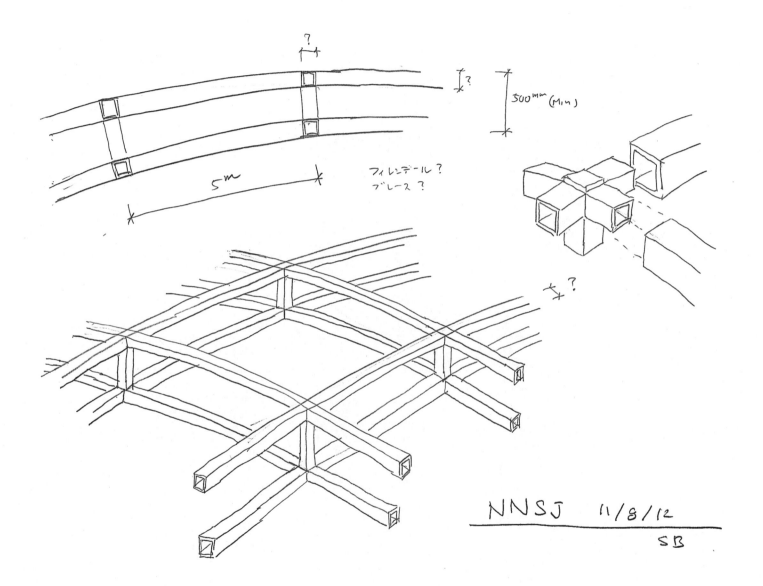

Kyoto University of Art and Design Disaster Relief Center
京都造形芸術大学 災害支援センター

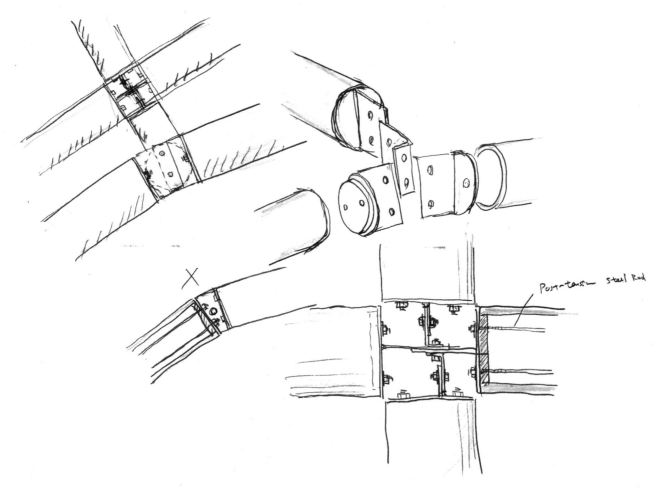

178

New Temporary House
新仮設住宅

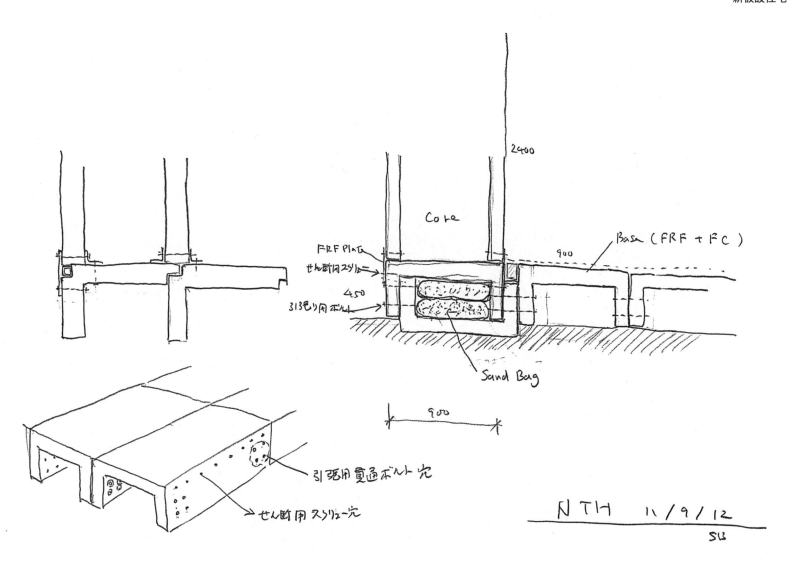

Doshisha University Kyotanabe Campus Chapel
同志社大学　京田辺キャンパス礼拝堂

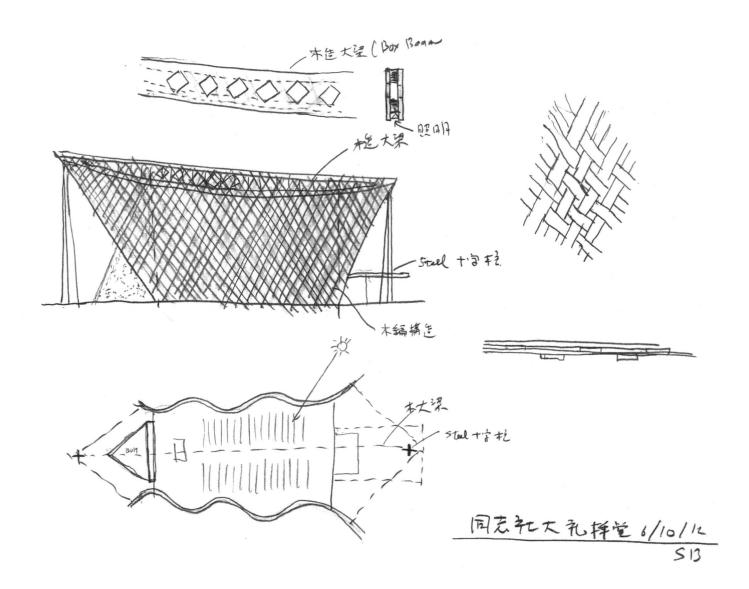

M+
エム・プラス

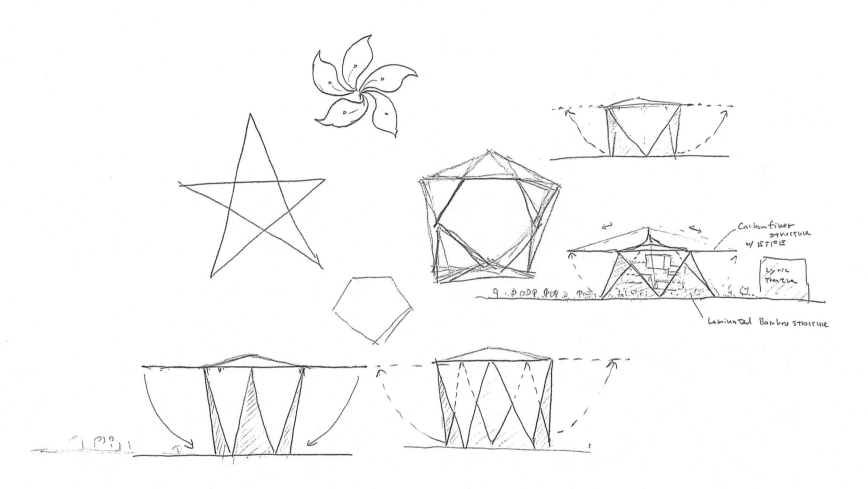

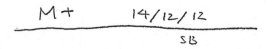

Onagawa Station / Onagawa Onsen Yupo'po
女川駅舎・女川温泉温浴施設ゆぽっぽ

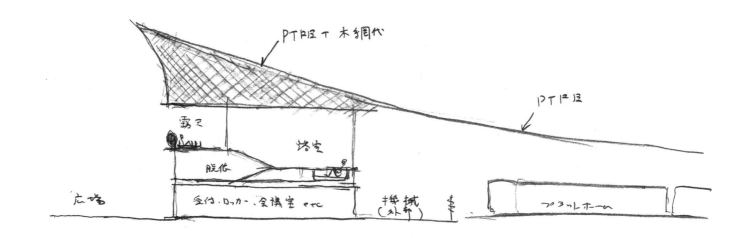

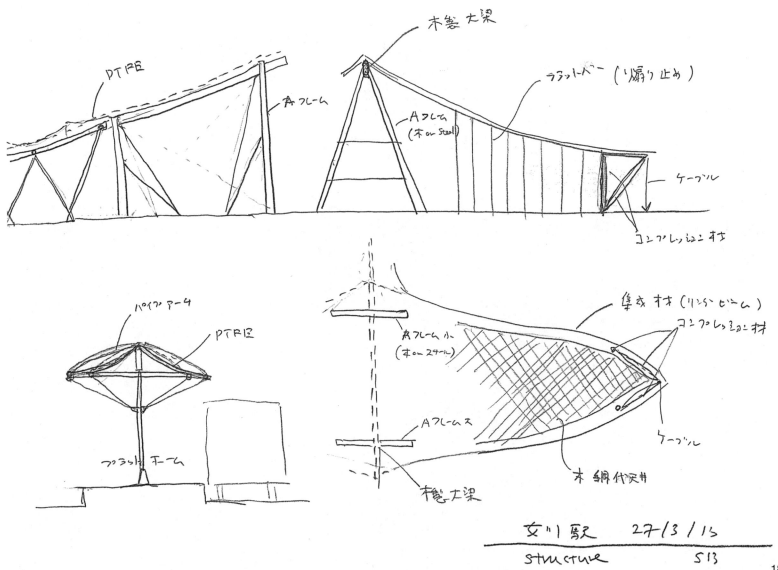

Tech Company HQ Campus Pavilion
テック企業本社キャンパス・パビリオン

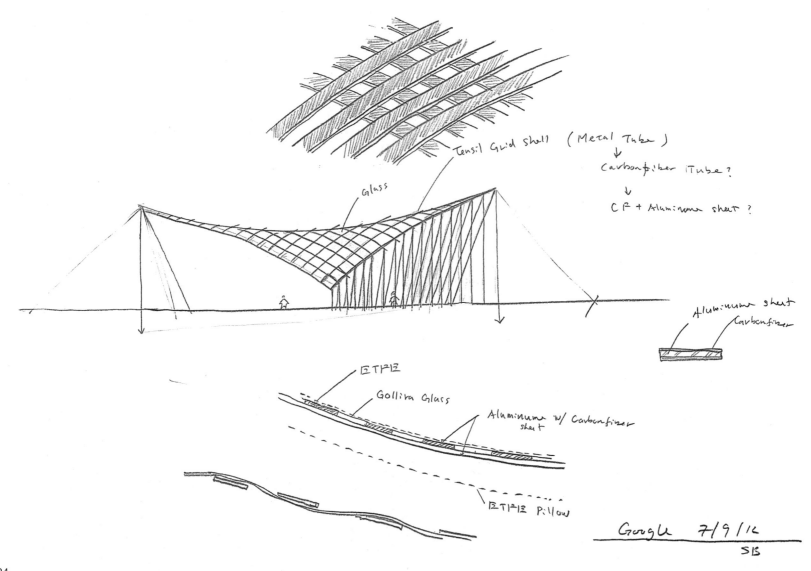

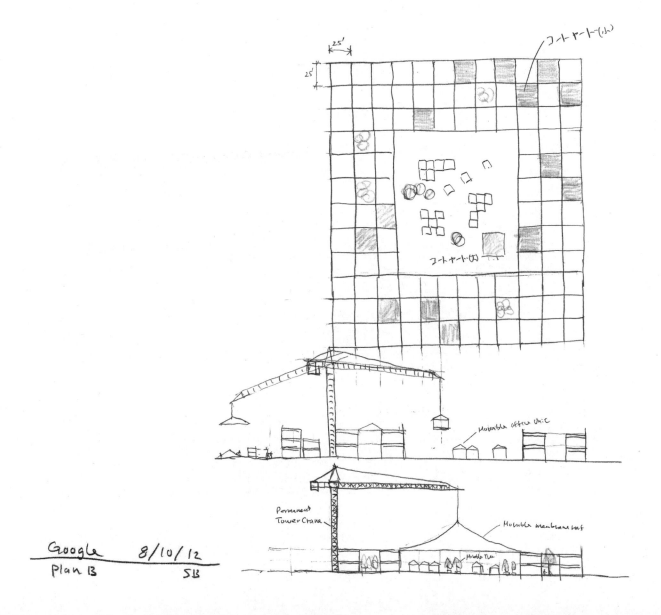

Garage Center for Contemporary Culture Temporary Pavilion
モスクワ仮設美術館　GARAGE

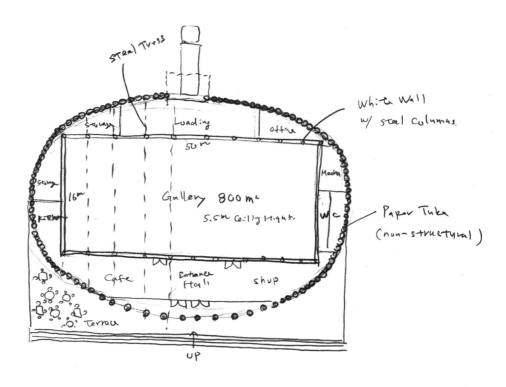

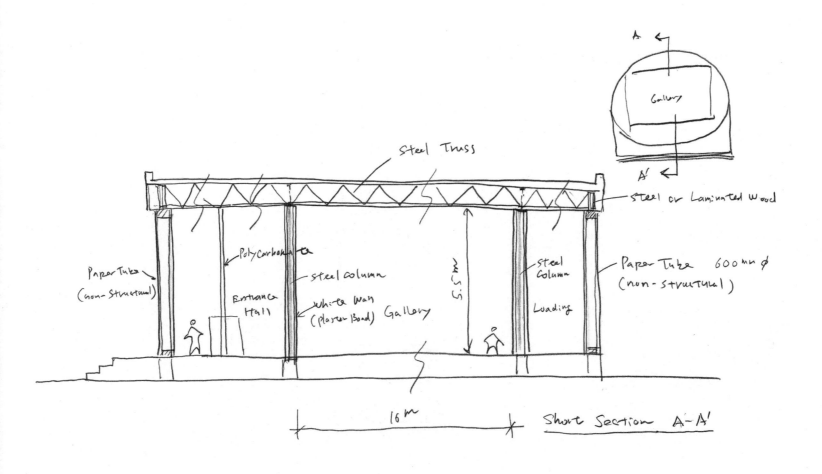

Madrid Paper Pavilion
マドリッド紙のパビリオン

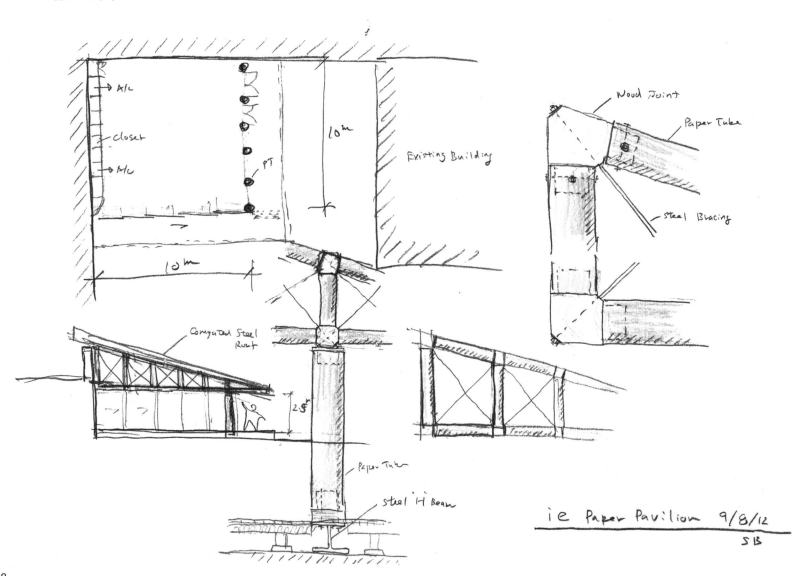

Solid Cedar House
無垢杉の家

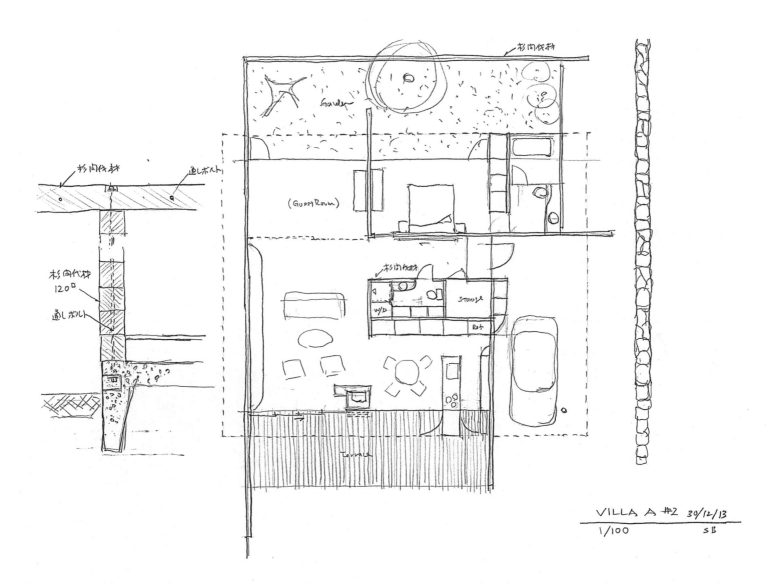

Abu Dhabi Art Pavilion
アブダビ・アート・パビリオン

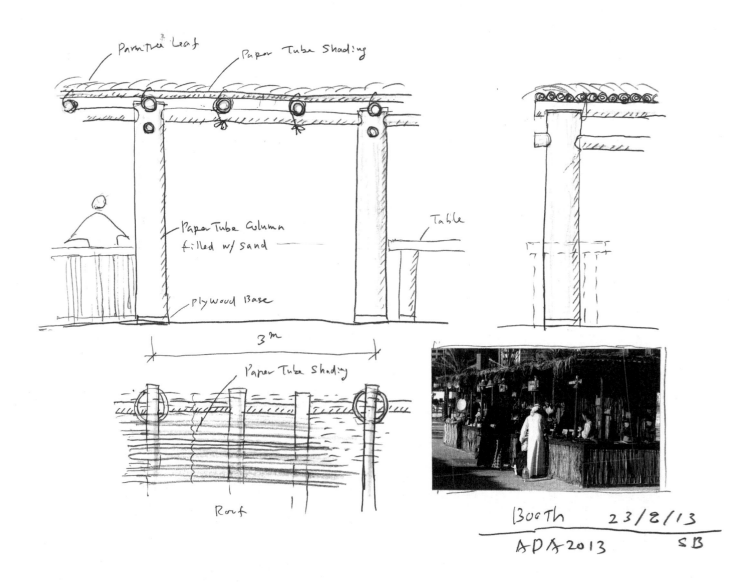

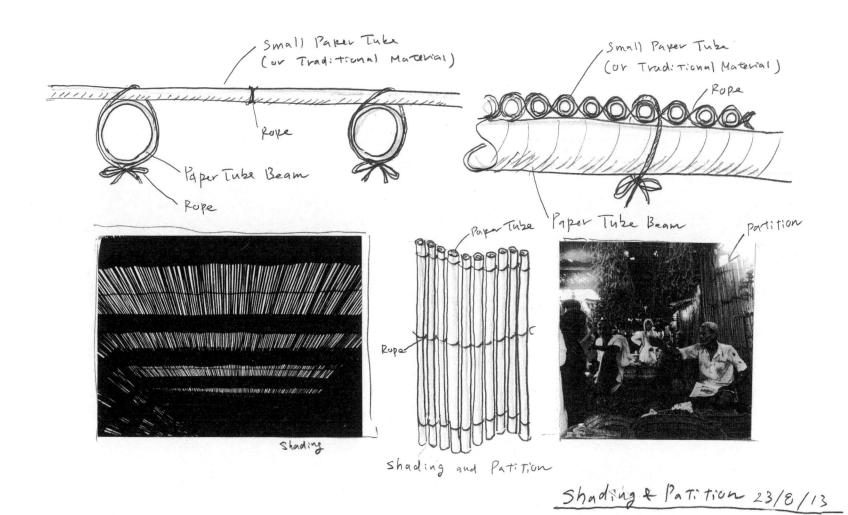

Abu Dhabi Art Pavilion
アブダビ・アート・パビリオン

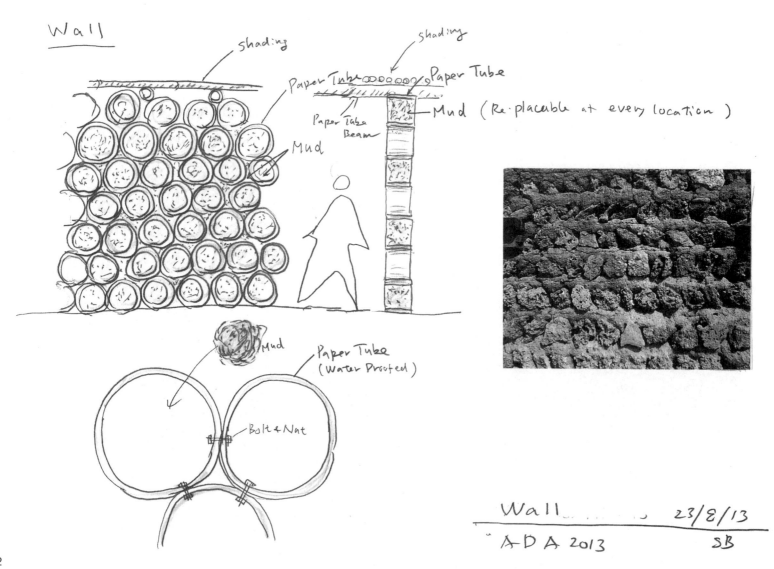

Wall 23/8/13
ADA 2013 SB

Swatch / Omega Campus
スウォッチ・オメガ本社

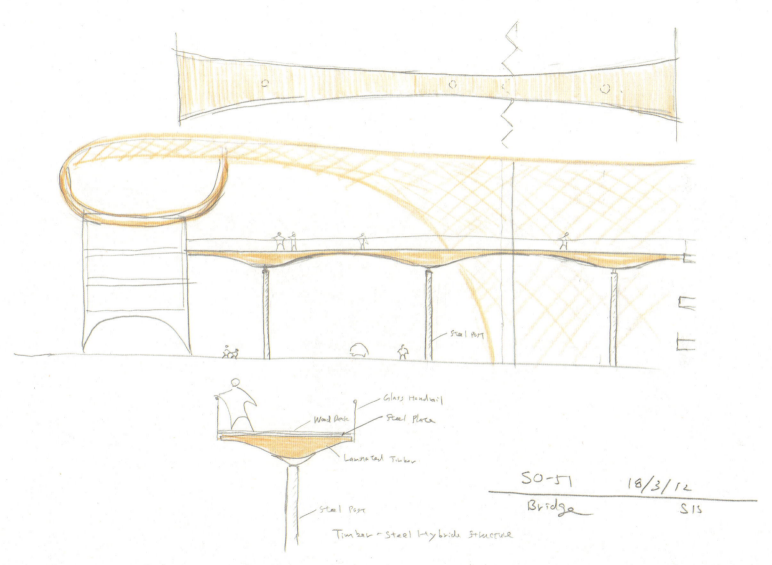

Mt. Fuji World Heritage Centre, Shizuoka
静岡県富士山世界遺産センター

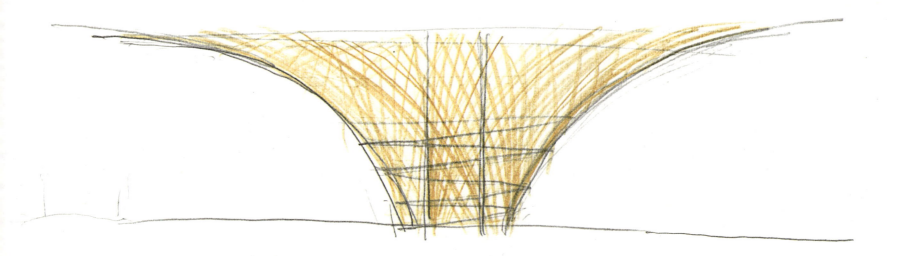

19/1/14　富士山世界遺産センター

Mt. Fuji Shizuoka Airport
富士山静岡空港

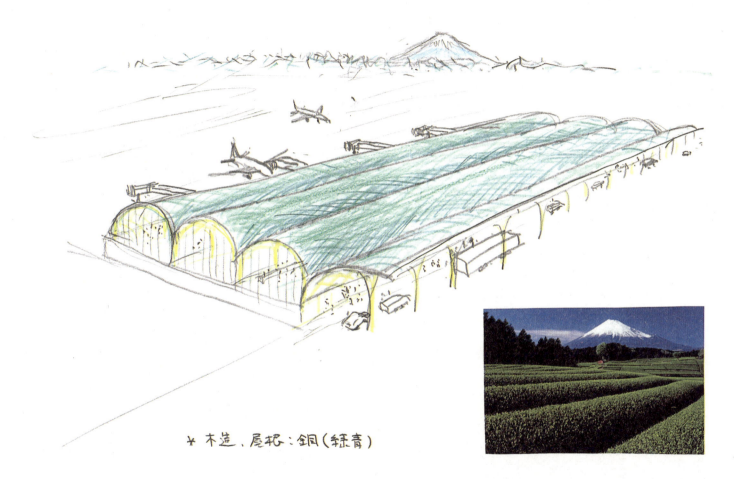

Roman's Spa
ローマンズ・スパ

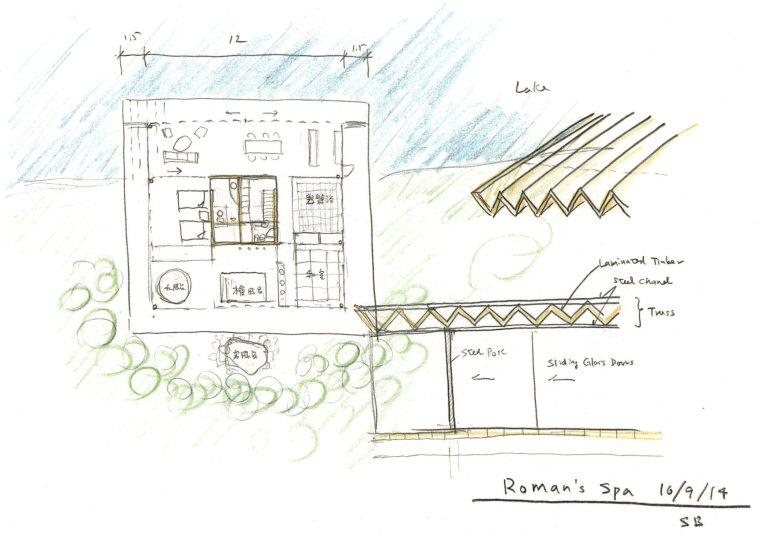

Roman's Spa 16/9/14
SB

Shishi-iwa House, Karuizawa
ししいわハウス

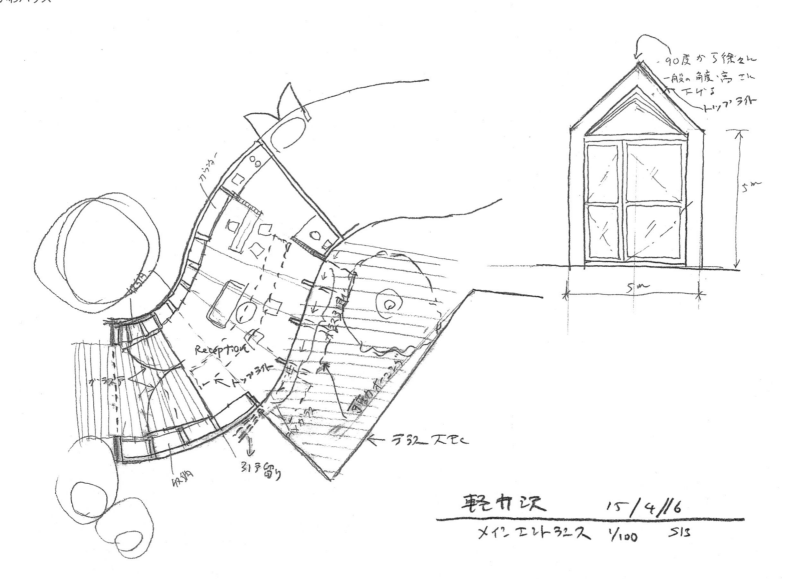

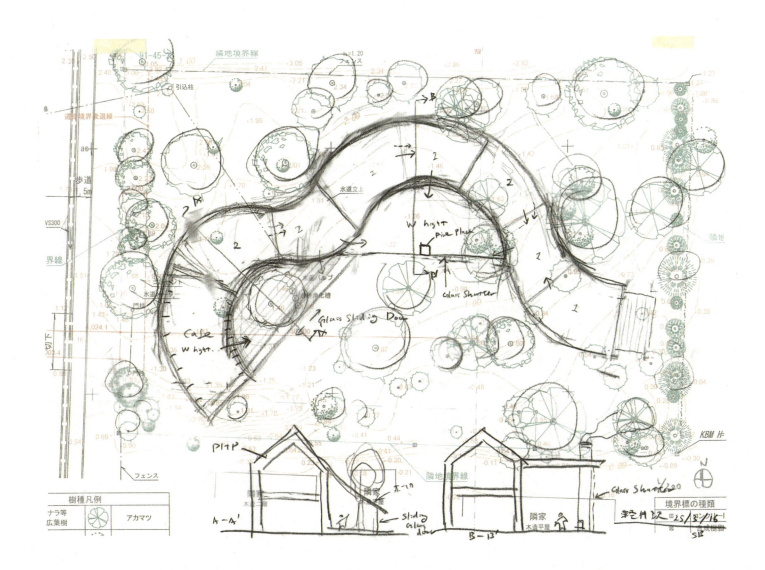

Self-Build House in Nepal
ネパール震災復興住宅

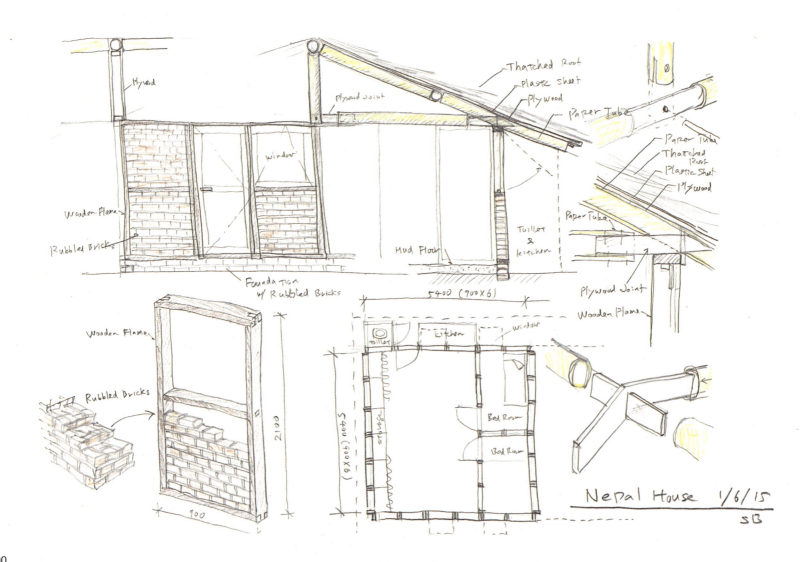

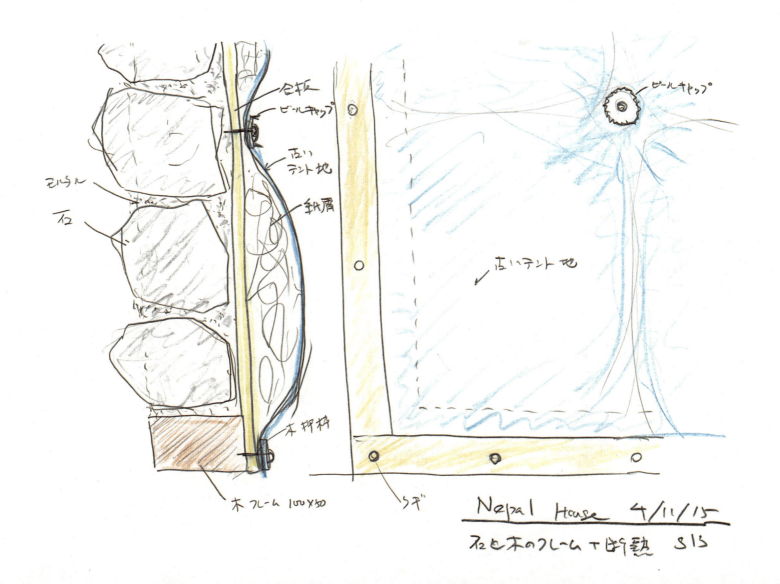

Nepal House 4/11/15
石と木のフレーム T断熱 S1:3

DMZ Bamboo Passage
DMZ 竹のパサージュ

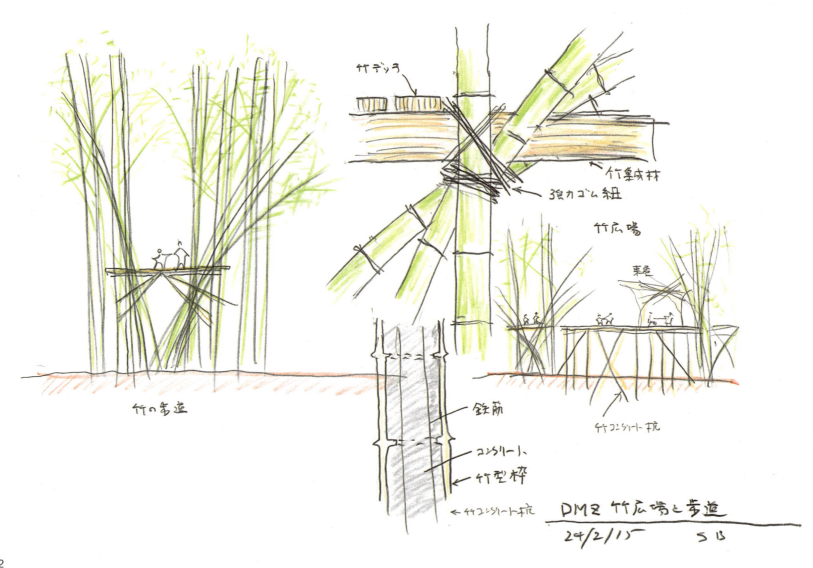

202

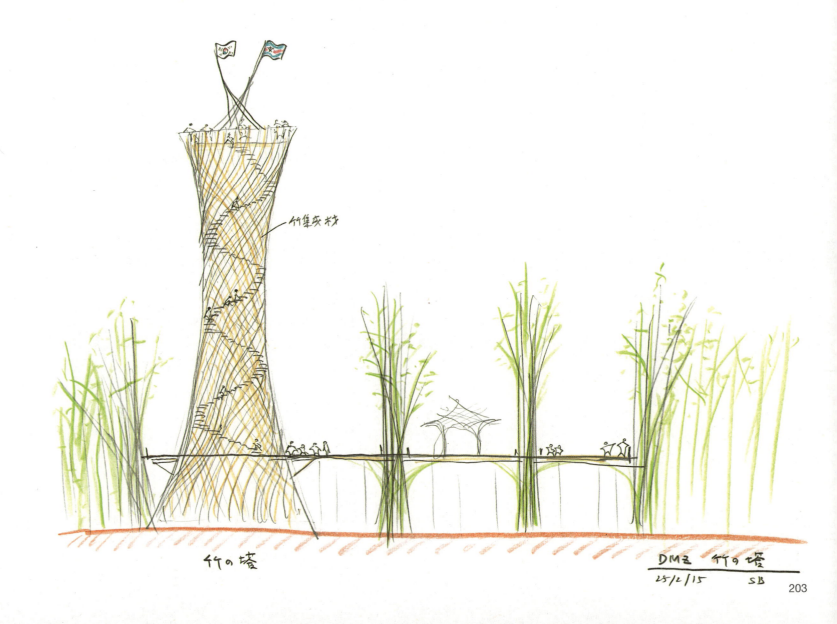

DMZ Bamboo Passage
DMZ 竹のパサージュ

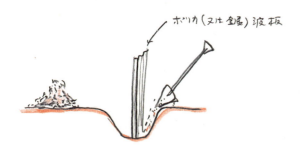

1. 波板を竹を植える境界に埋める。

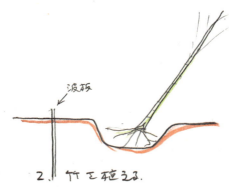

2. 竹を植える。

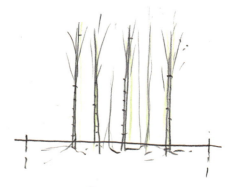

3. ある程度の長さ太さになるのを待つ。(初めに何メートルの竹を植えるかによる。)

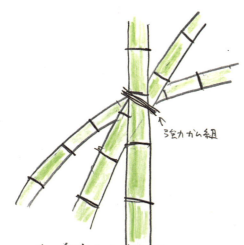

4. 何本かを束ねて強力ゴム紐(?)で結ぶ。

5. 竹集成材梁を軸に竹を固定する。

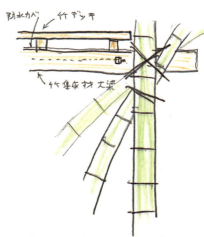

6. 竹集成材大梁に小梁や筋かいを入れ、竹のデッキを張る。

DMZ 竹の構造
組立てプロセス 25/2/15 S13

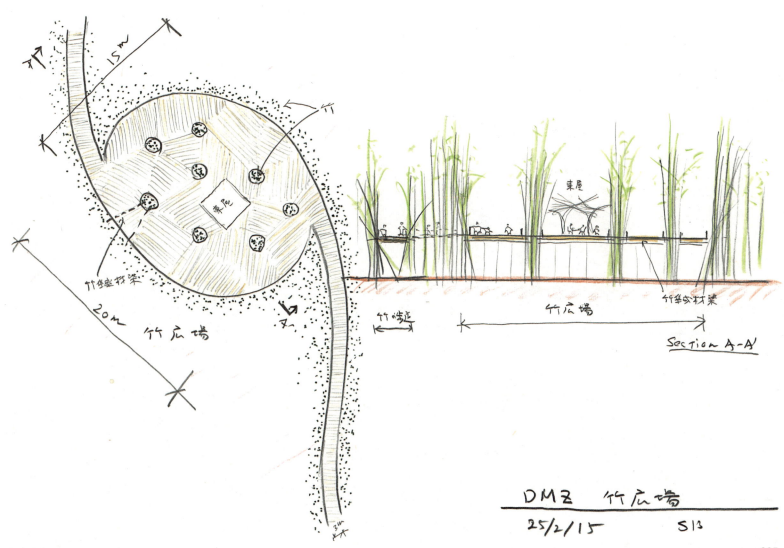

DMZ 竹広場
25/2/15   S13

Terrace House
テラスハウス

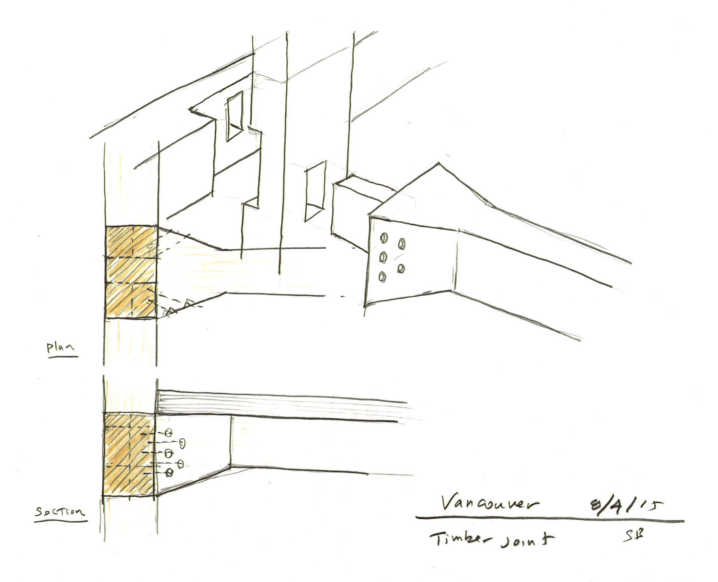

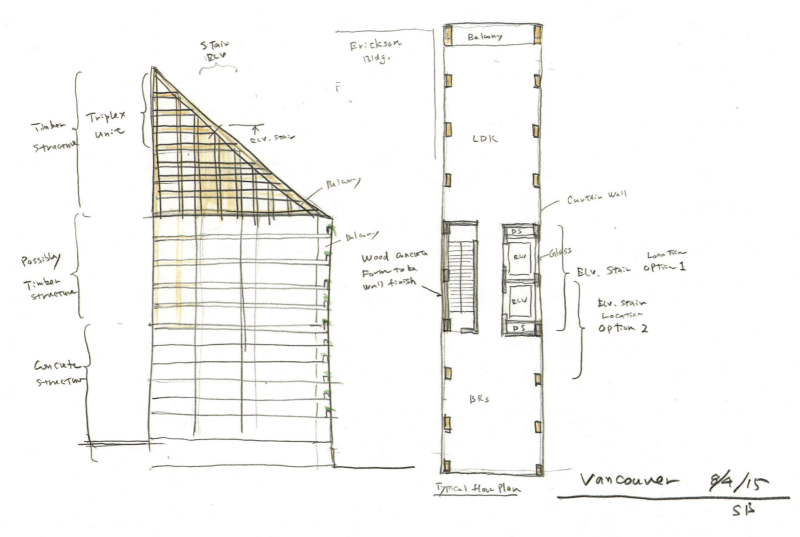

Expo 2020 Dubai Mobility Signature Pavilion
ドバイ国際博覧会 2020　モビリティパビリオン

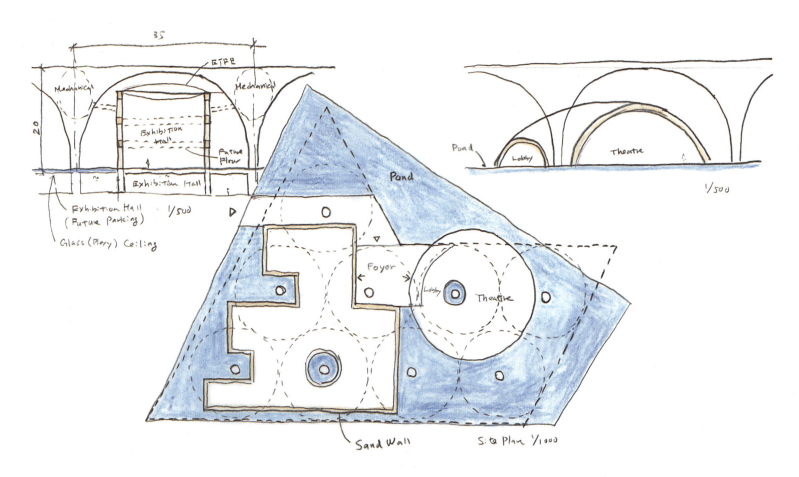

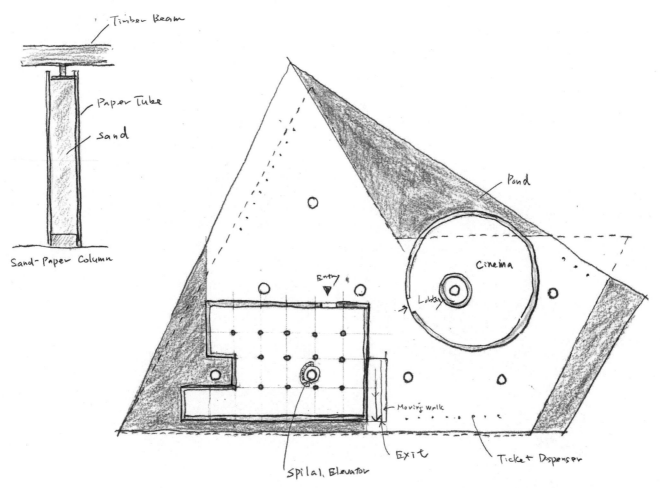

Expo 2020 Dubai Mobility Signature Pavilion
ドバイ国際博覧会 2020　モビリティパビリオン

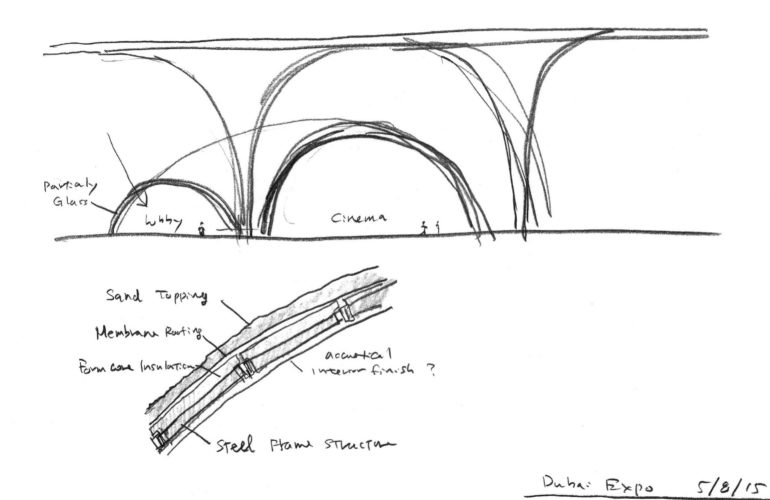

210

Temporary Church for the Philippines
仮設の教会　フィリピン

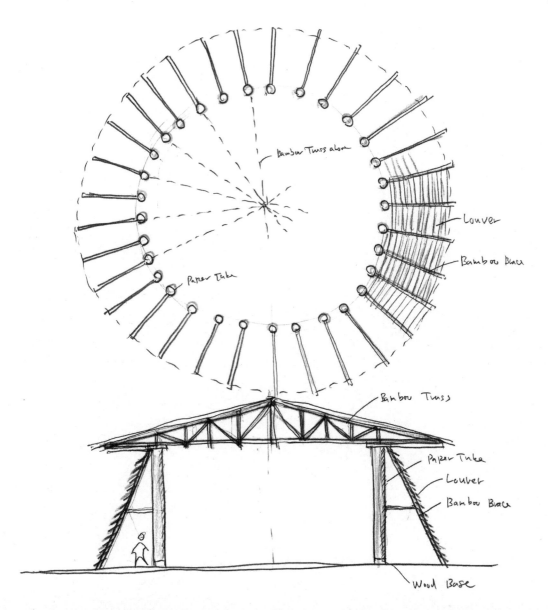

Triangle House
三角の家

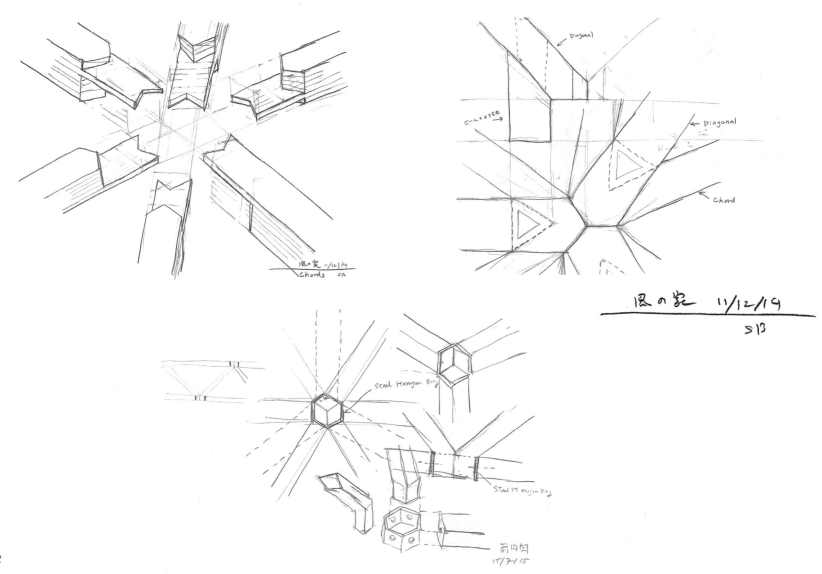

Tainan Art Museum
台南市美術館

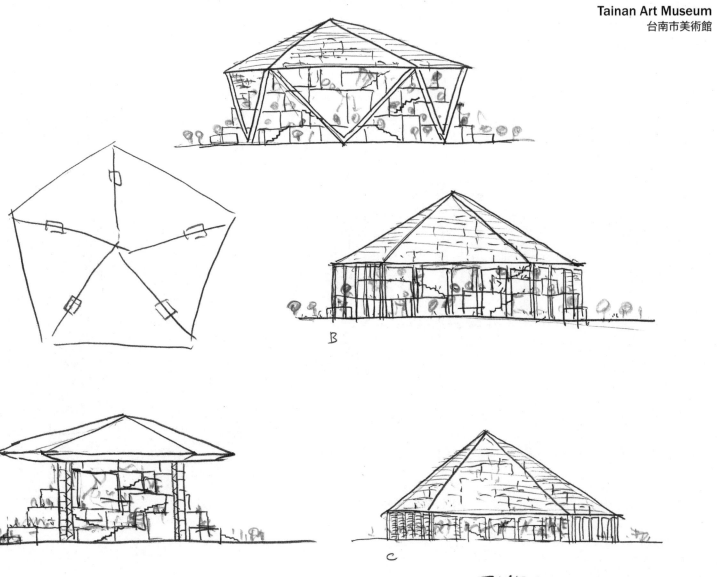

TMFA 7/8/14

Zenith
ゼニス

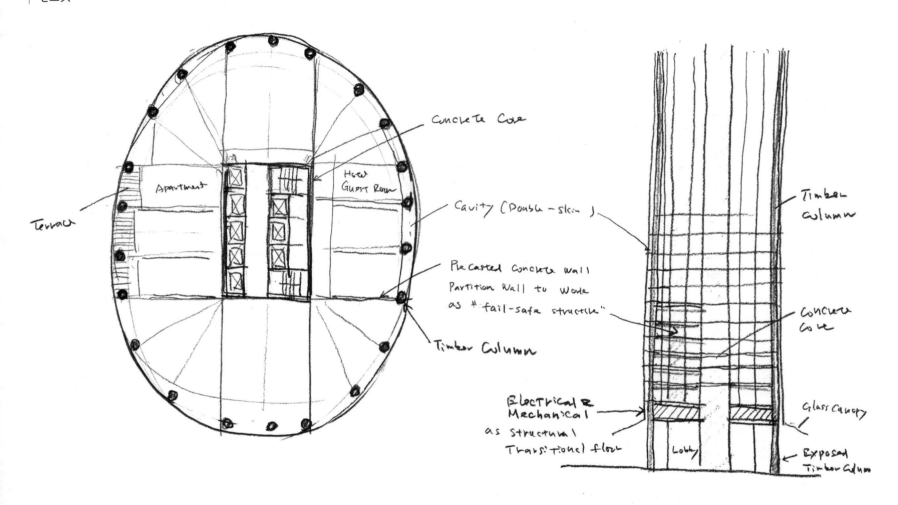

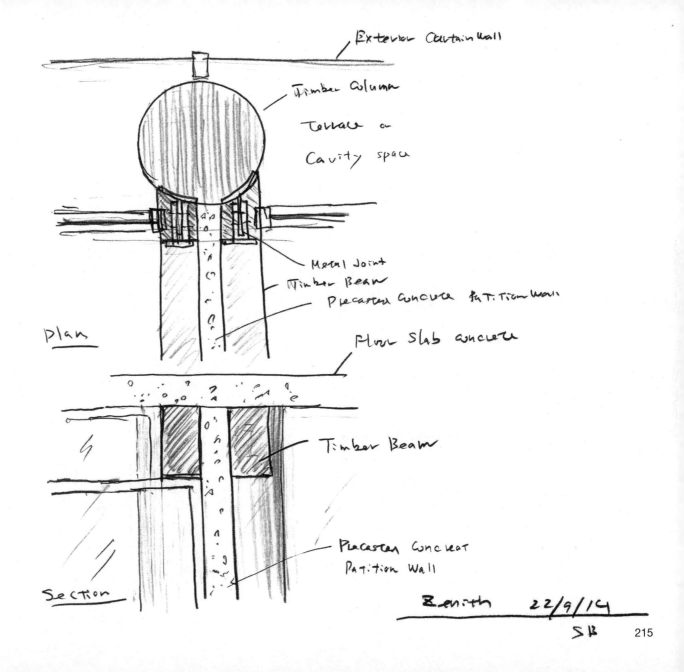

Shonai Hotel Suiden Terrasse
ショウナイホテル スイデンテラス

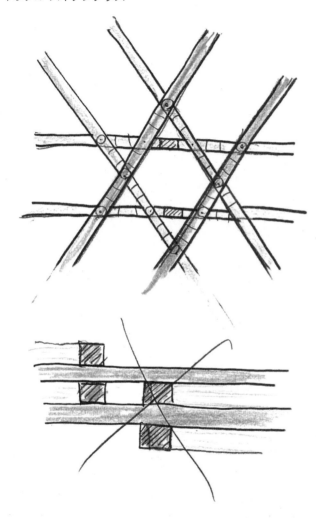

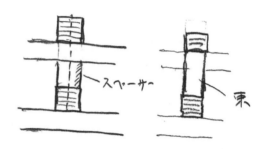

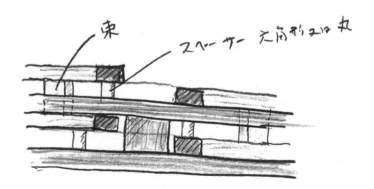

Bath House 13/2/17
spybel SB

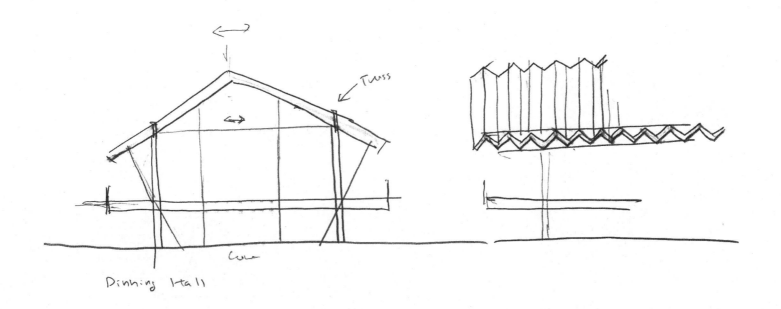

Dinning Hall

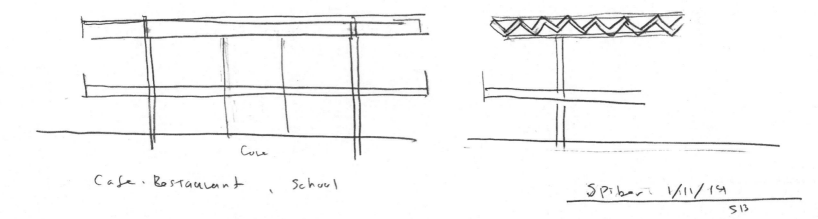

Cafe, Restaurant, School

Spibert 1/11/19
513

Shonai Hotel Suiden Terrasse
ショウナイホテル スイデンテラス

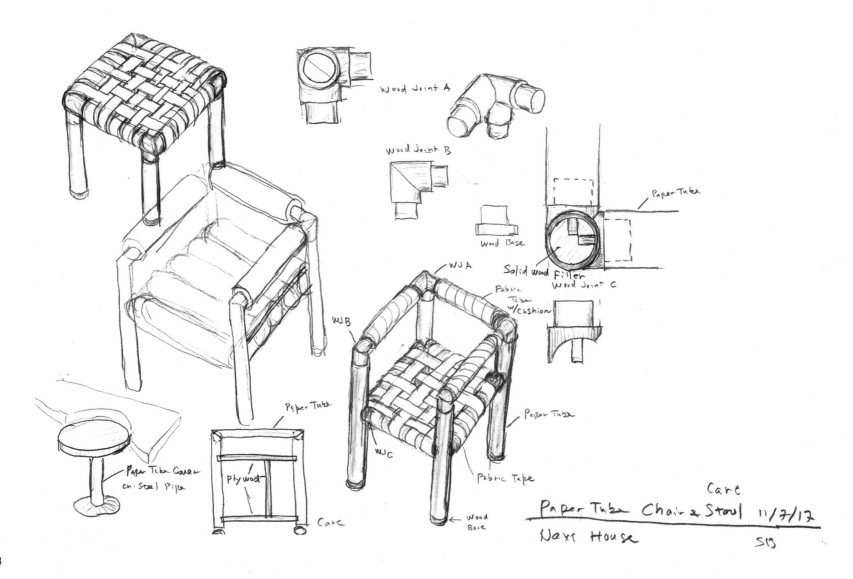

Monaco Cable Car Mid Station
モナコケーブルカー駅

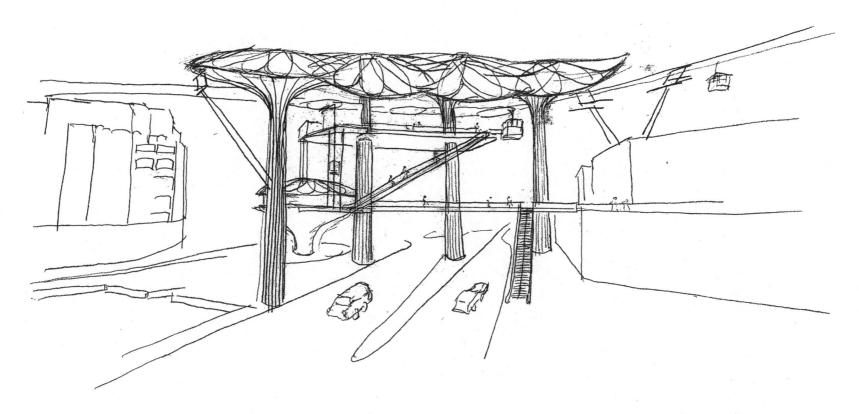

Monaco Mid-Station 18/12/15
SB

Monaco Cable Car Mid Station
モナコケーブルカー駅

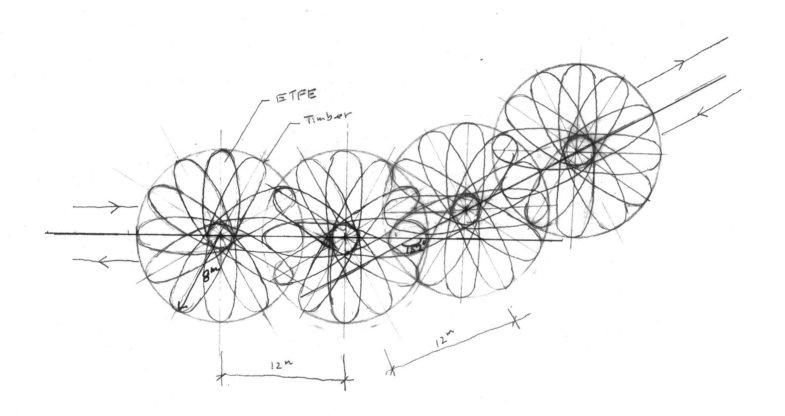

220

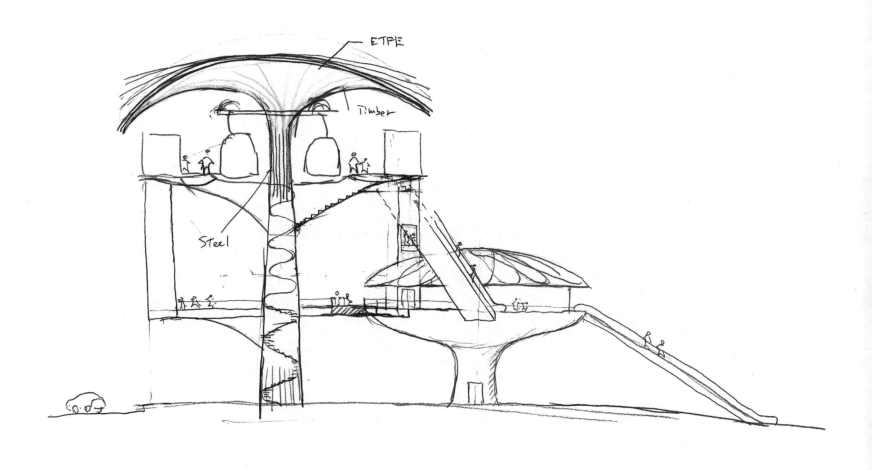

Monaco Mid-Station 18/12/15
S13

Monaco Cable Car Mid Station
モナコケーブルカー駅

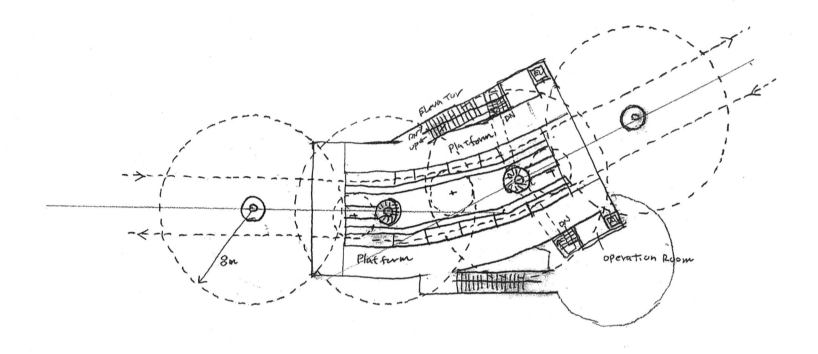

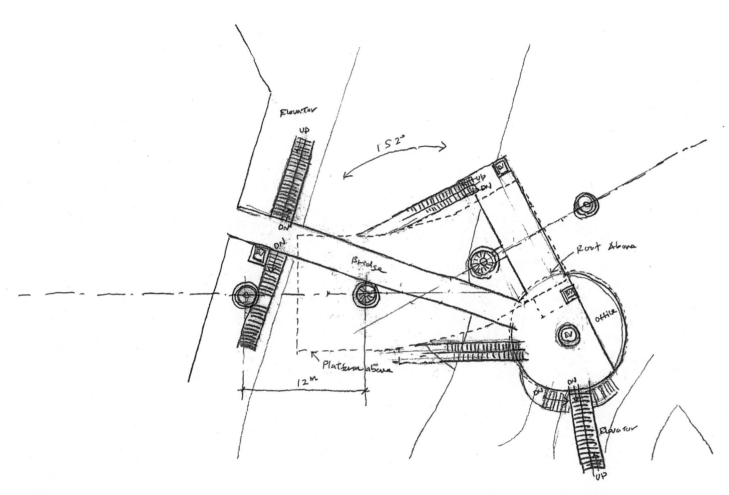

Monaco Mid-station 17/12/15
Bridge Level 1/300 S13

Monaco Cable Car Mid Station
モナコケーブルカー駅

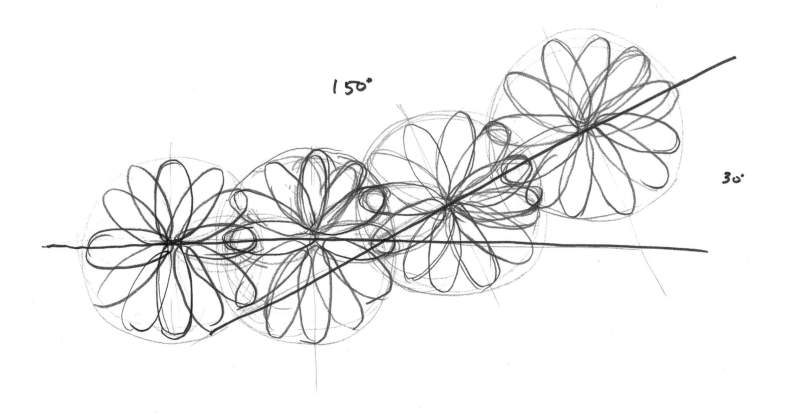

Monaco Cable Car Mid Station
モナコケーブルカー駅

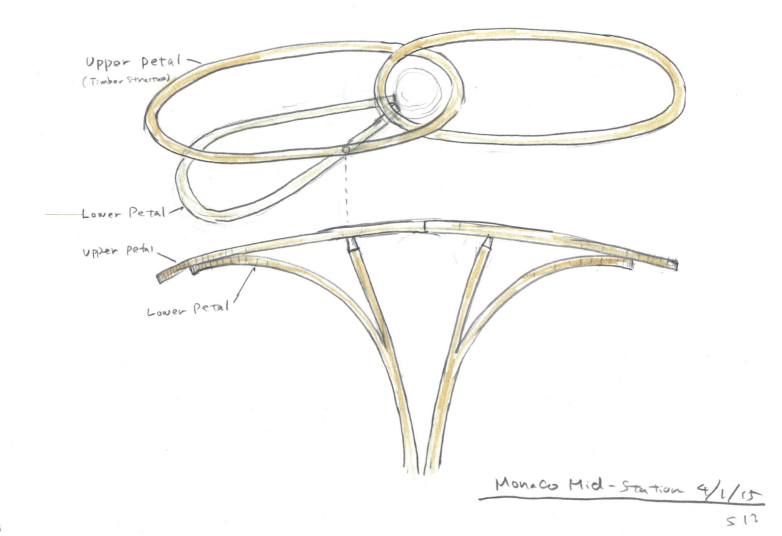

Sully Morland's Concert & Performance Hall
シュリー・モルラン・コンサート＆パフォーマンスホール

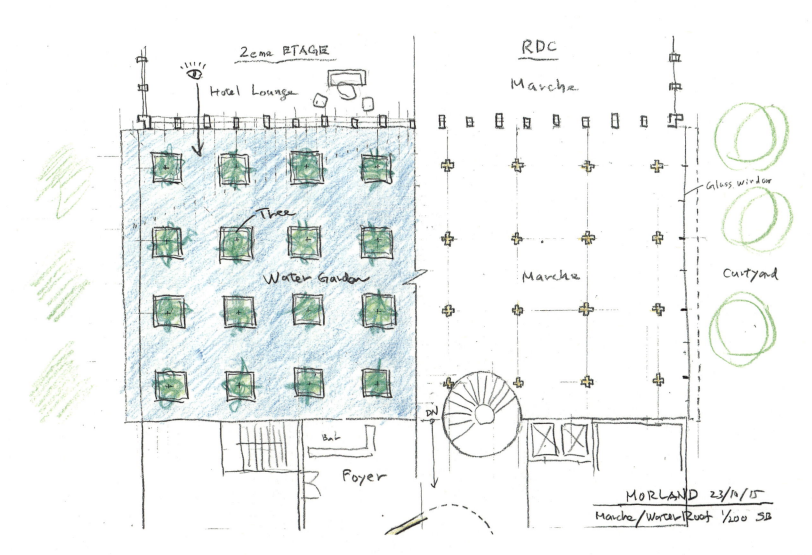

Sully Morland's Concert & Performance Hall
シュリー・モルラン・コンサート＆パフォーマンスホール

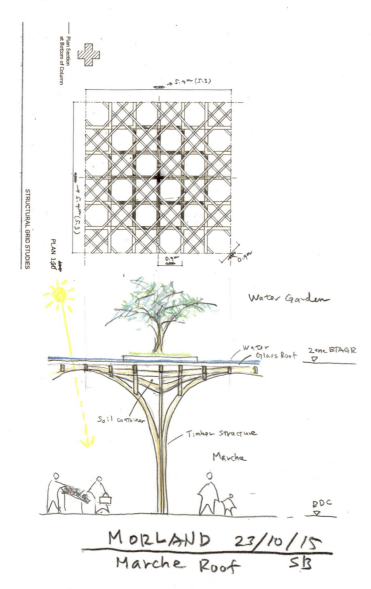

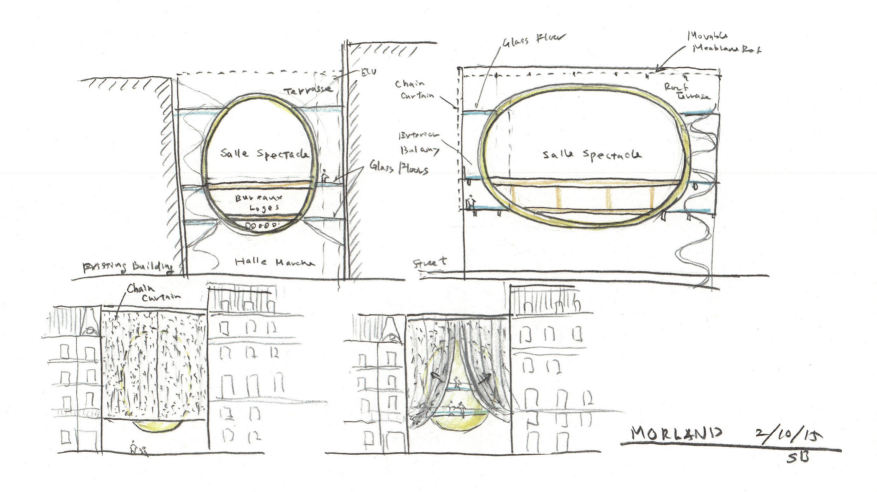

Sully Morland's Concert & Performance Hall
シュリー・モルラン・コンサート＆パフォーマンスホール

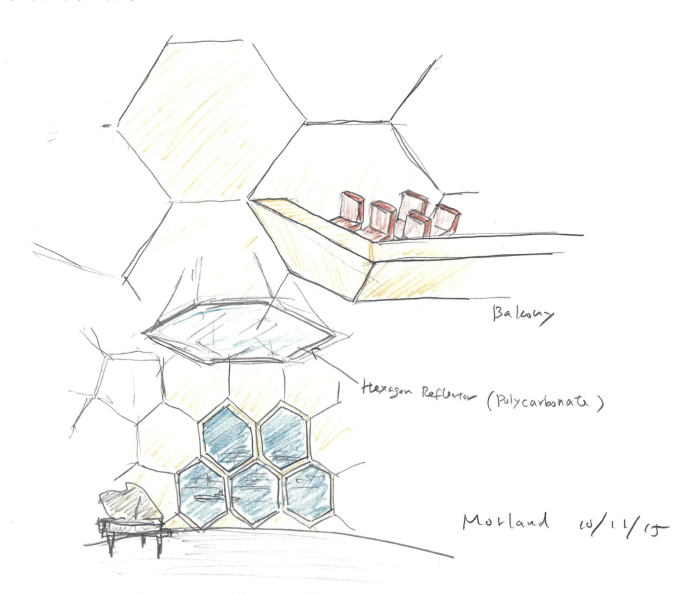

Kur Park Nagayu
クアパーク長湯

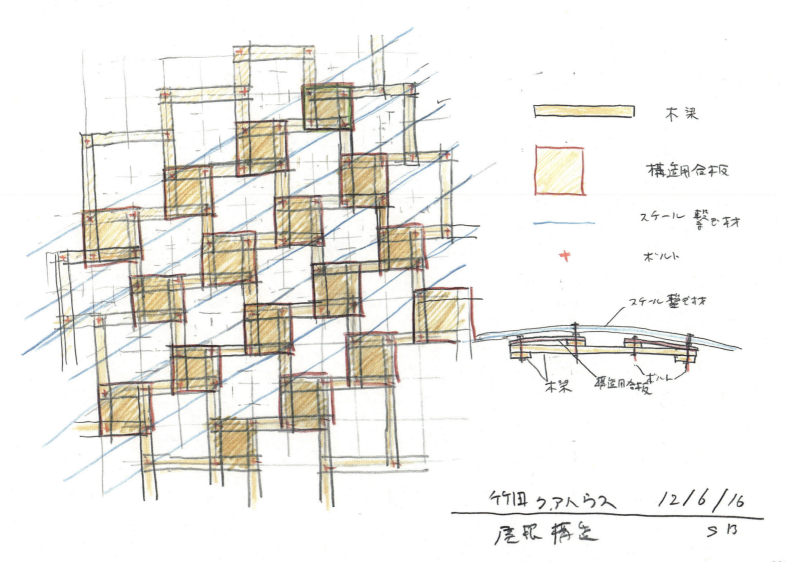

Kur Park Nagayu
クアパーク長湯

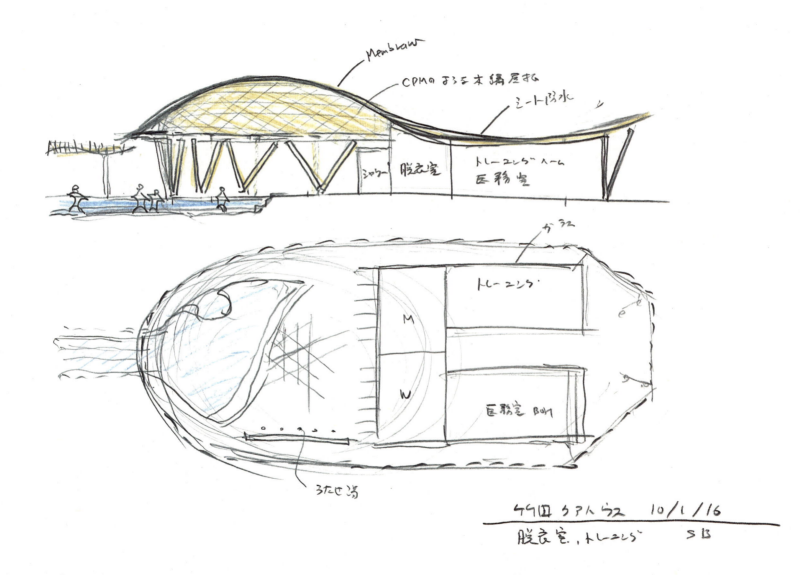

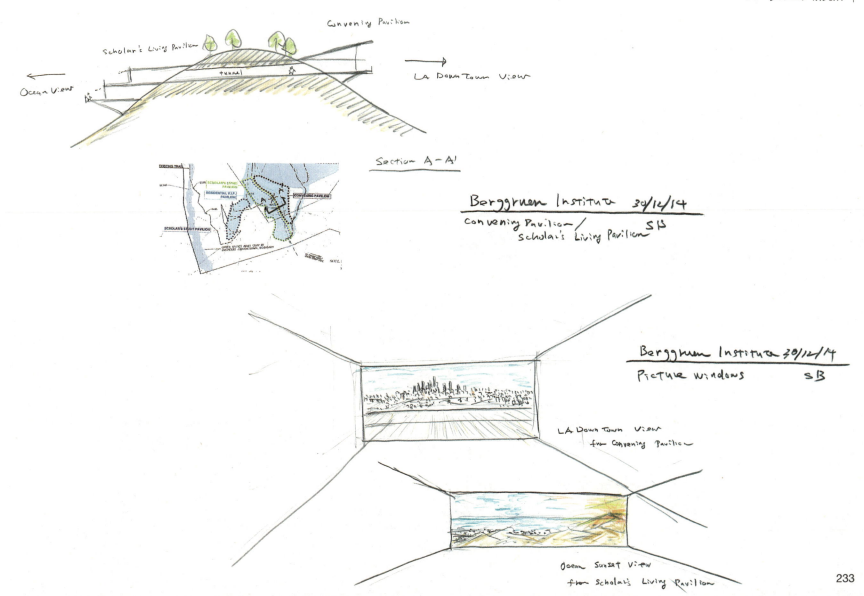

Paper Shelter for Nepal
ネパール復興住宅

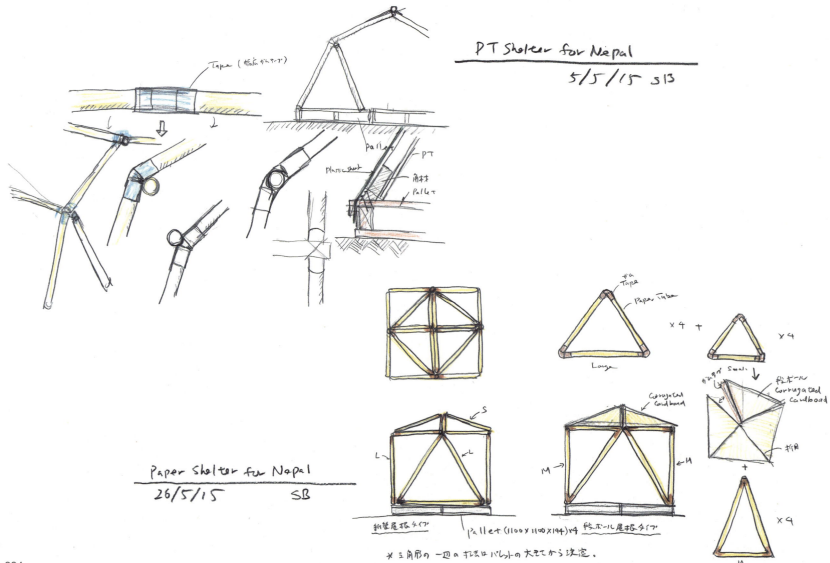

Haesley Hamlet
ヘスリー・ハムレット

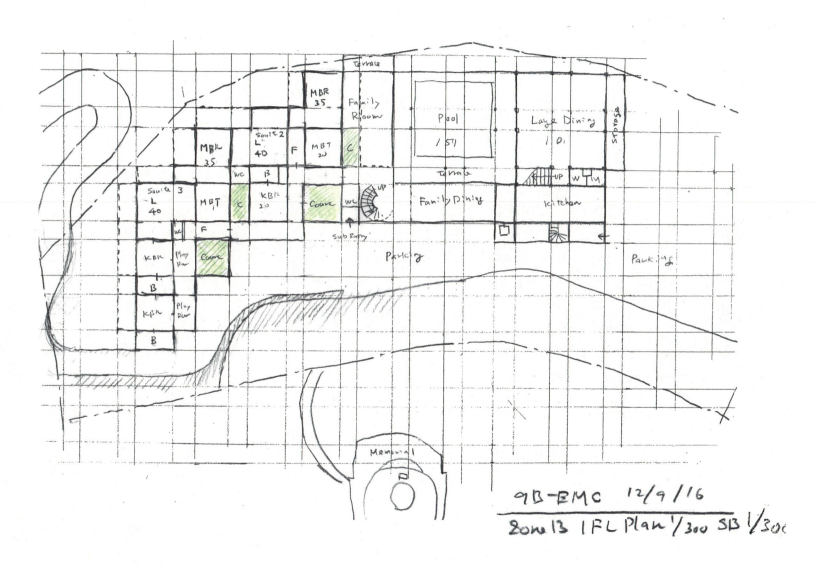

Haesley Hamlet
ヘスリー・ハムレット

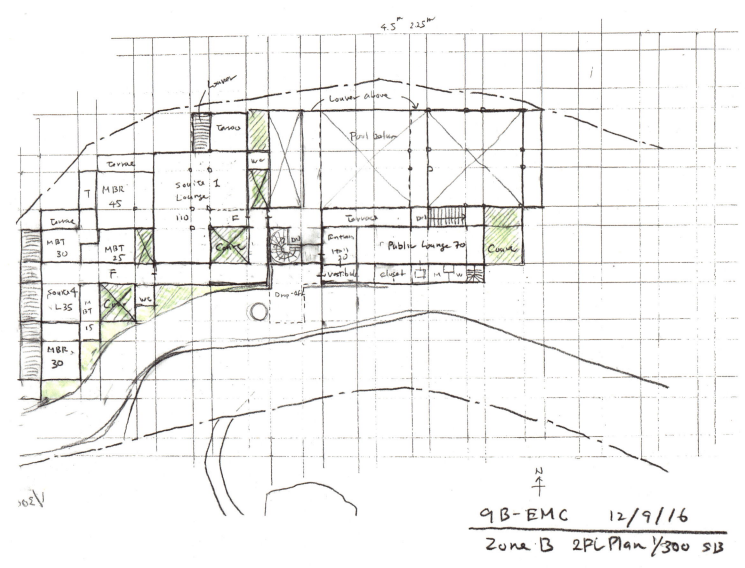

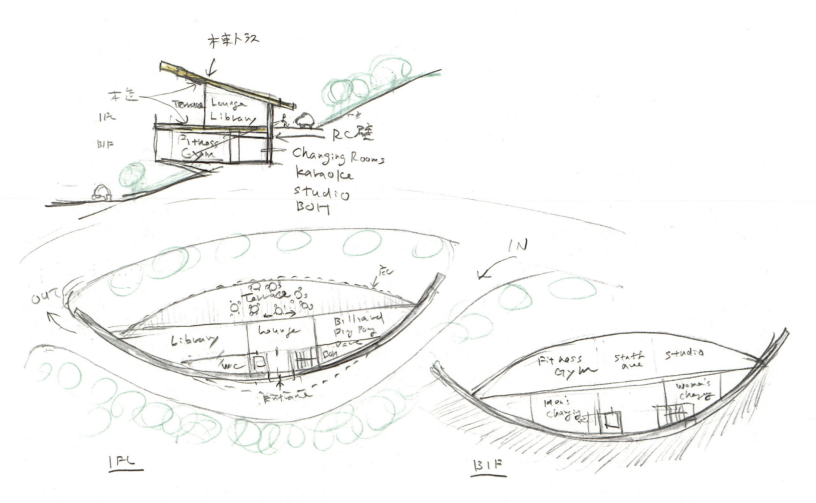

Haesley Hamlet
ヘスリー・ハムレット

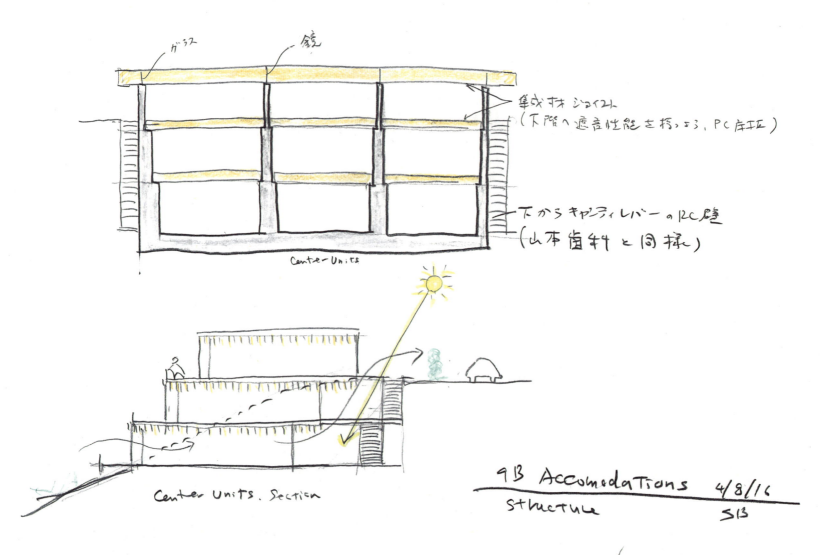

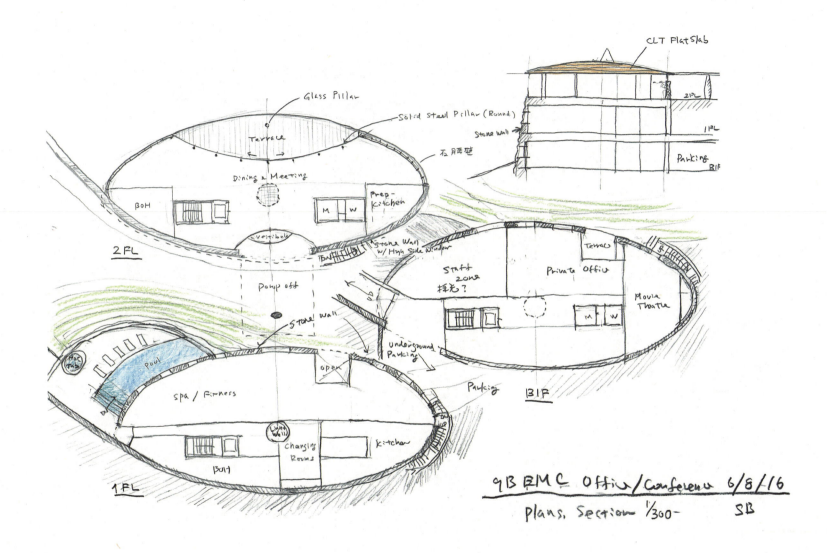

Haesley Hamlet
ヘスリー・ハムレット

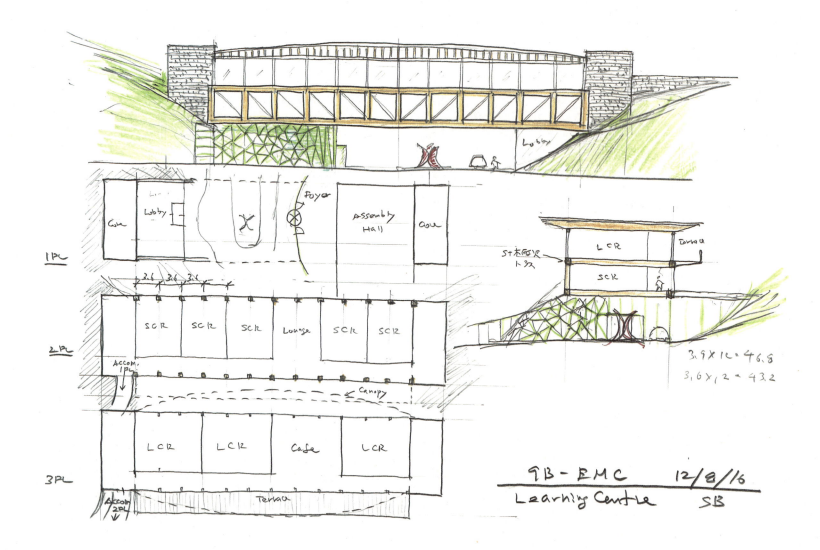

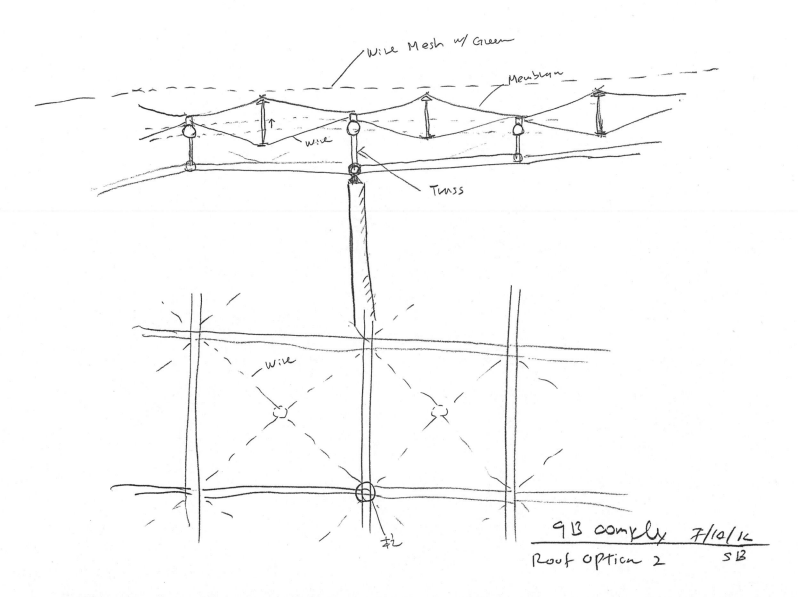

Haesley Hamlet
ヘスリー・ハムレット

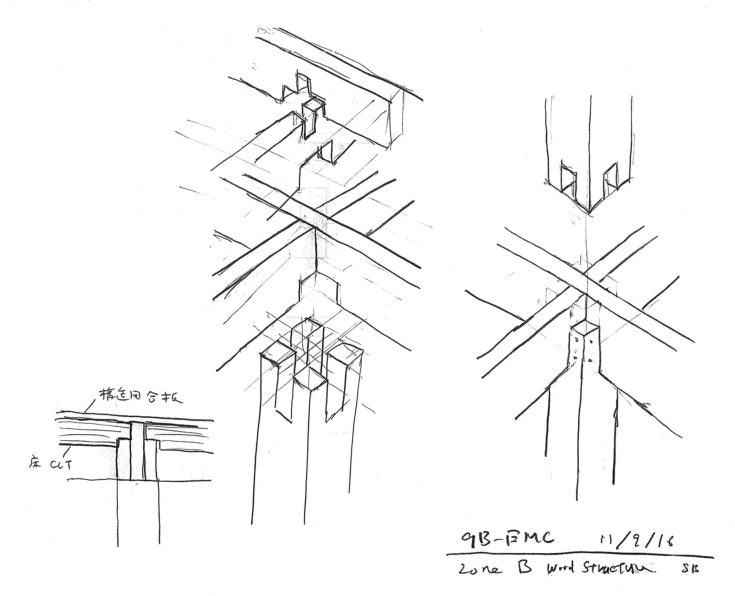

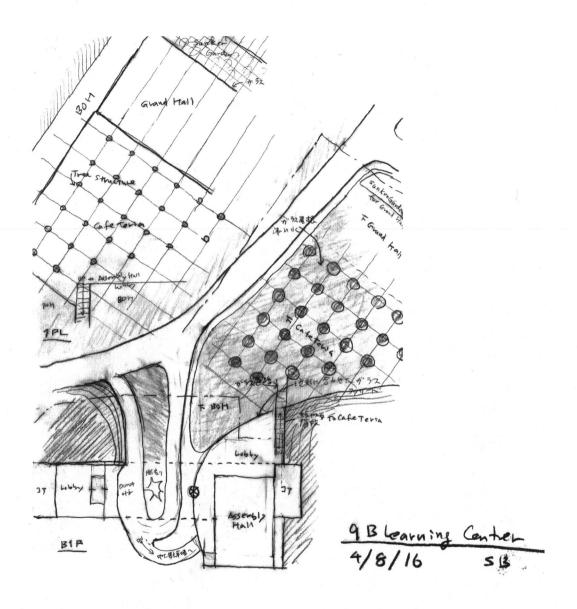

Art Biotop – Suite Villa
アートビオトープ・スイートヴィラ

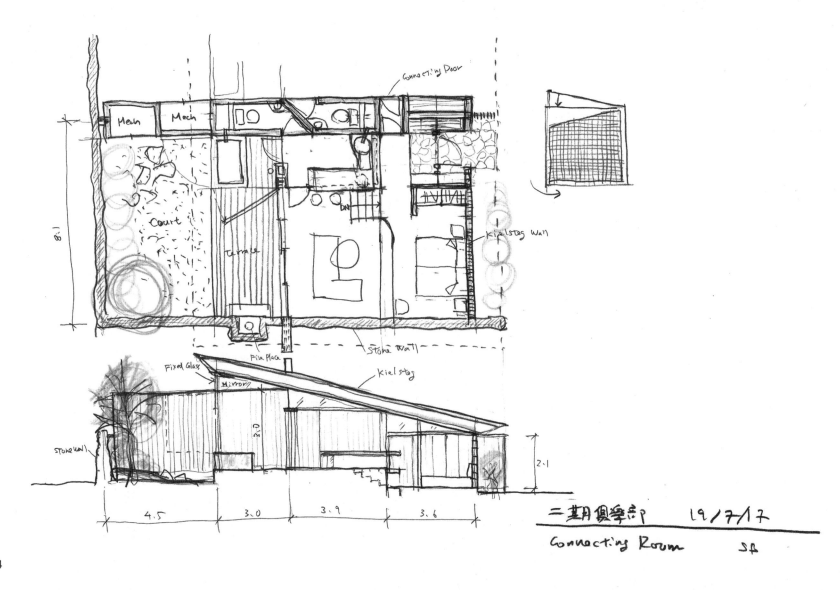

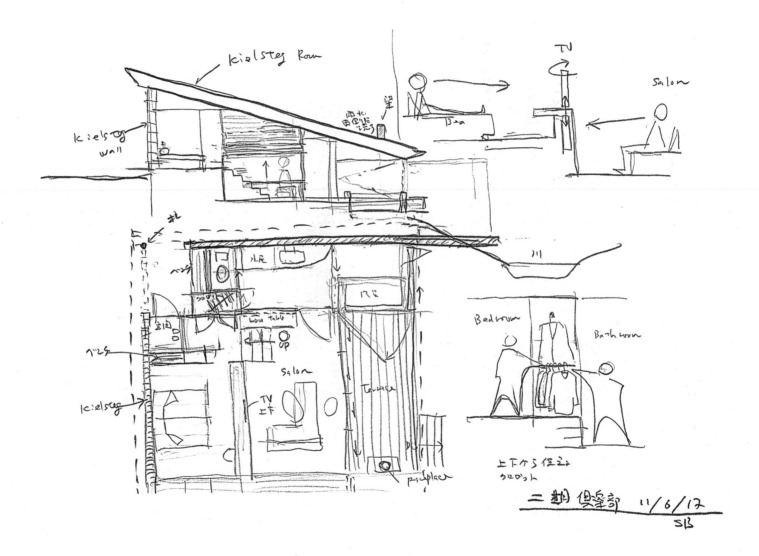

Kentuck Knob Reception Pavilion
ケンタック・ノブ　レセプション・パビリオン

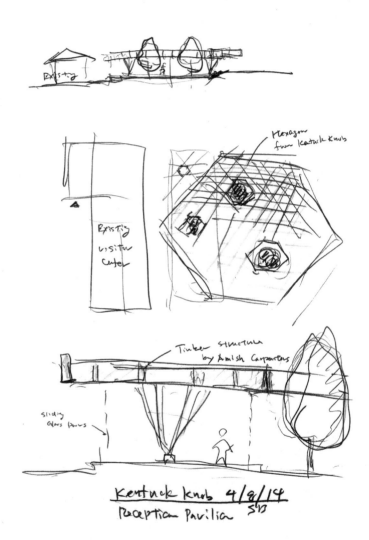

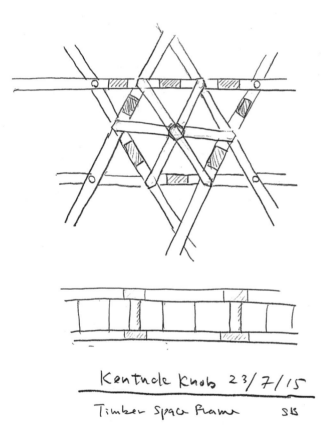

House in Auckland
オークランドの家

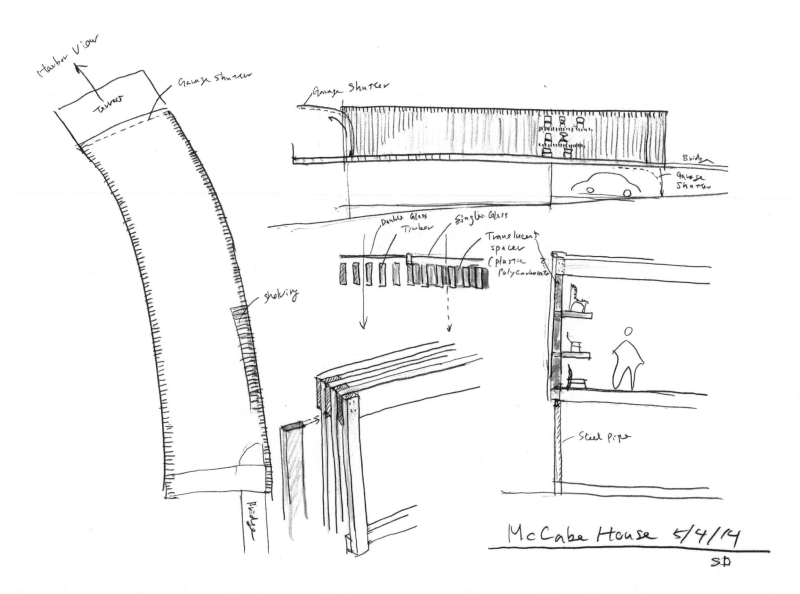

McCabe House 5/4/14
S.D.

NSY/Victoria Street
NSY/ヴィクトリア・ストリート

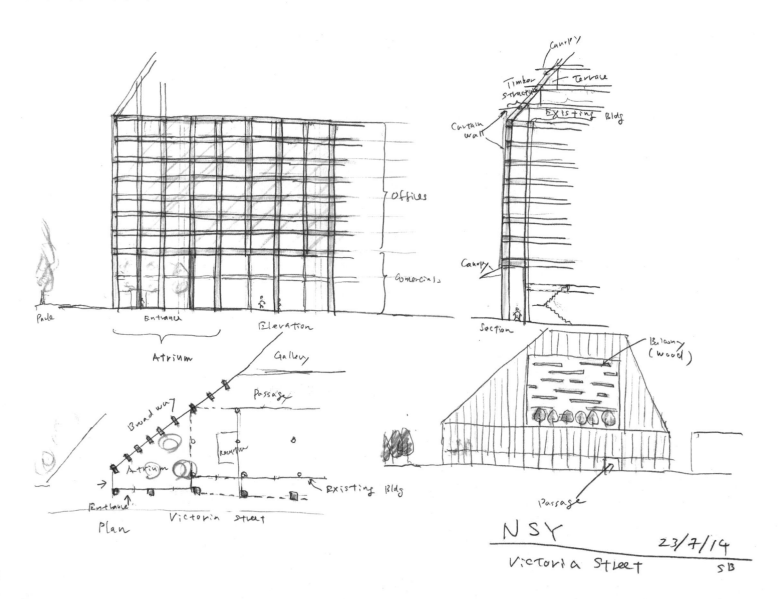

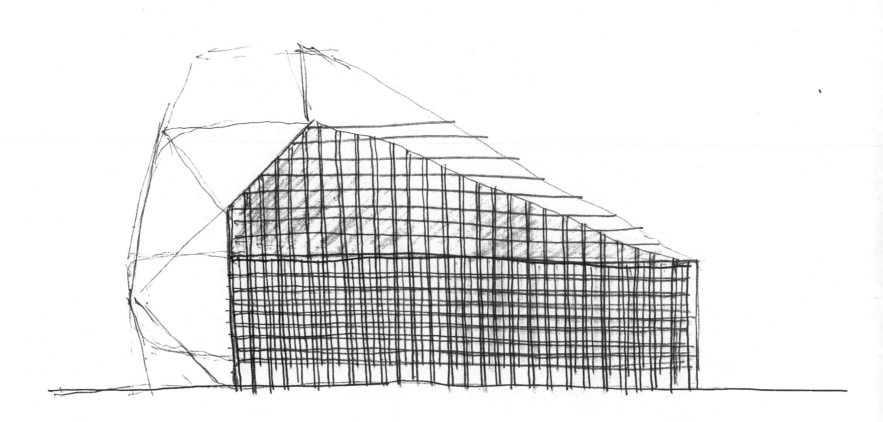

249

Le Monde Headquarters
ル・モンド本社

Enternity

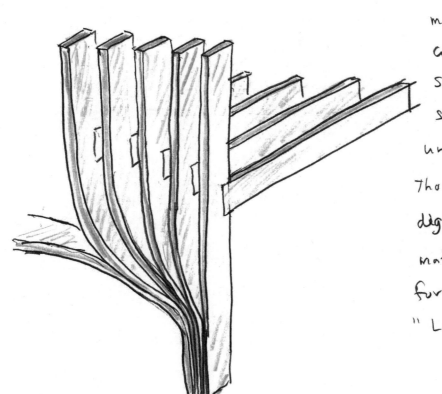

Both Concrete and Steel are structural materials which are consumed from limited sources. Wood is only structural material with unlimited sources.

Though the advance of current digital technology, the printed matter on paper should be kept for ever as the spirit of "Le Monde" is eternal.

Yufu City Tourist Information Center
由布市ツーリストインフォメーションセンター

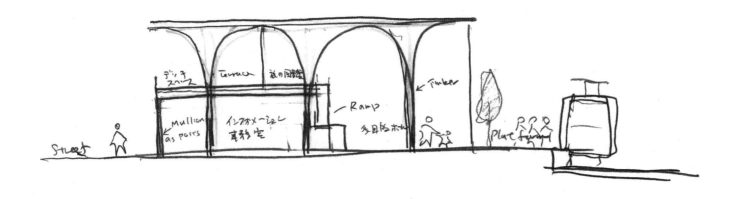

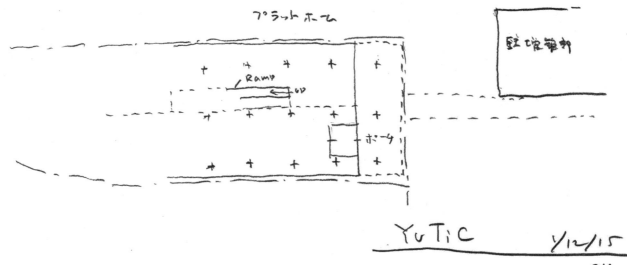

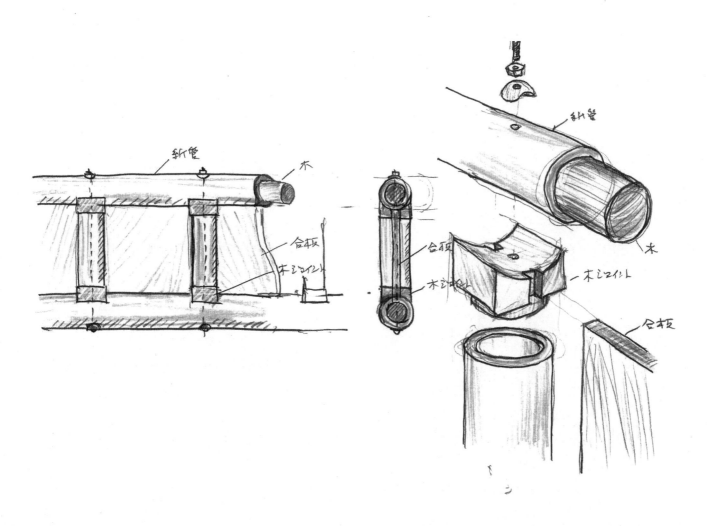

由布院ツーリストインフォメーションセンター
新管トラス   8/9/15 SB

Chrystie Street Residences
クリスティー・ストリート集合住宅

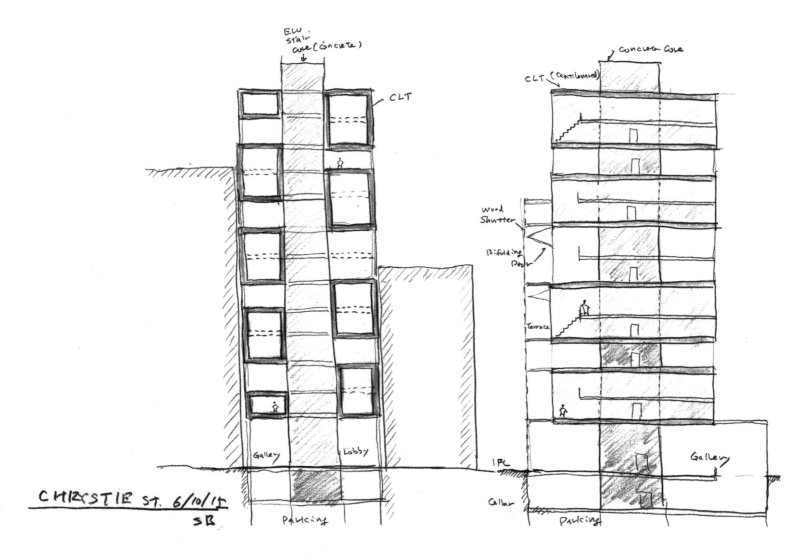

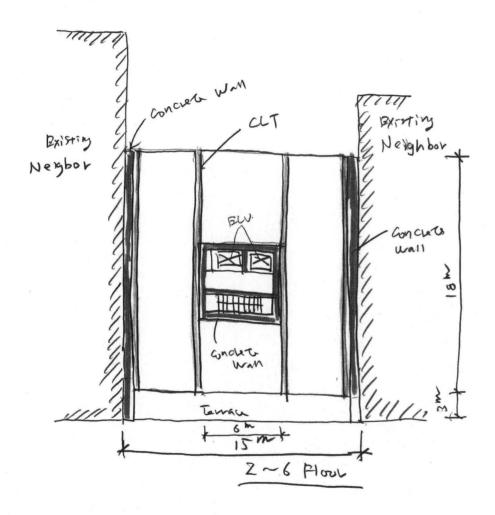
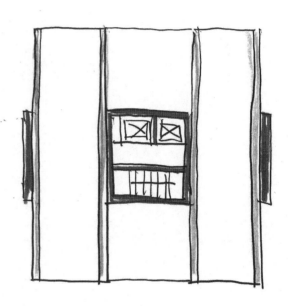

CHRYSTIE ST. 11/10/15
Floor plans   SB

Oita Prefectural Sports Arena
大分県立屋内スポーツ施設

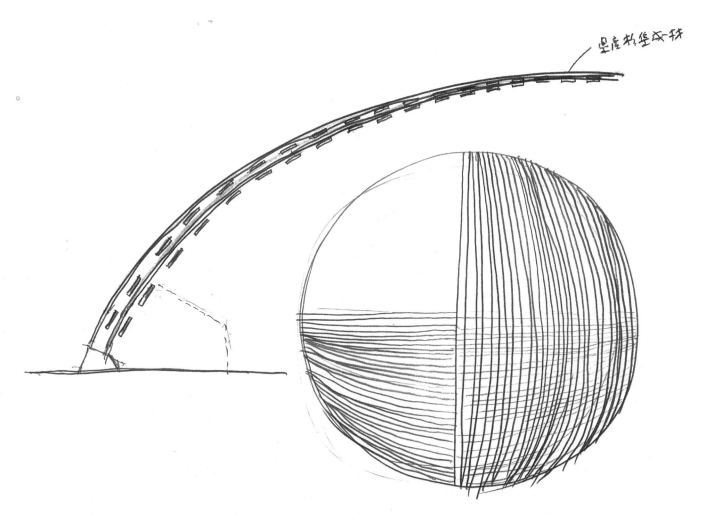

256

Mokuzai/Bouscat
モクザイ / ブスキャ

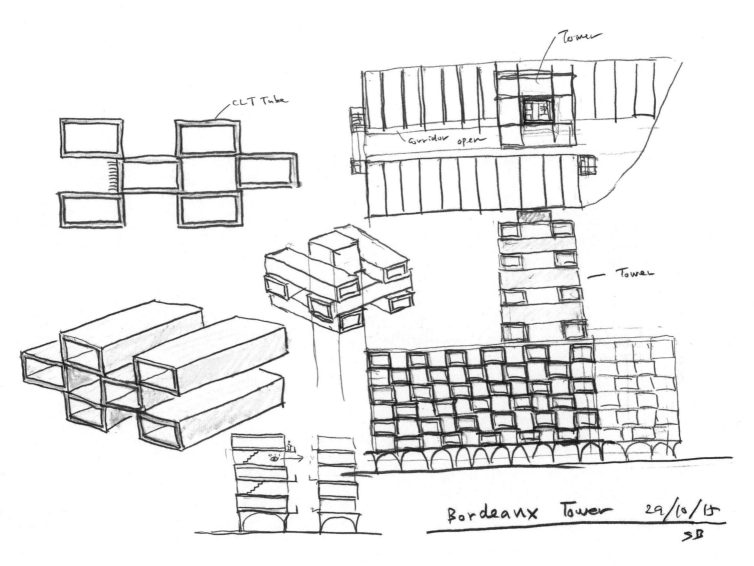

Camper Mallorca
カンペール　マヨルカ

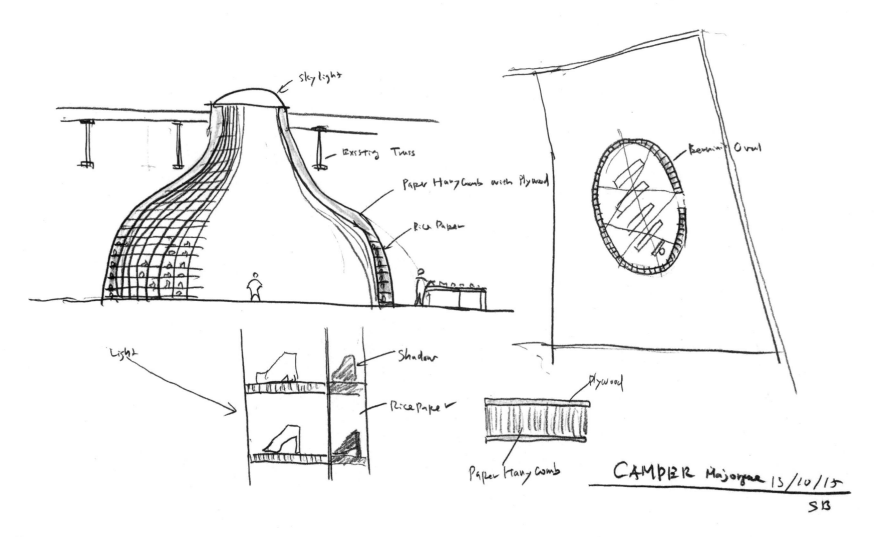

Varna One Table
ヴァルナ・ワン・テーブル

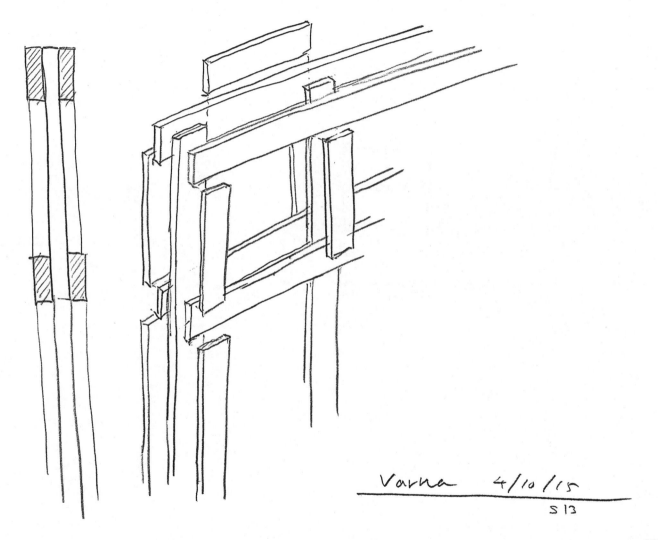

Varna One Table
ヴァルナ・ワン・テーブル

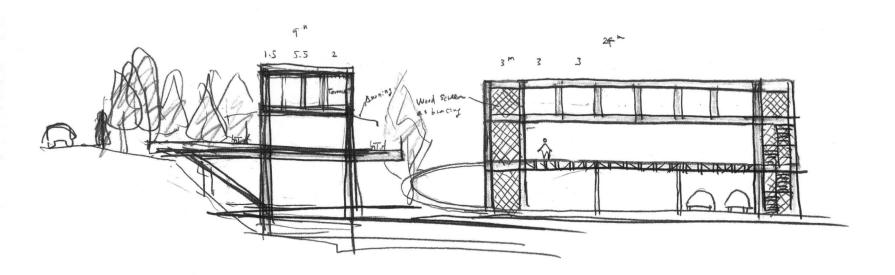

260

Potters Fields House
ポッターズ・フィールズ・ハウス

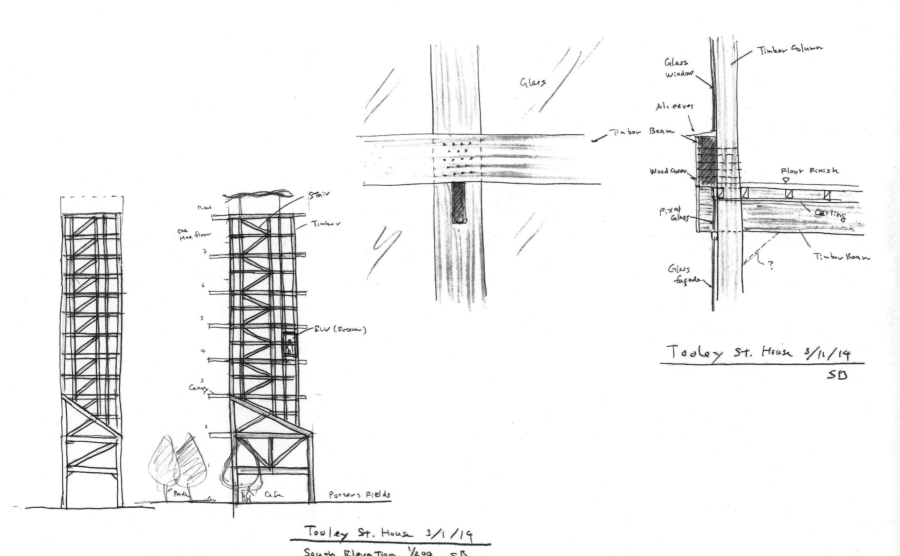

Sebastiao Salgado Exhibition
セバスチャン・サルガド展

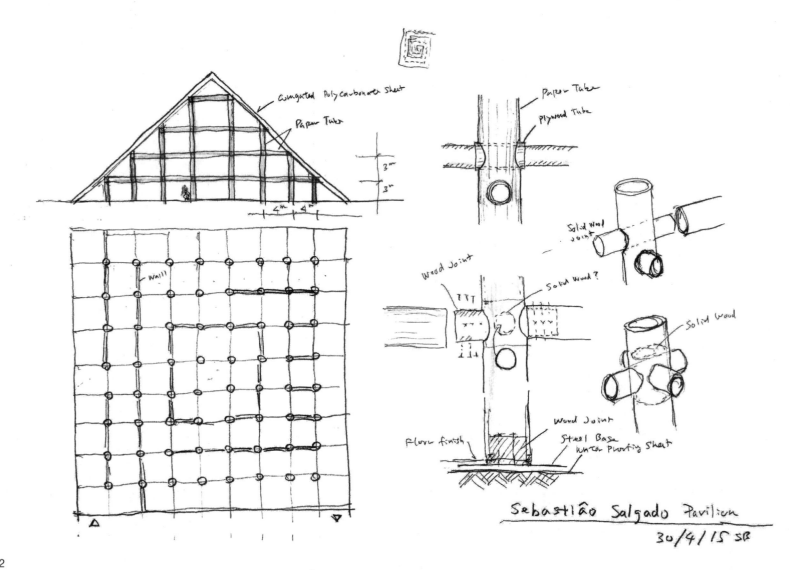

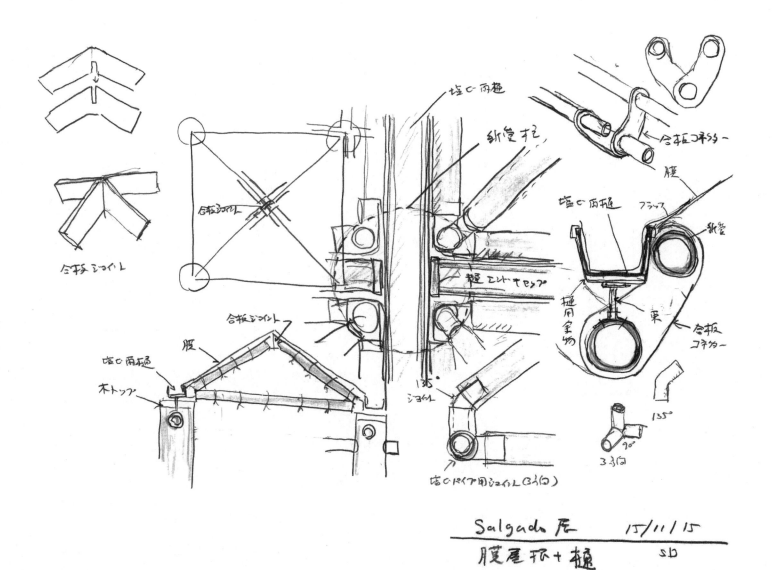

Sebastiao Salgado Exhibition
セバスチャン・サルガド展

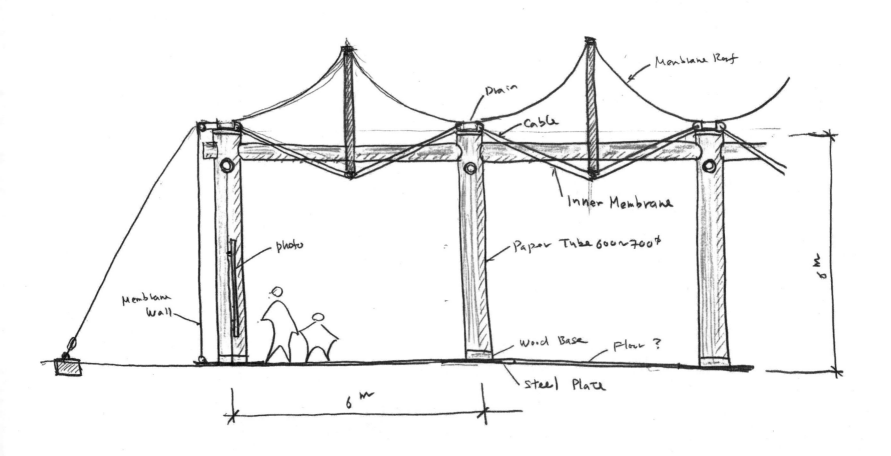

SBC Dome (SFC)
SBC ドーム

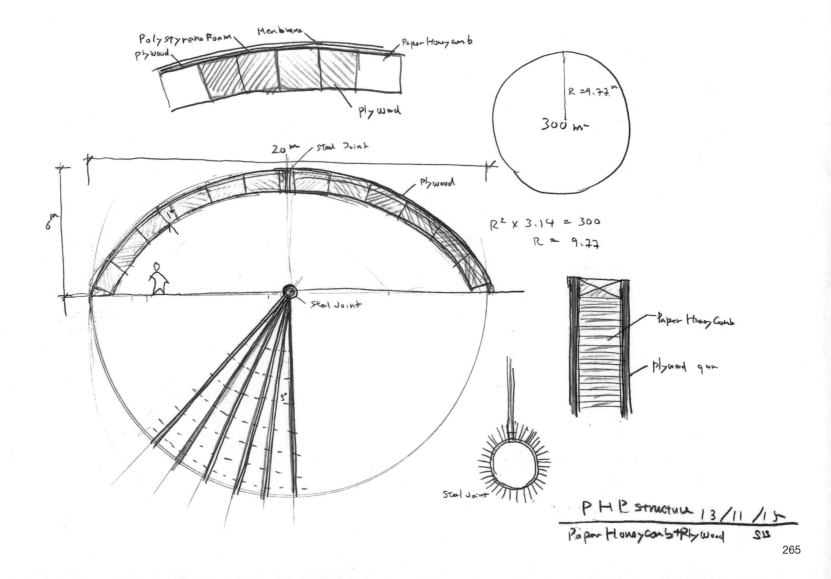

Wooden Prefabricated Temporary Housing for Kumamoto
熊本地震木造仮設住宅

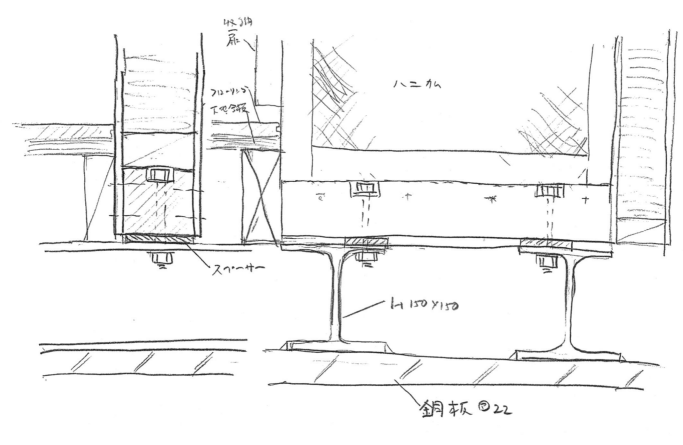

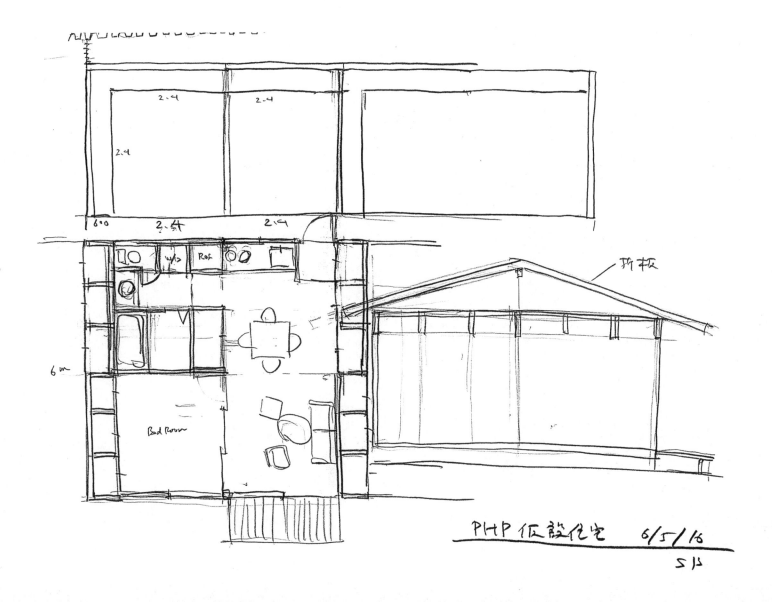

PHP仮設住宅 6/5/10

Wooden Prefabricated Temporary Housing for Kumamoto
熊本地震木造仮設住宅

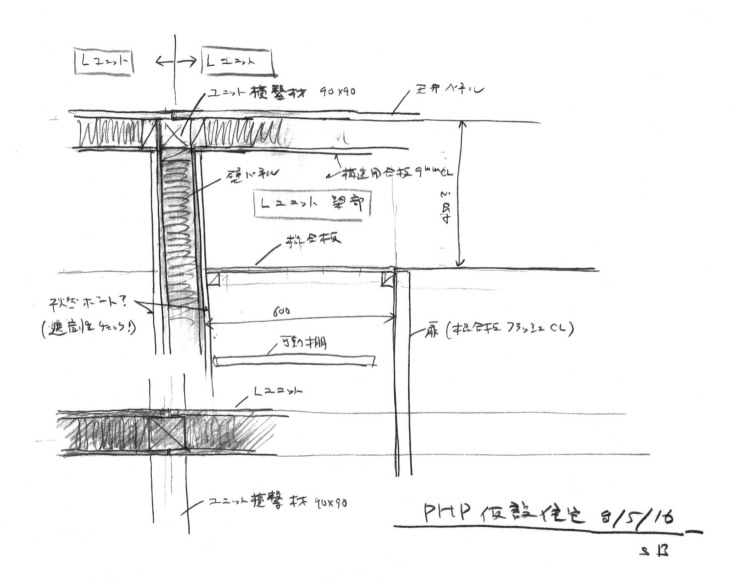

Europaris Tower
ユーロパリス・タワー

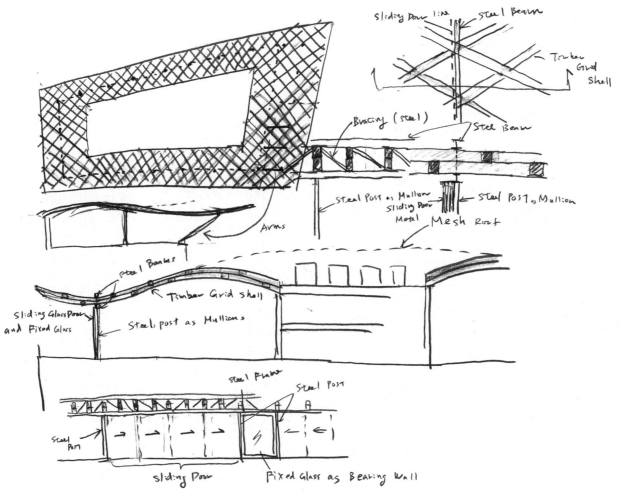

Europaris Tower
Roof Structure
26/4/16
SB

Europaris Tower
ユーロパリス・タワー

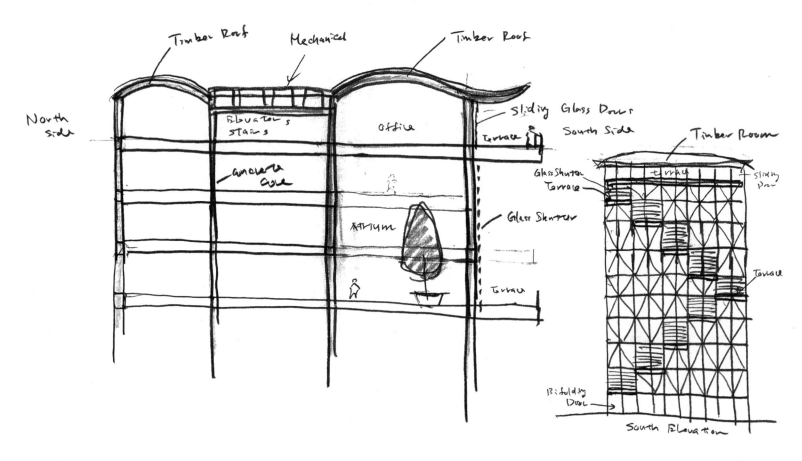

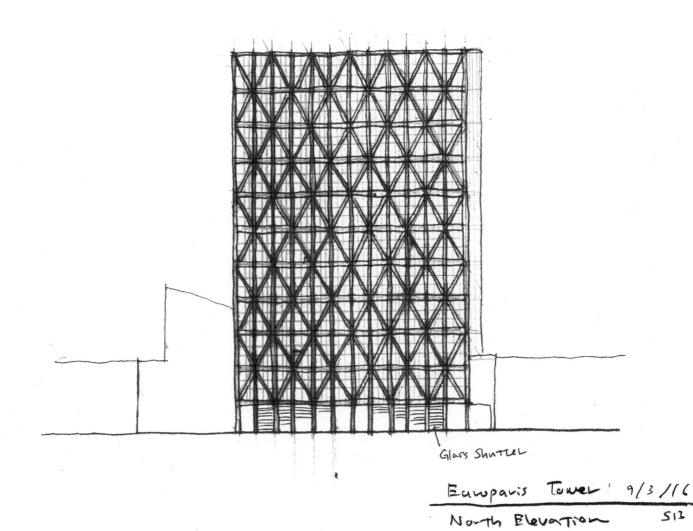

Glass Shuttel

Europaris Tower   9/3/16
North Elevation   S12

Europaris Tower
ユーロパリス・タワー

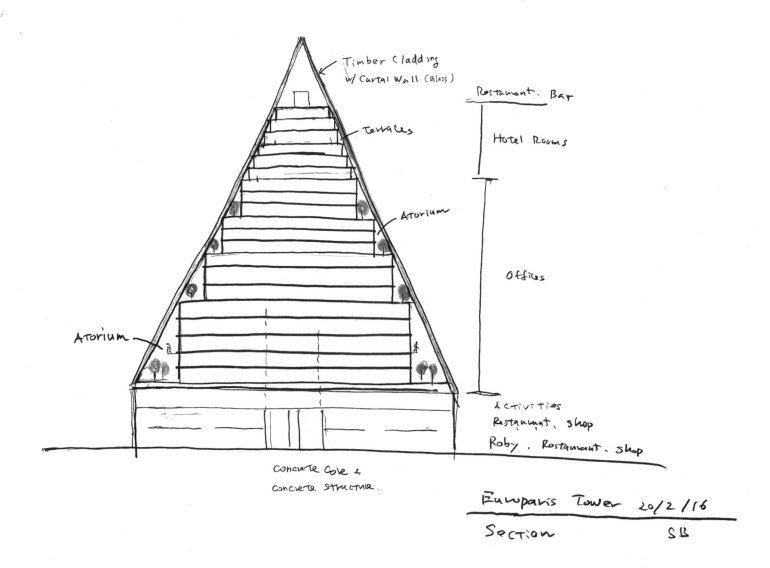

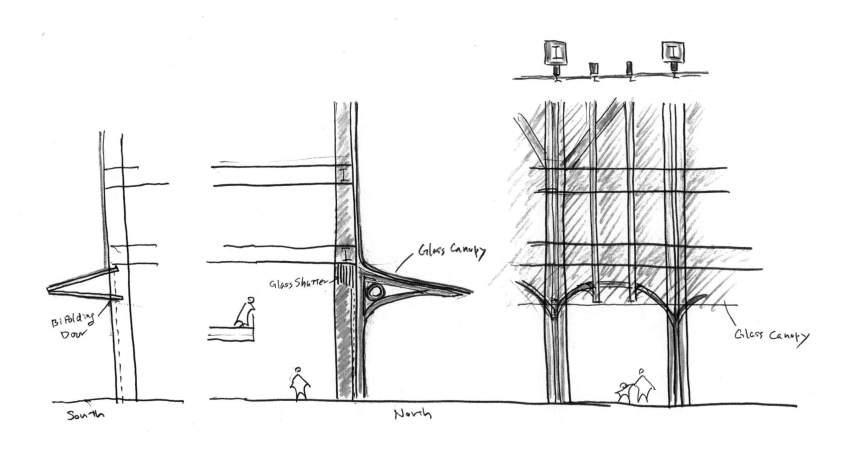

Europaris Tower
ユーロパリス・タワー

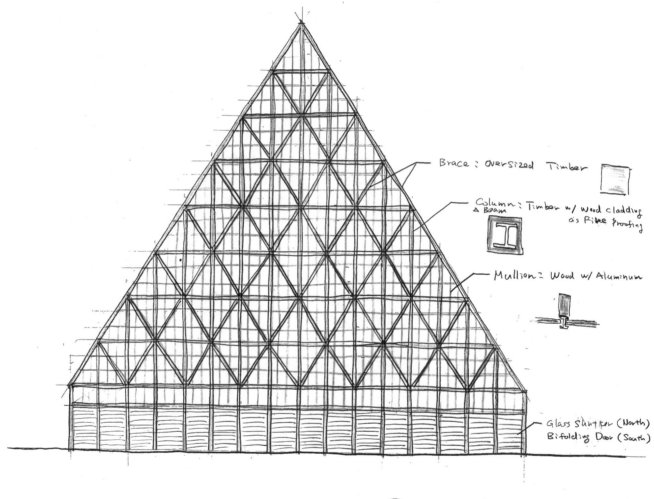

Maison du Peuple
メゾン・デュ・ププル

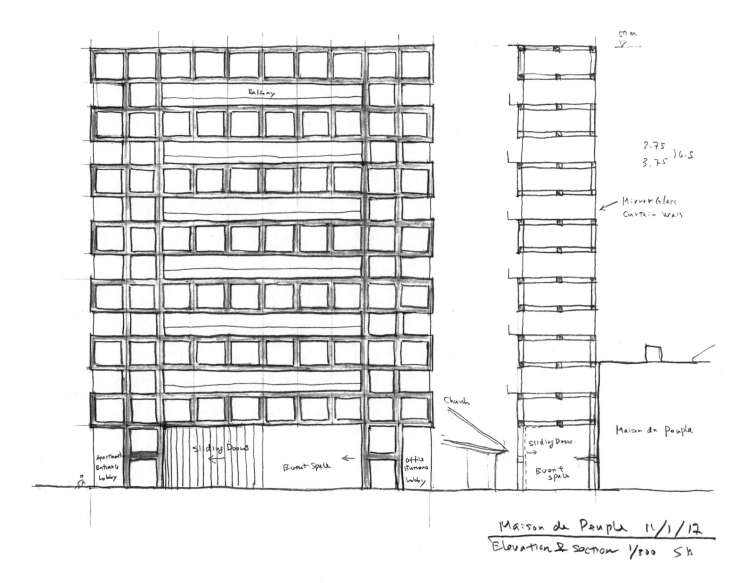

Maison du Peuple
メゾン・デュ・ププル

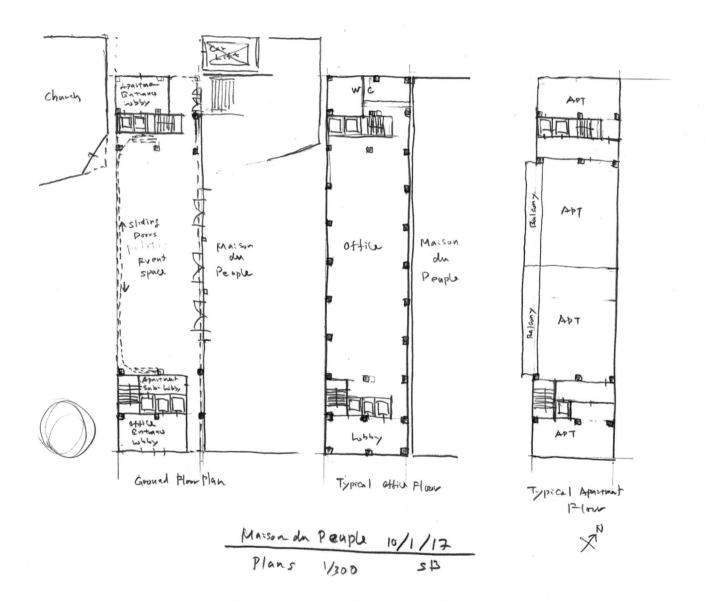

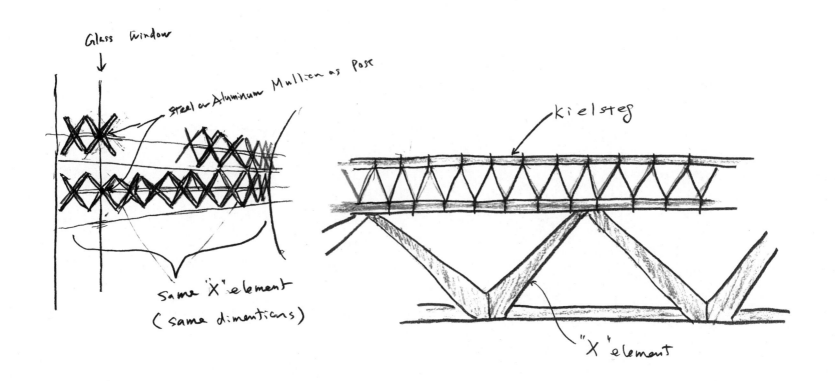

Team 7
ティームセブン新社屋

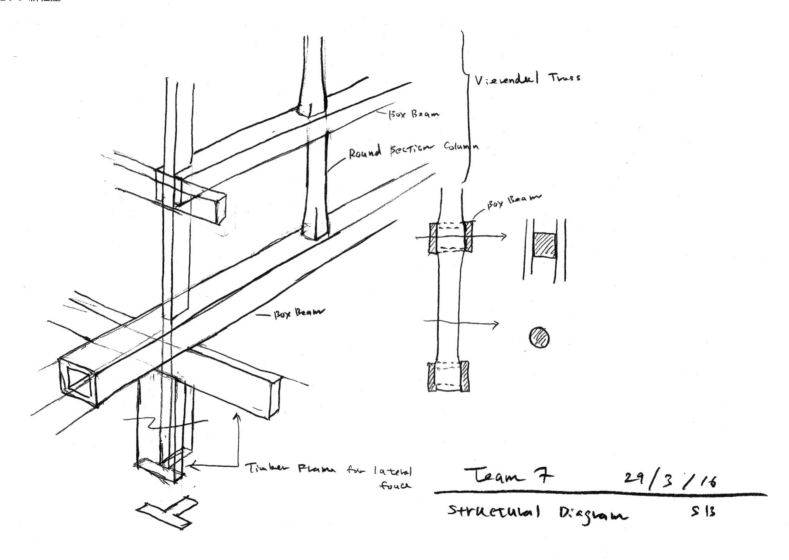

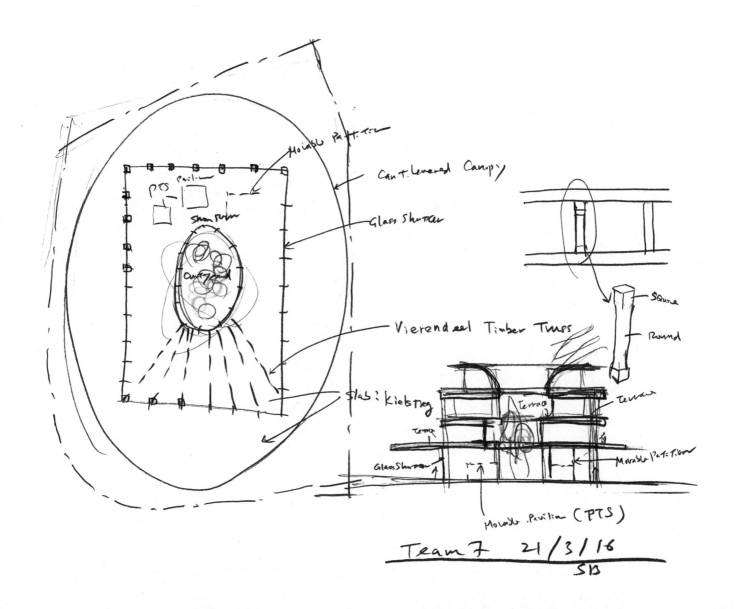

Team 7
ティームセブン新社屋

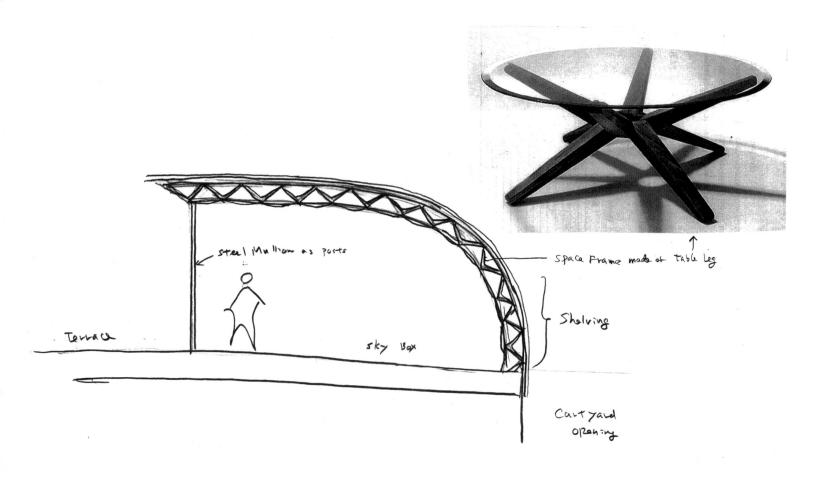

steel Mullion as posts
Space Frame made of Table Leg
Shelving
Terrace
Sky Box
Courtyard opening

Team 7   25/3/16
3rd Floor Roof   SB

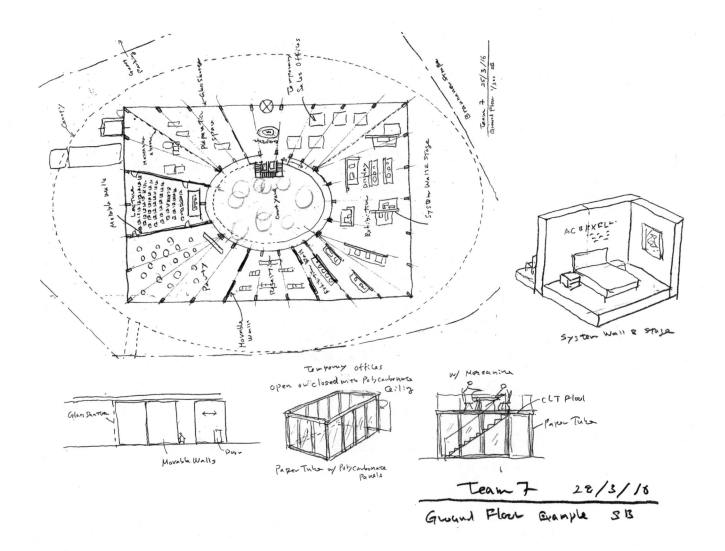

Team 7
ティームセブン新社屋

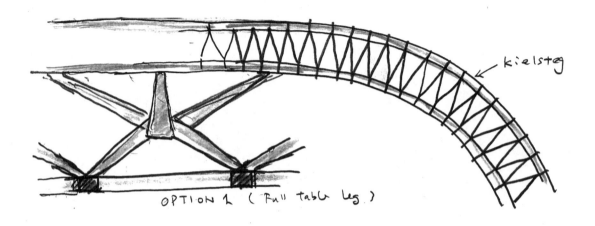

OPTION 1 (Full table leg)

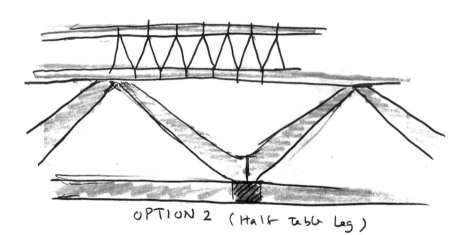

OPTION 2 (Half table leg)

Team 7　　26/3/16
Space Frames　　SB

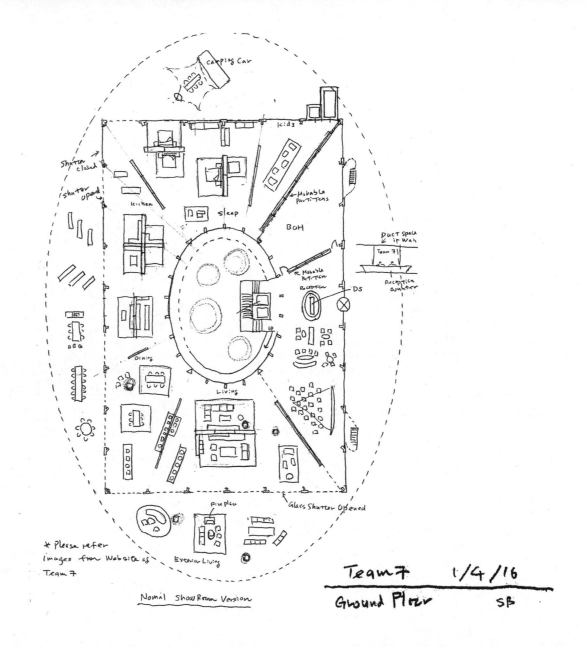

Team 7
ティームセブン新社屋

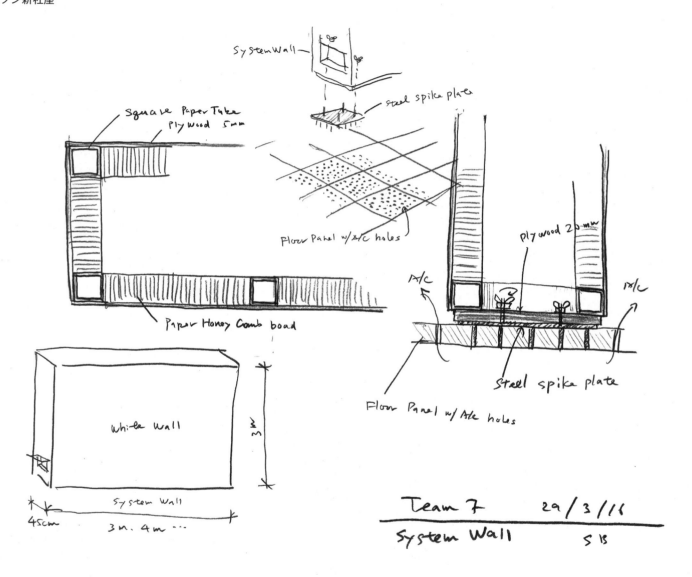

House Vision 2016

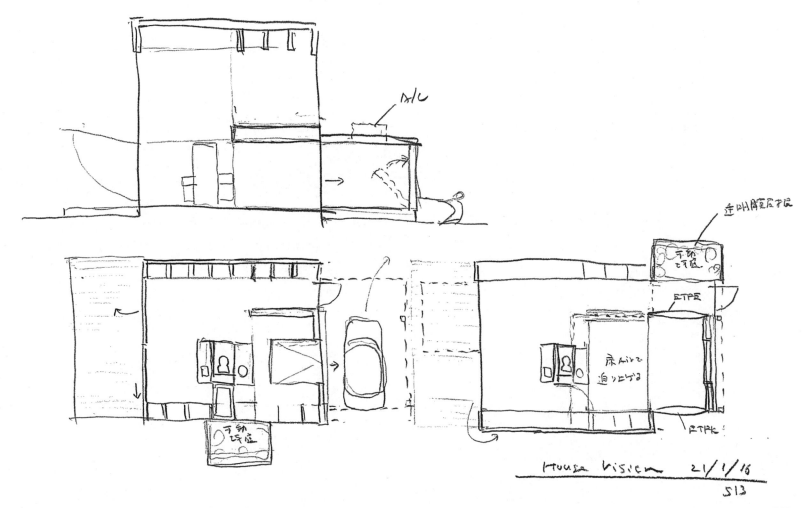

House Vision 2016

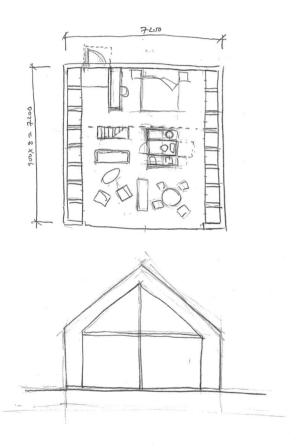

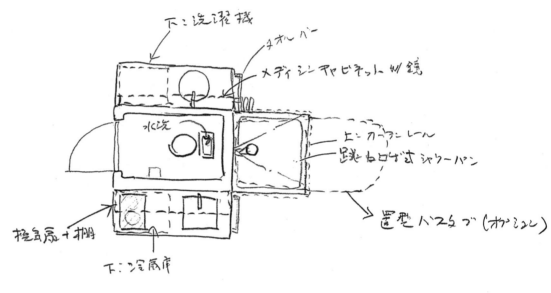

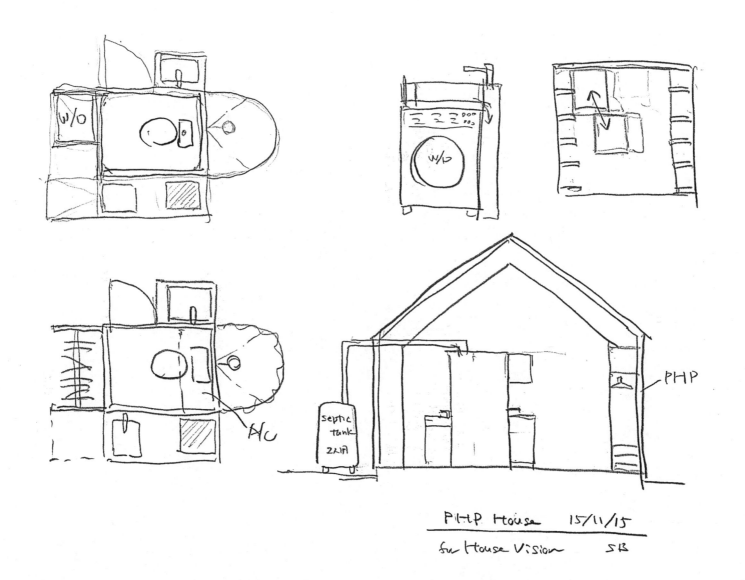

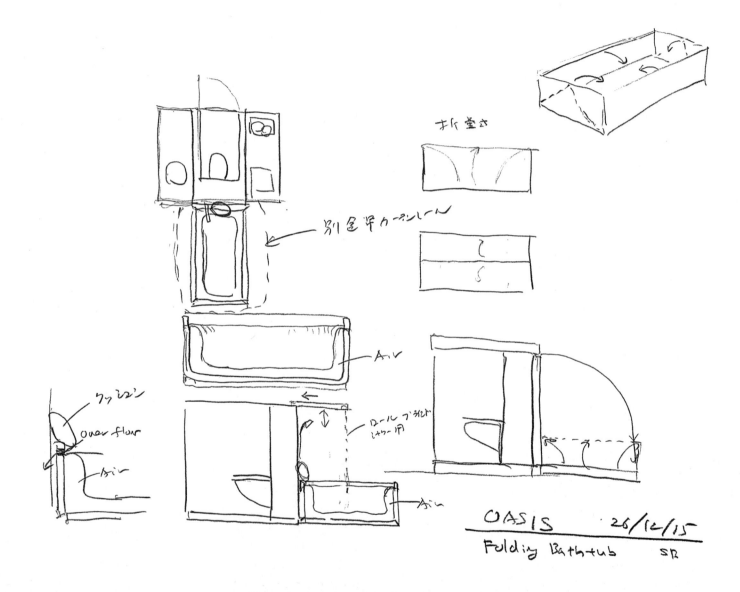

Human Future Pavilion
ヒューマン・フューチャー・パビリオン

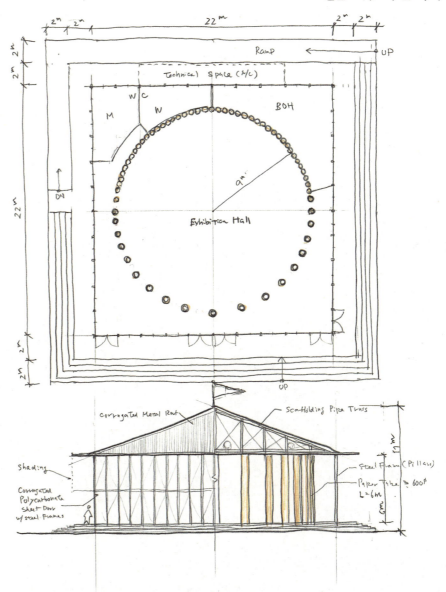

Amaravati Pavilion 14/11/17
Plan, Elevation & Section 1/200 SB

Paper Tube Hut
紙管の小屋

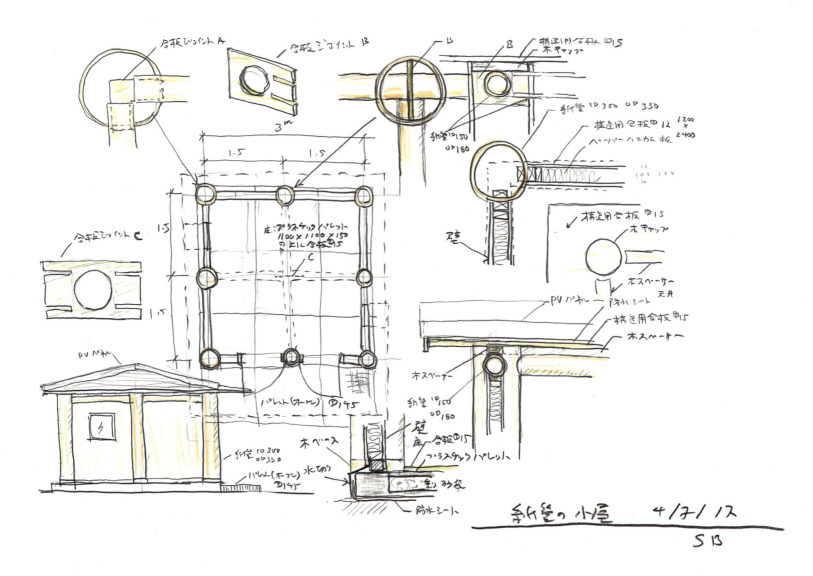

Aubervilliers
オーベルヴィリエ

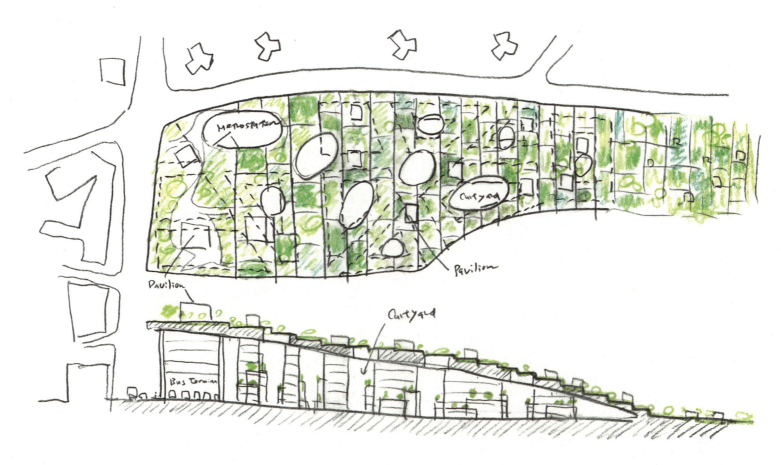

Novartis Pavilion
ノバルティス・パビリオン

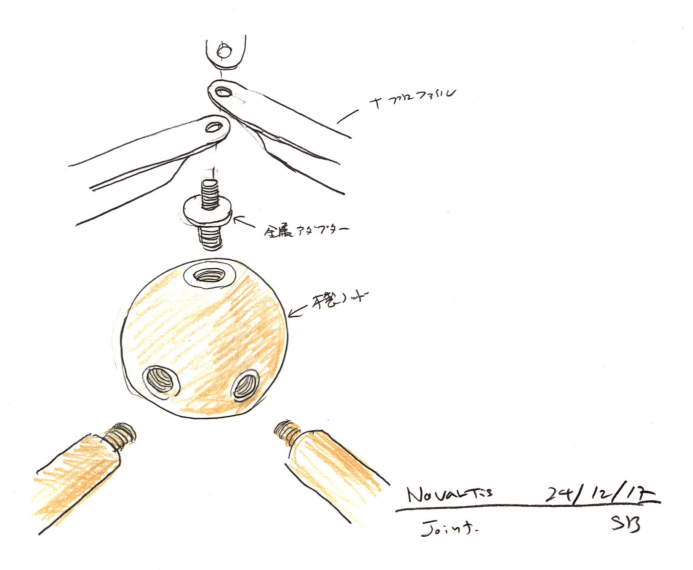

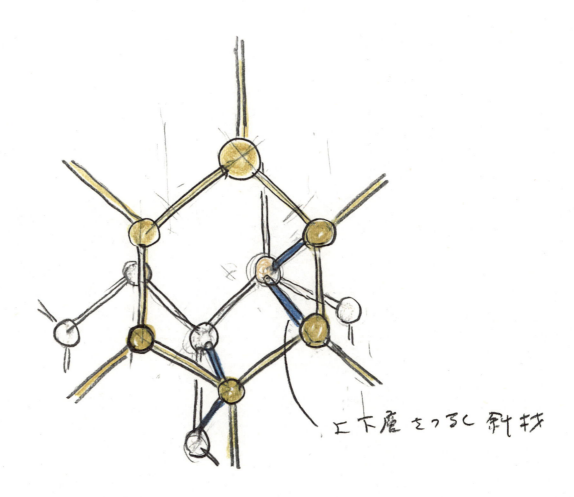

上下層をつなぐ斜材

Novartis 19/12/12
SB

Novartis Pavilion
ノバルティス・パビリオン

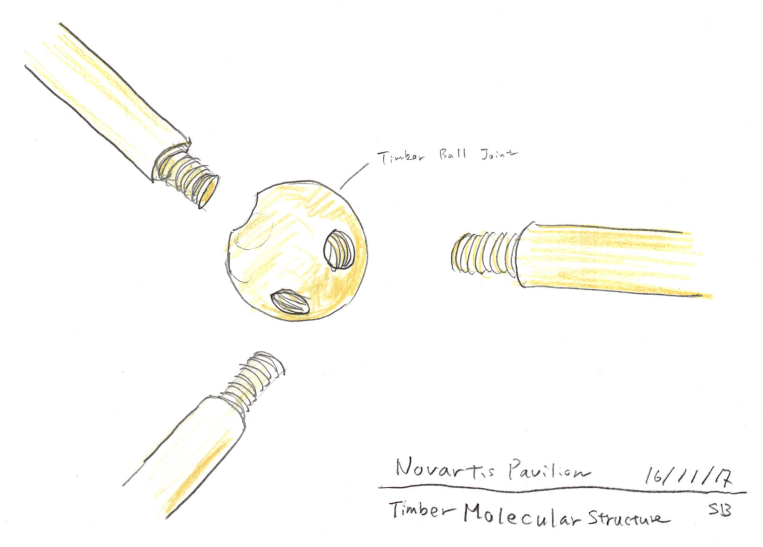

294

Paper Temporary House Ecuador
紙の仮設住宅 エクアドル

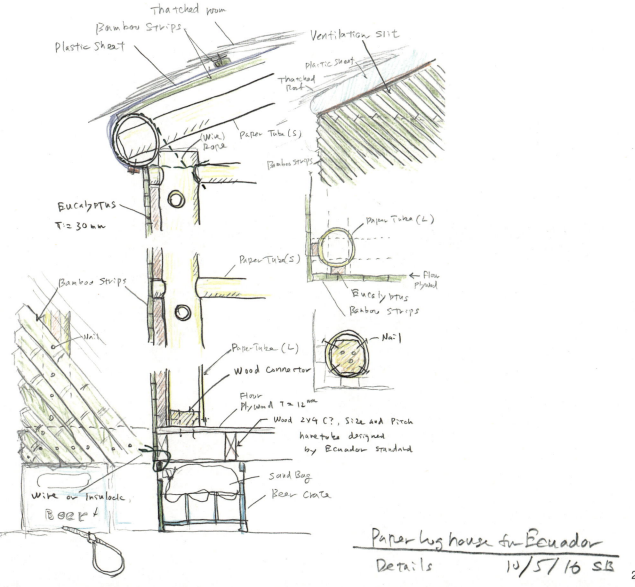

Paper Temporary House Ecuador
紙の仮設住宅　エクアドル

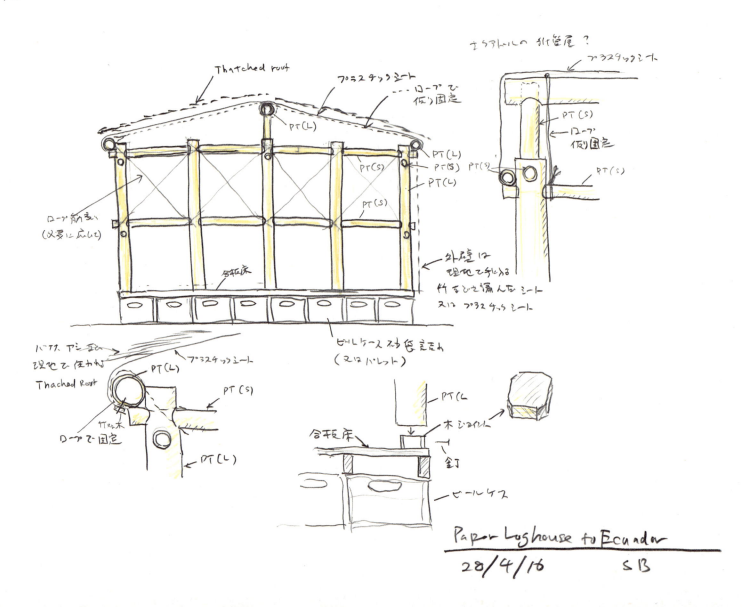

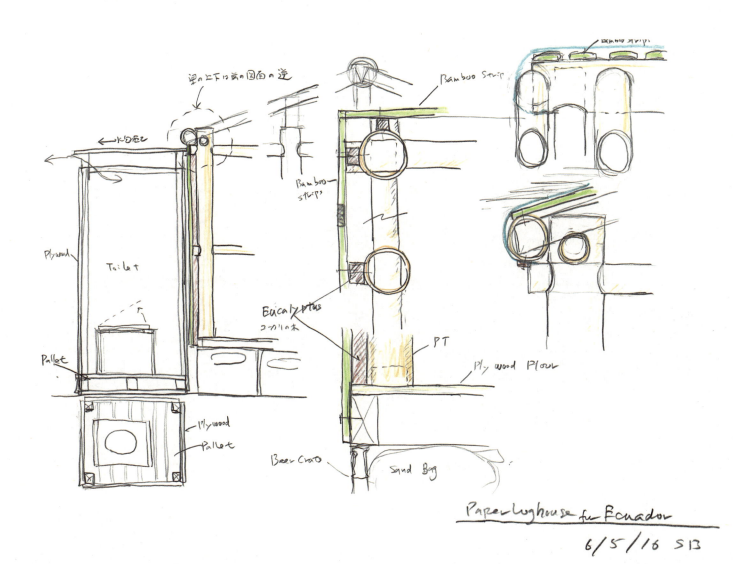

Place Mazas
プラス・マザ

298

Morikami Museum
モリカミ美術館

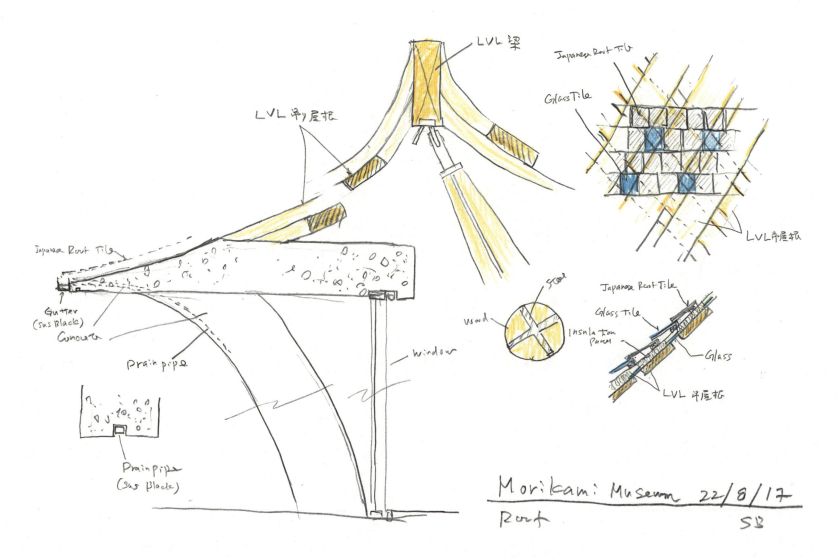

Morikami Museum
モリカミ美術館

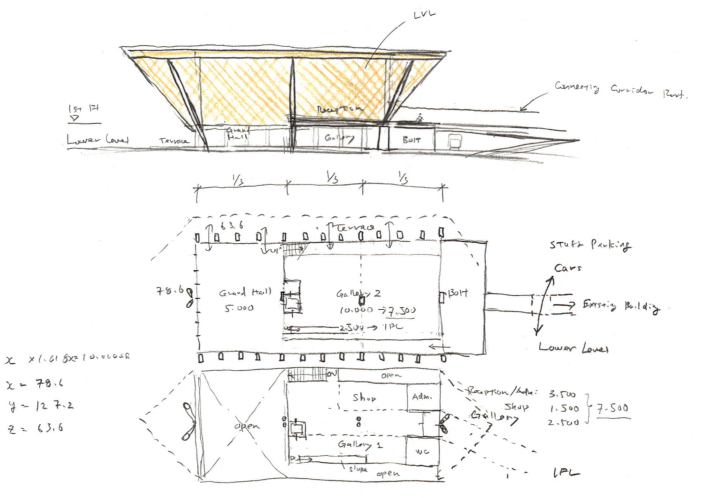

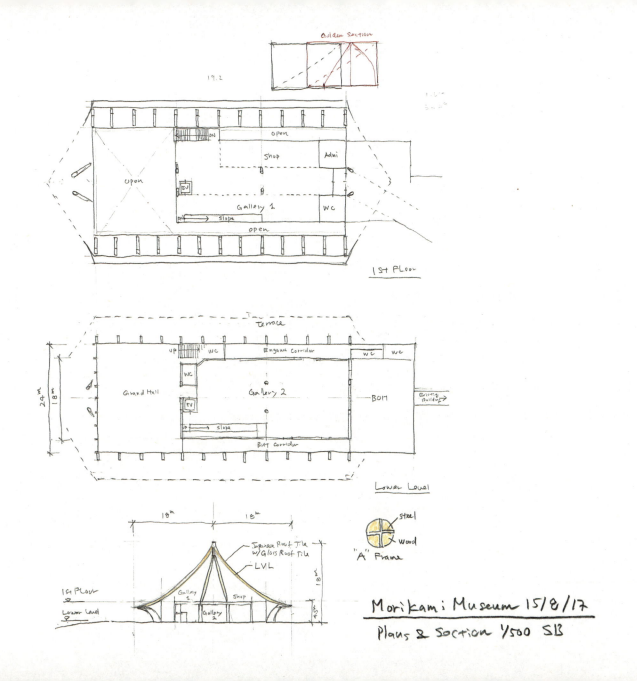

Morikami Museum
モリカミ美術館

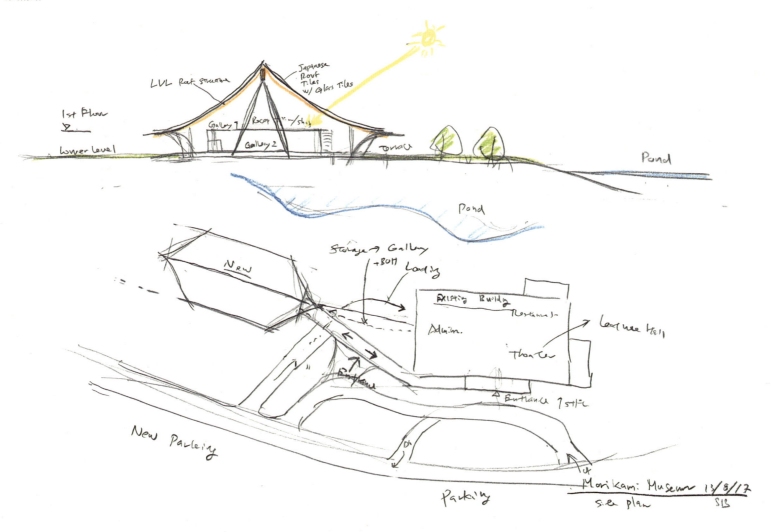

Setagaya City Hall
世田谷区本庁舎

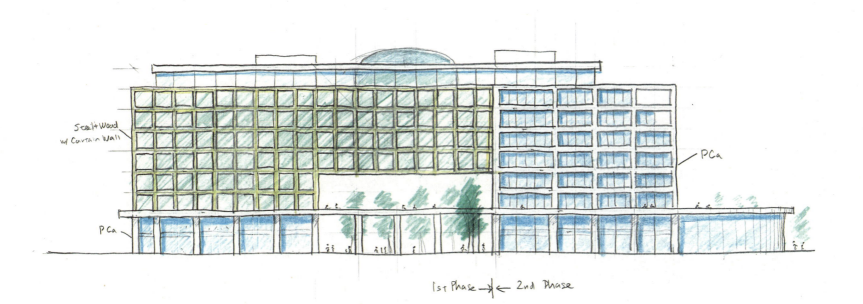

Setagaya City Hall
世田谷区本庁舎

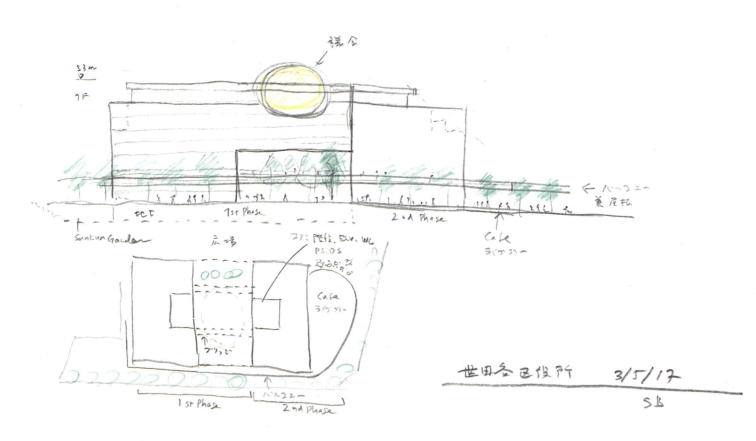

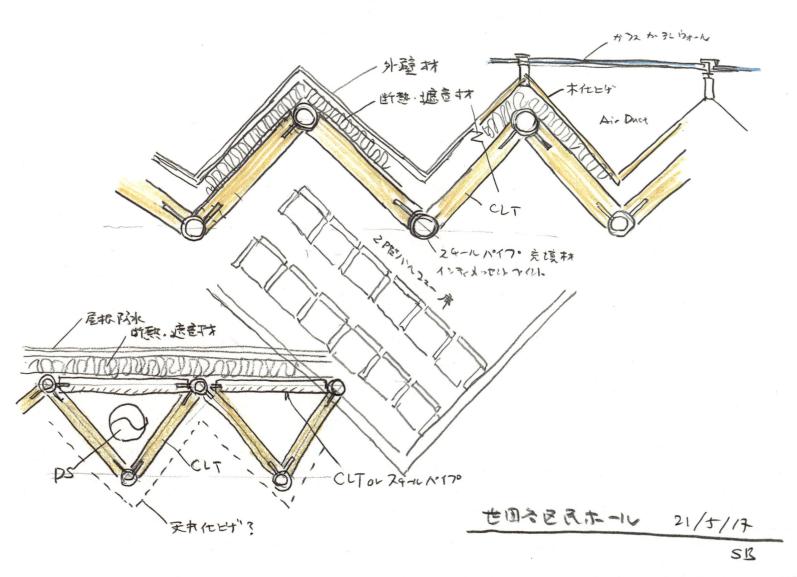

Kyoto City University of Arts Campus Relocation
京都市立芸術大学 移転整備

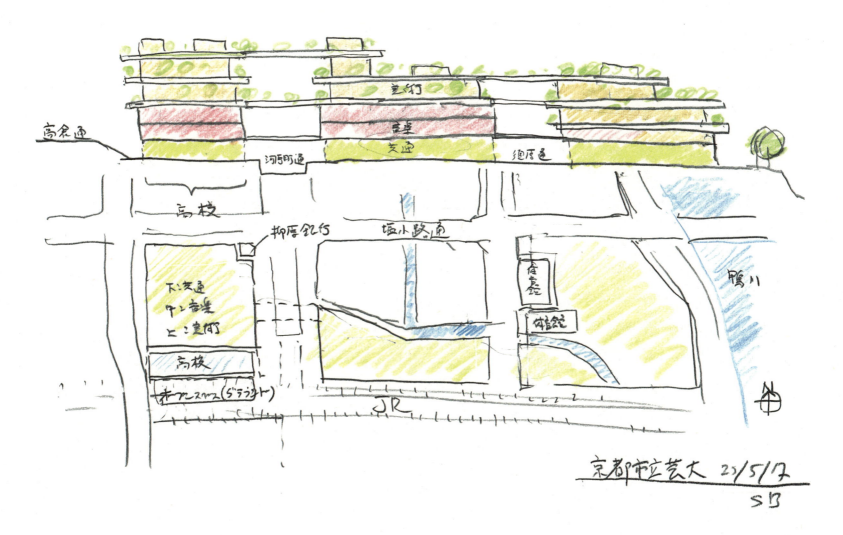

Kyoto City University of Arts Campus Relocation
京都市立芸術大学 移転整備

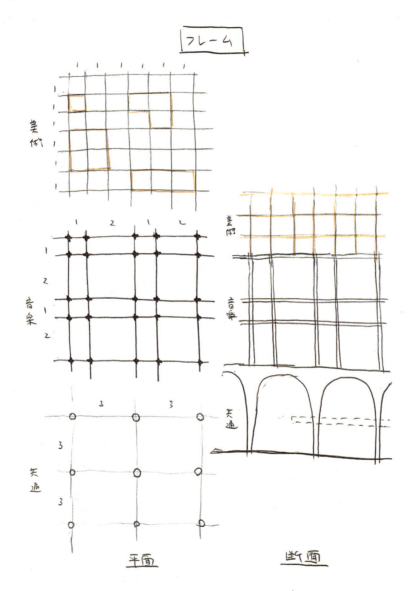

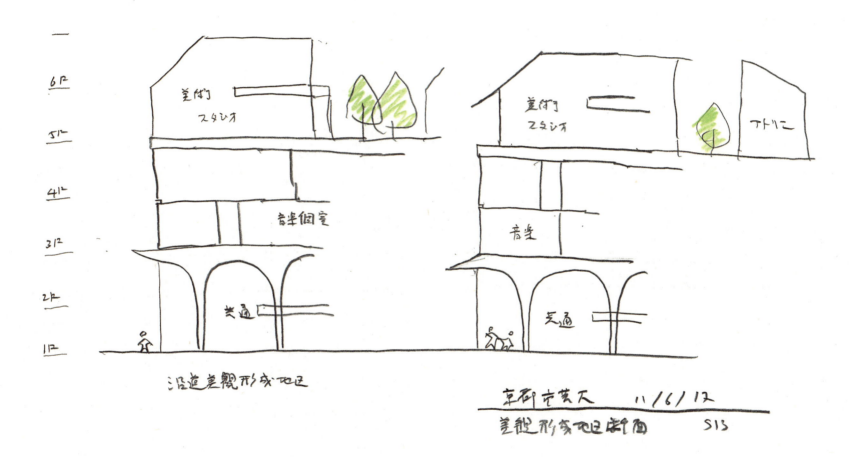

Kyoto City University of Arts Campus Relocation
京都市立芸術大学 移転整備

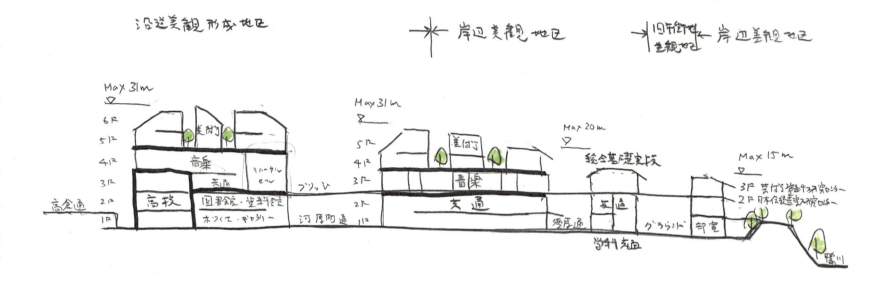

310

Mermaid Pavilion
マーメイド・パビリオン

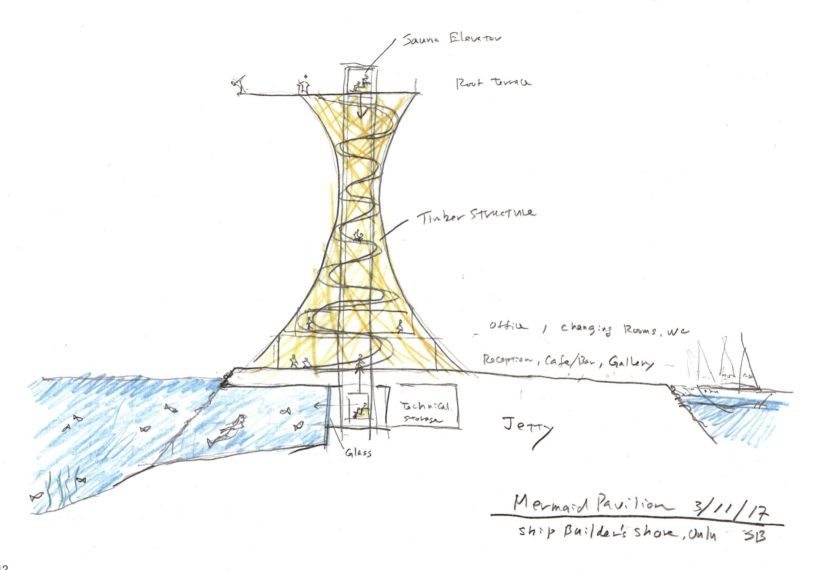

Underwater Garden Restaurant
水中農園

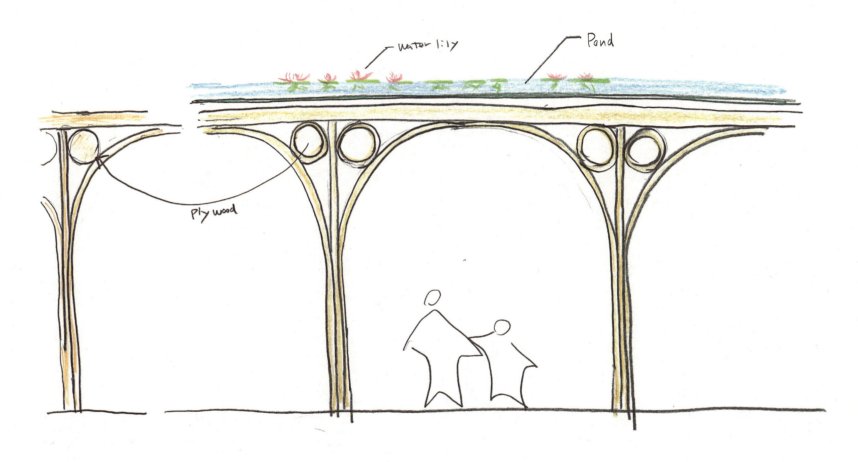

水中農園　29/1/18
Timber Structure　SB

Zenbo Seinei
禅坊 靖寧

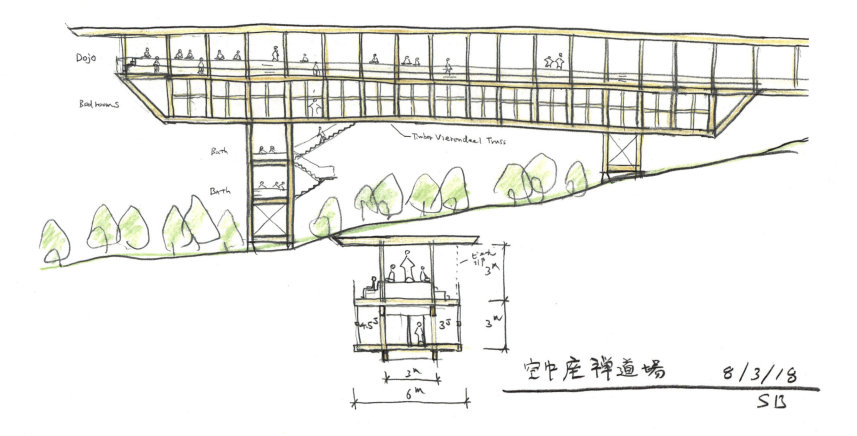

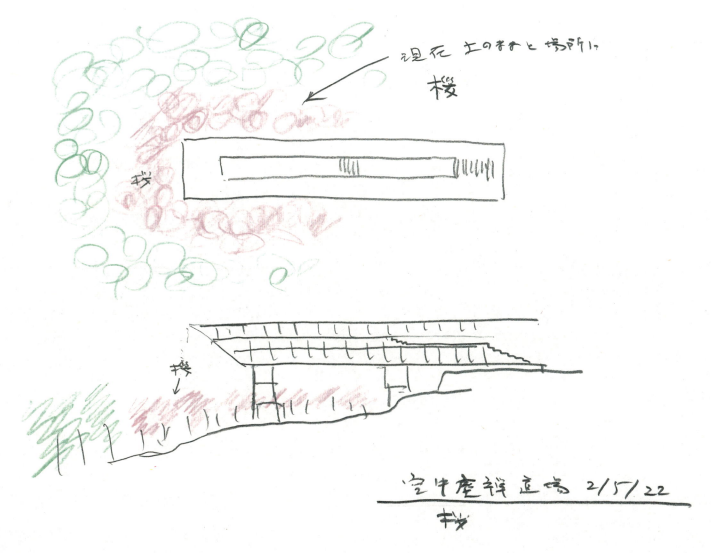

SIMOSE
下瀬美術館

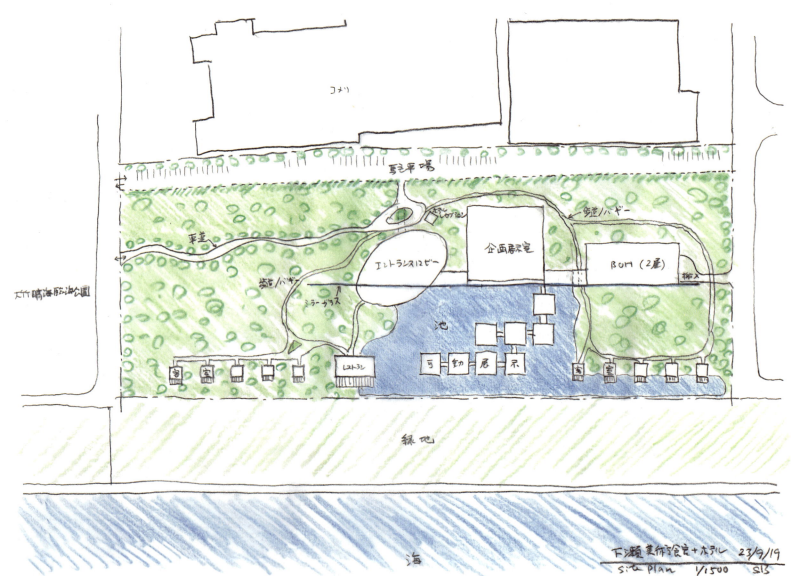

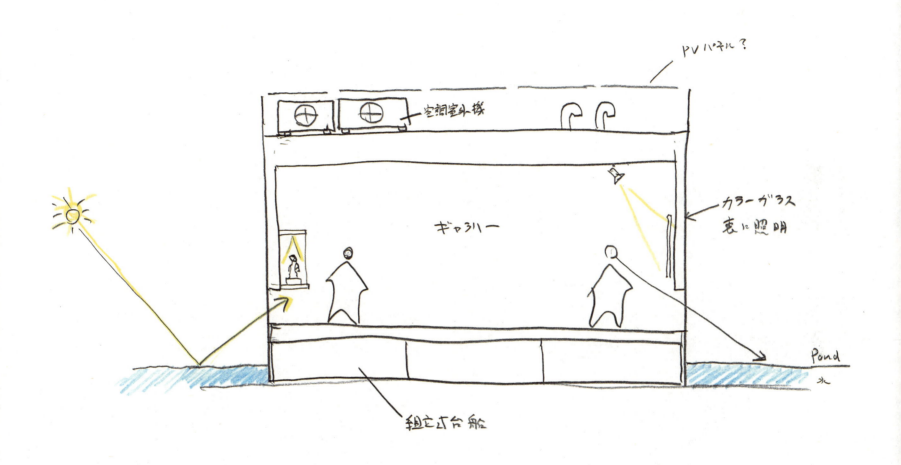

SIMOSE
下瀬美術館

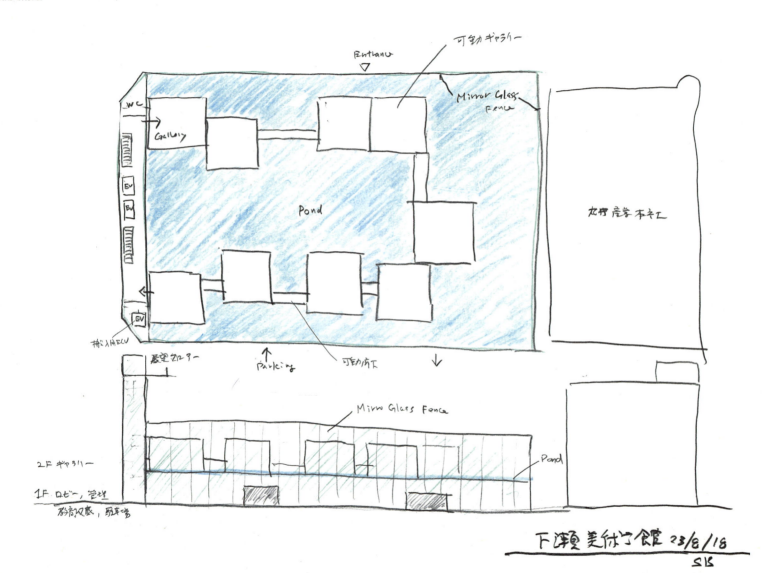

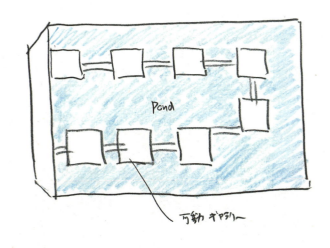

Pond

可動ギャラリー

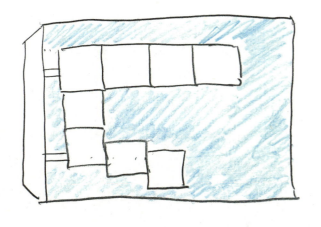

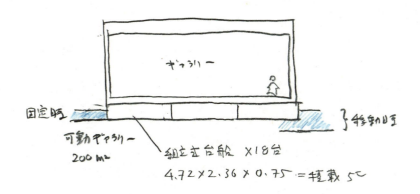

ギャラリー

固定時

可動ギャラリー
200m²

組立台船 ×18台
4.72×2.36×0.75 = 積載 5t

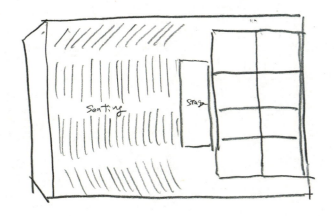

Seating　Stage

下瀬美術館　23/8/18
SB

SIMOSE
下瀬美術館

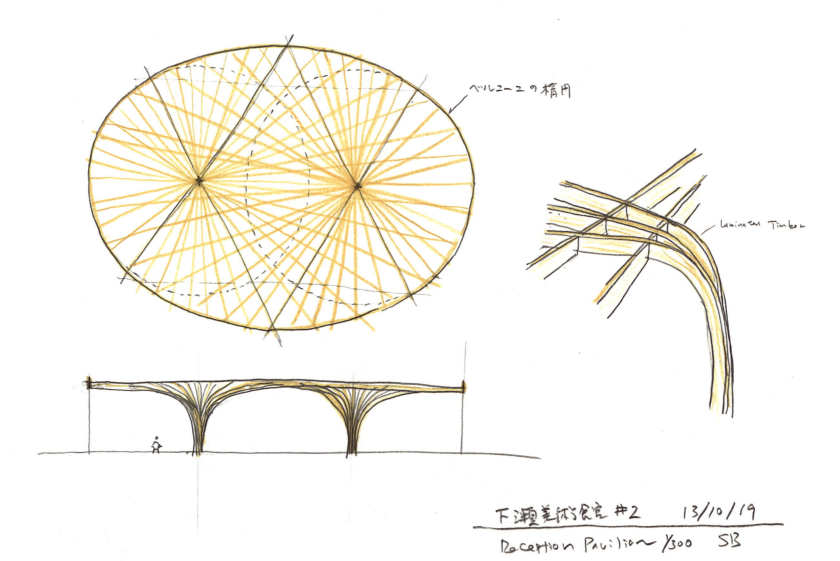

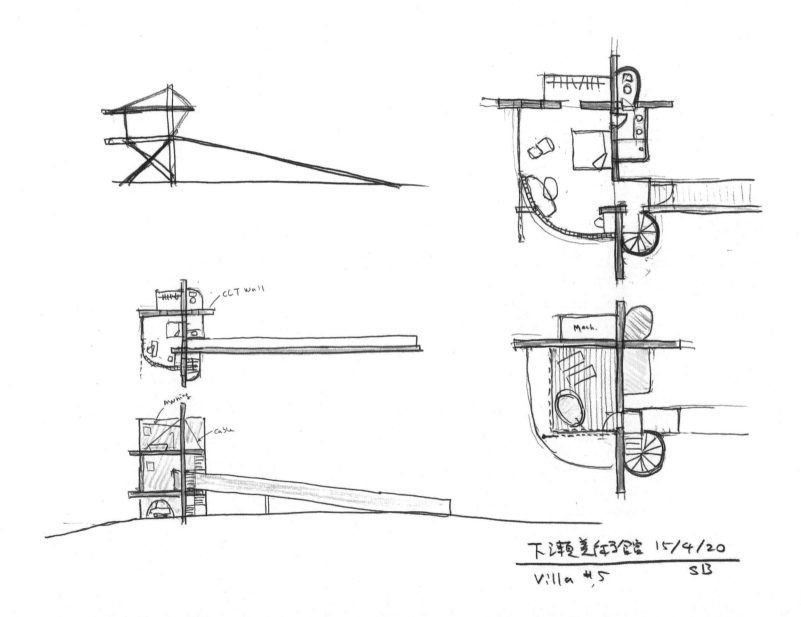

Taketa City Historical Museum & Community Center
竹田市歴史文化交流拠点施設

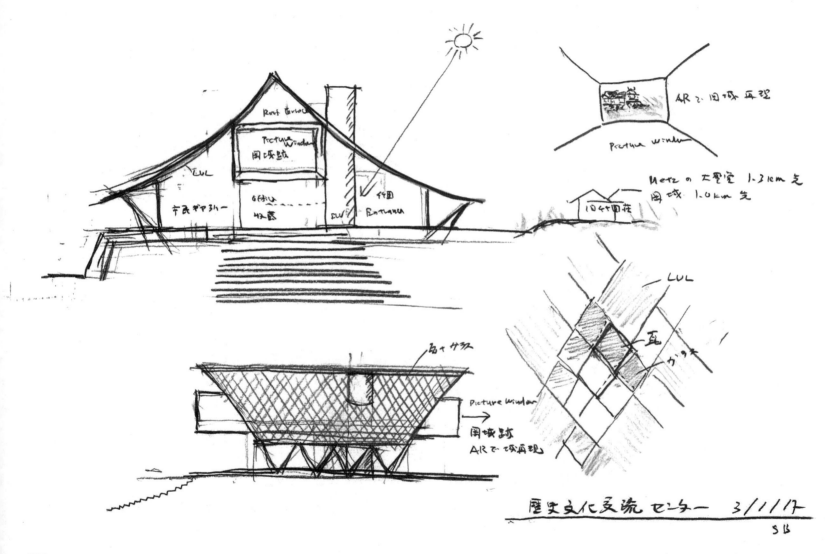

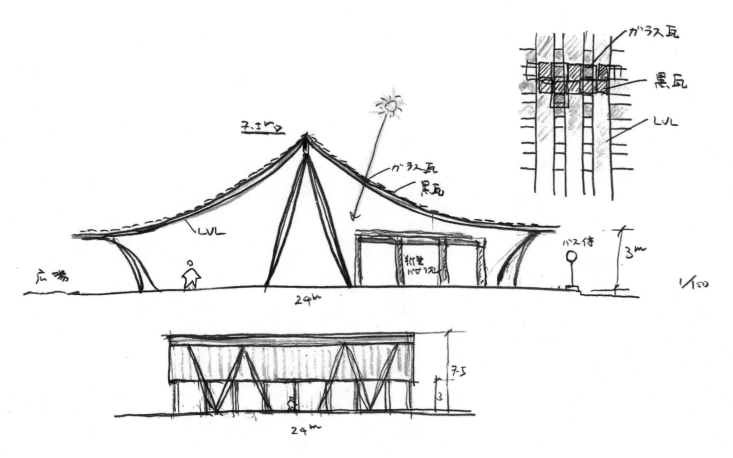

Taketa City Historical Museum & Community Center
竹田市歴史文化交流拠点施設

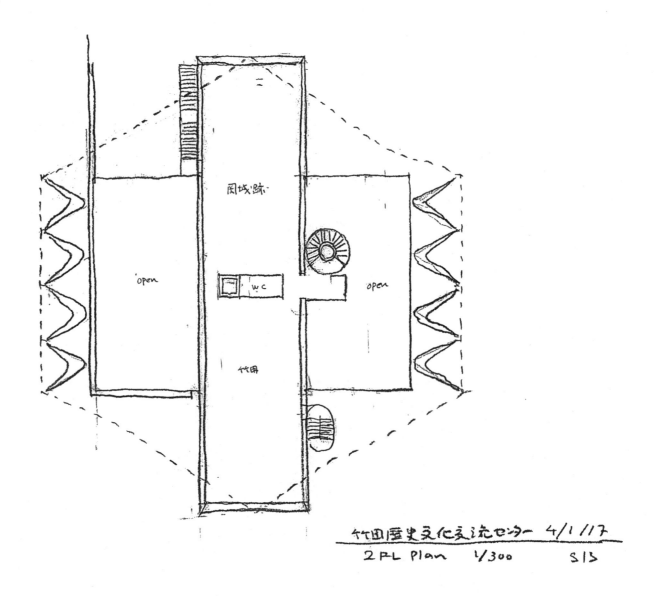

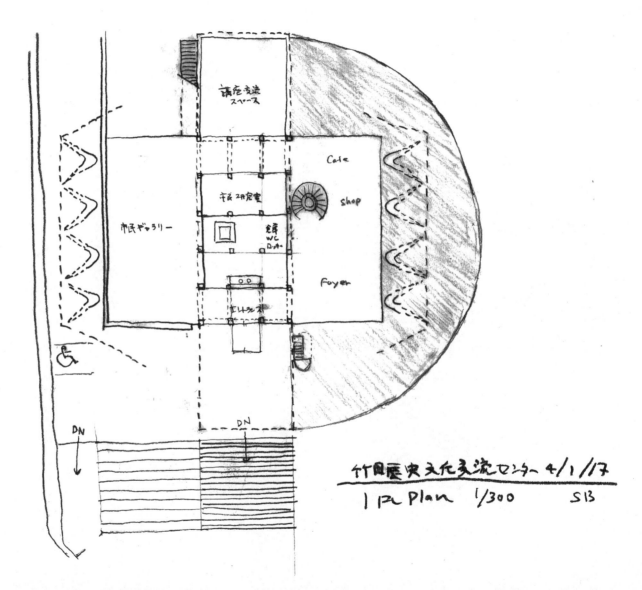

Taketa City Historical Museum & Community Center
竹田市歴史文化交流拠点施設

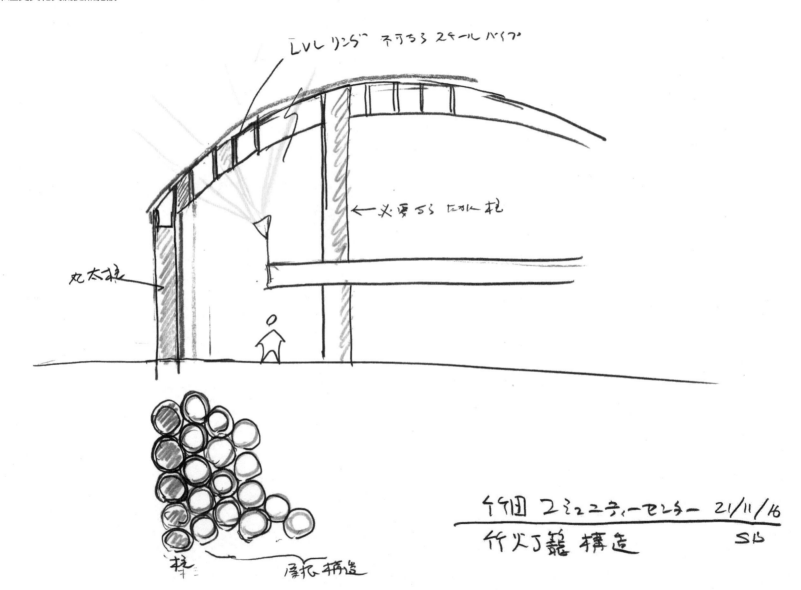

Pilot Houses for Kalobeyei New Settlement
カロベイエイ難民居住区のためのパイロットハウス

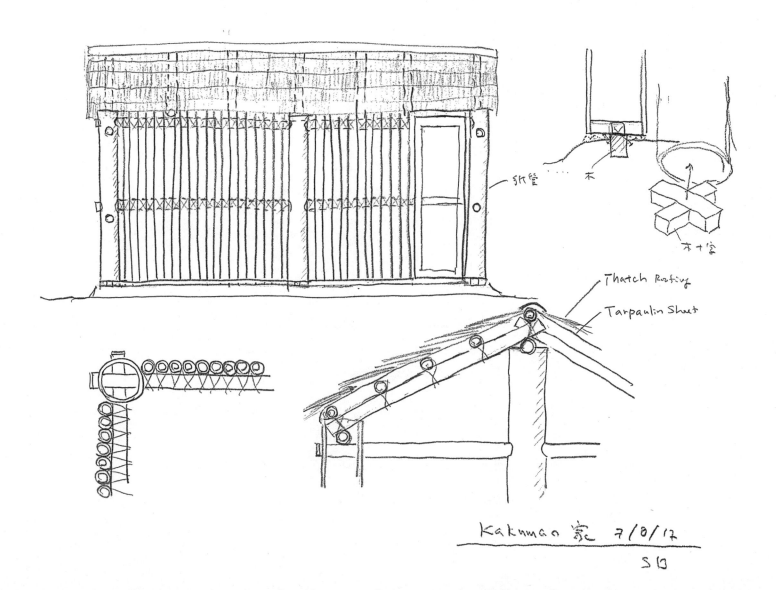

Triangle Lattice House
三角格子の家

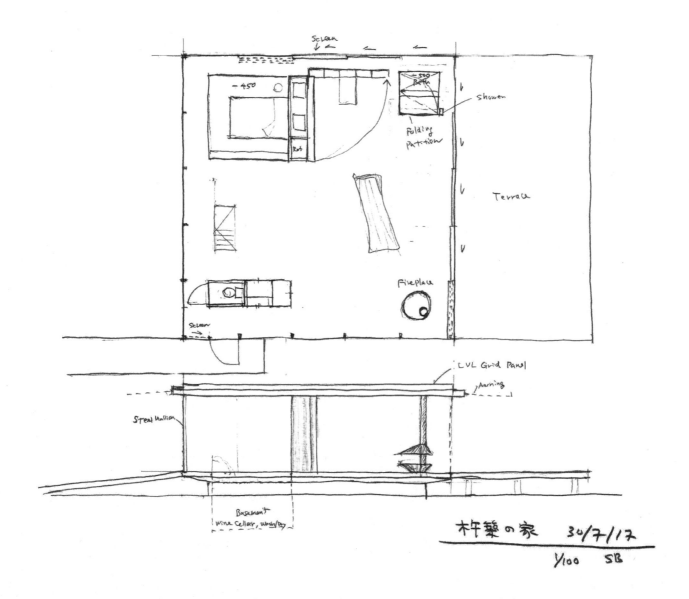

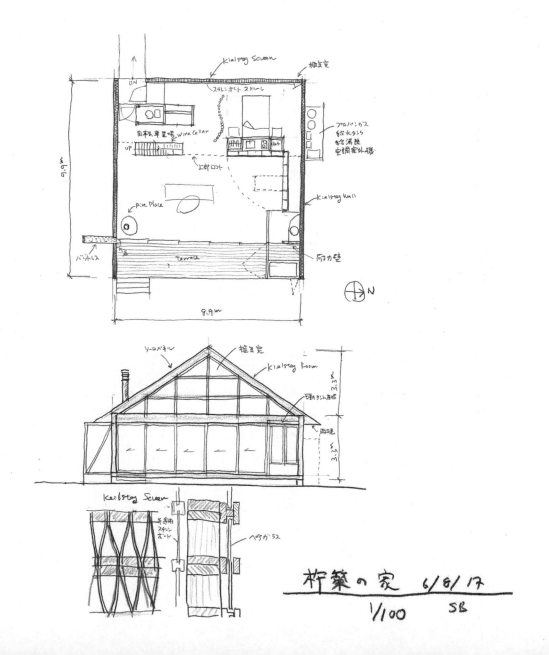

Loro Piana Façade
ロロ・ピアーナ　ファサード

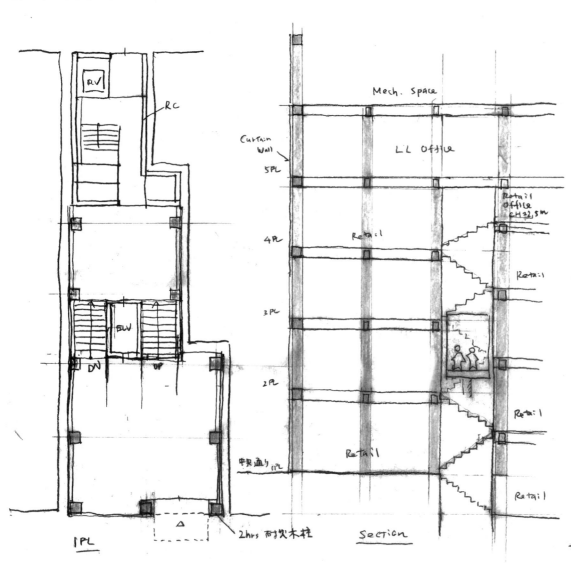

New Kagawa Prefectural Sports Arena
新香川県立体育館

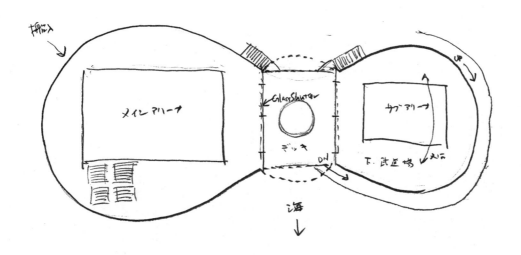

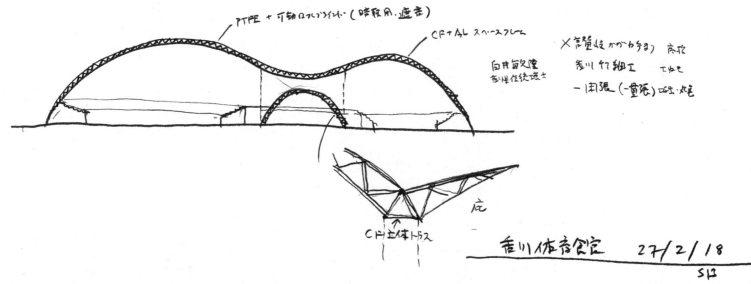

Kumoi-dori District Redevelopment
雲井通5丁目地区再開発

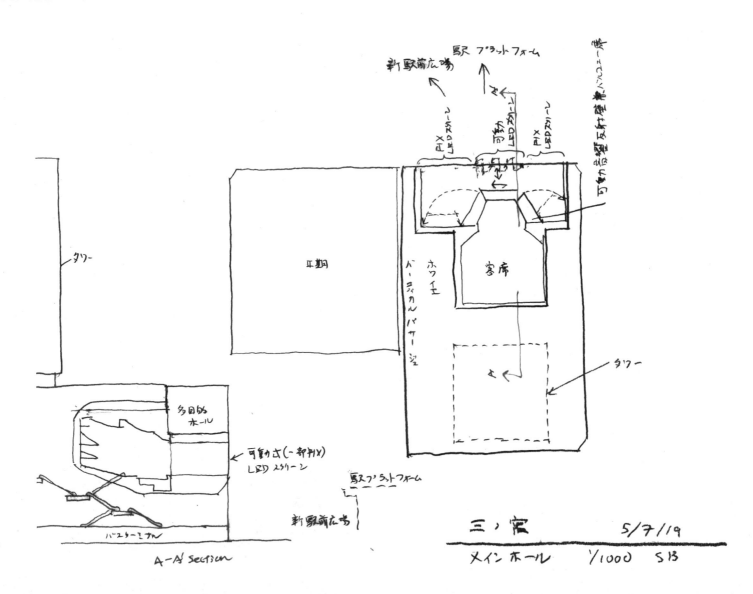

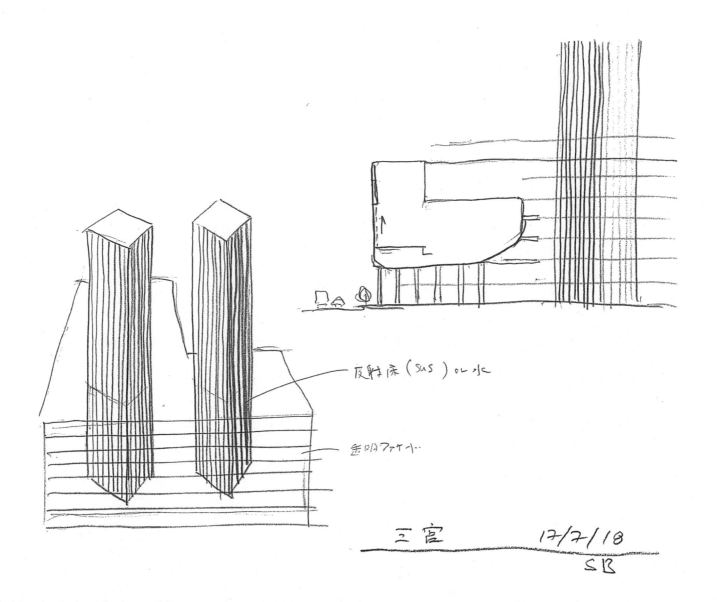

反射床（SUS）or 水

透明ファサード

三宮　12/7/18
SB

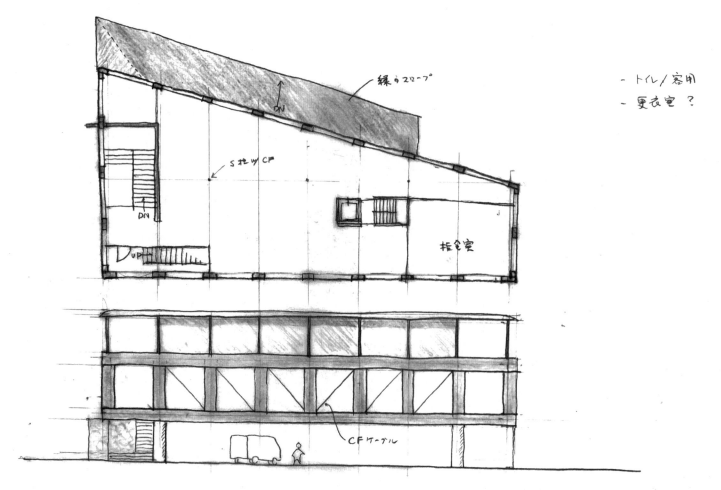

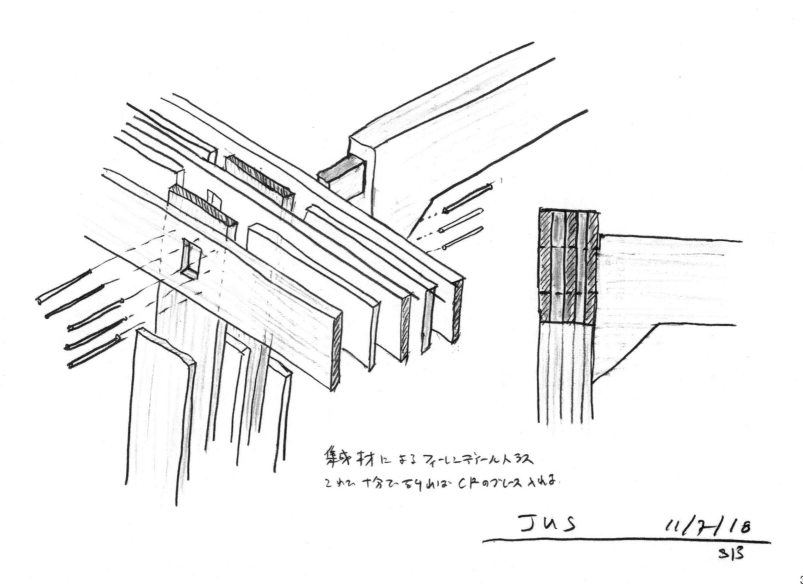

集成材による フィーレンディールトラス
これで十分であれば CFのブレス入れる

JUS 11/7/18
313

Shishi-iwa House 2
ししいわハウス2

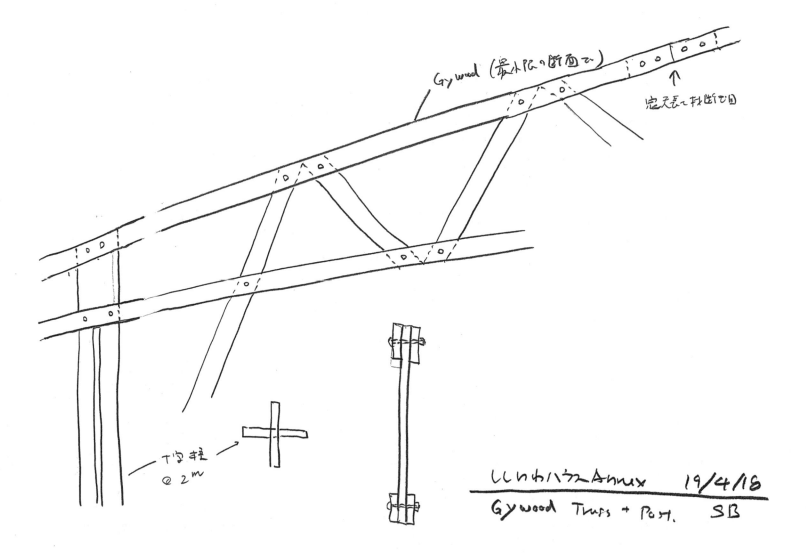

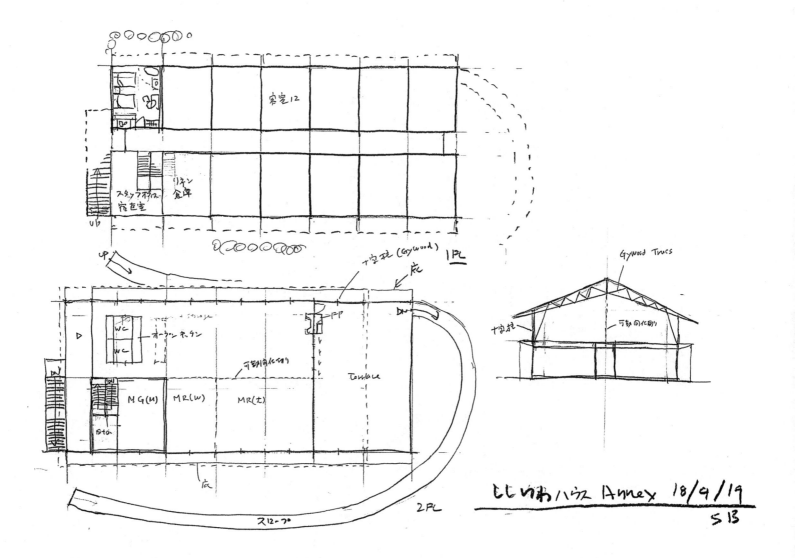

Paper Green House
紙の温室

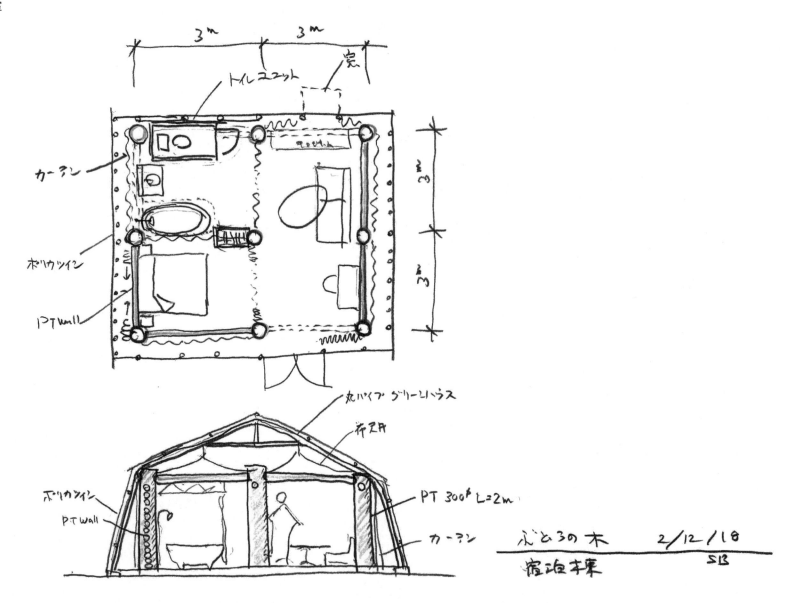

338

LV Pavilion
LV パビリオン

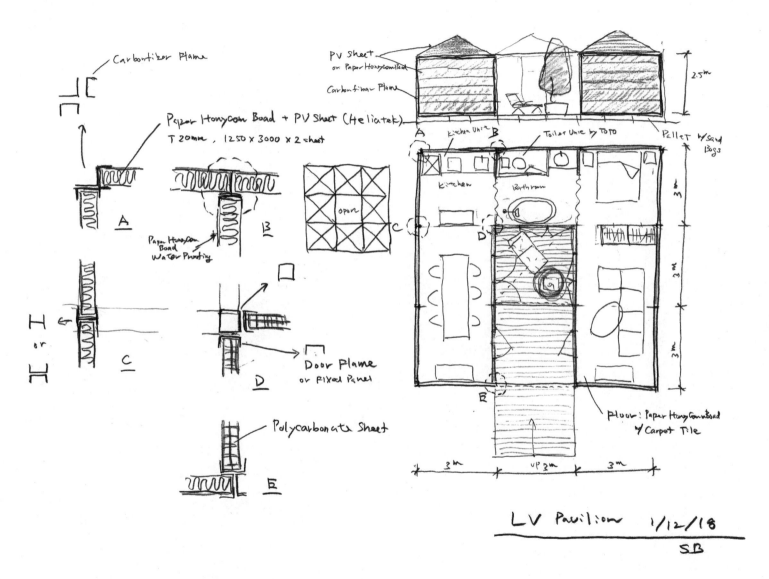

LV Pavilion
LV パビリオン

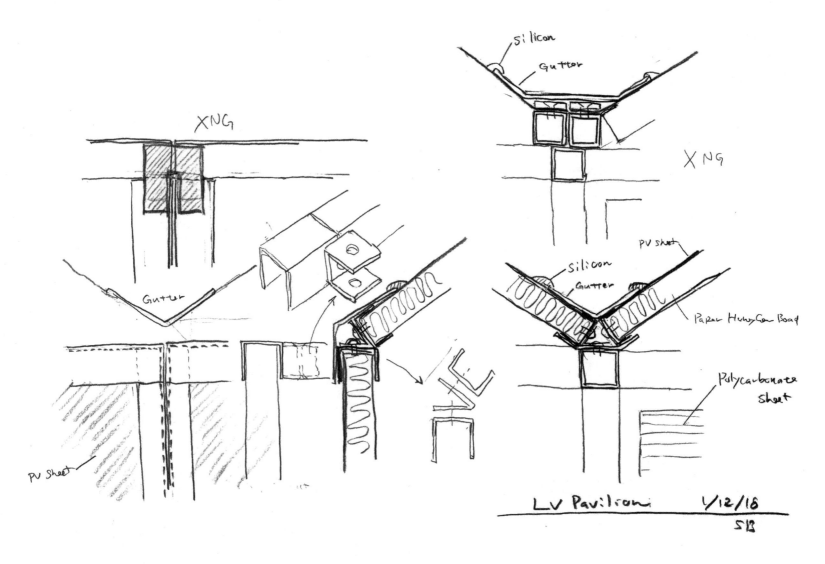

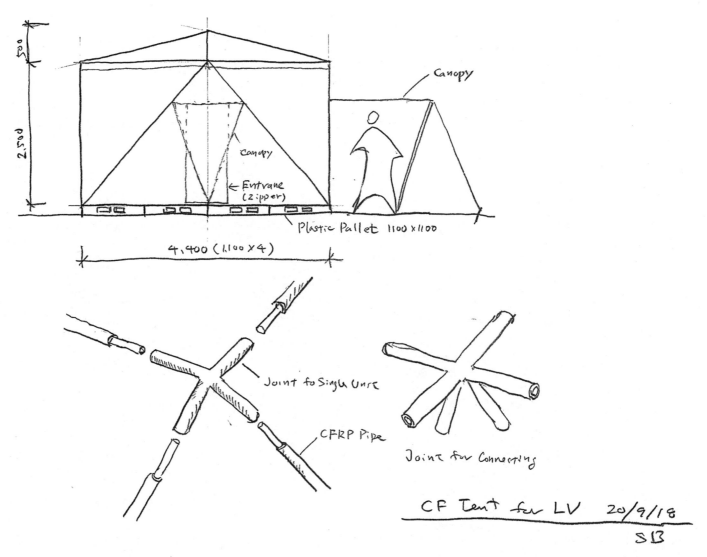

LV Pavilion
LV パビリオン

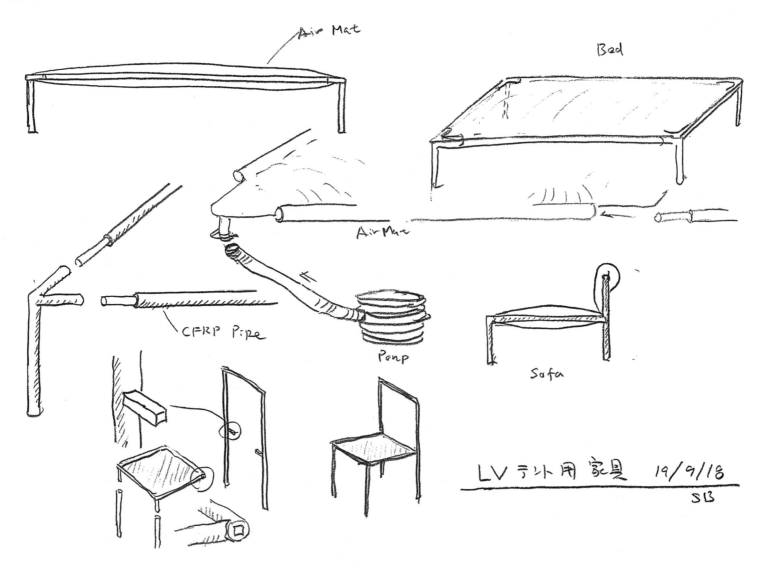

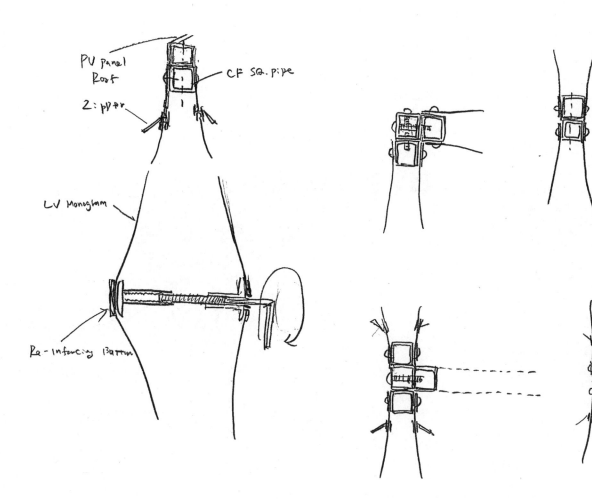

LV Pavilion 18/10/18

SB

Kentucky Owl Park
ケンタッキー・アウル・パーク

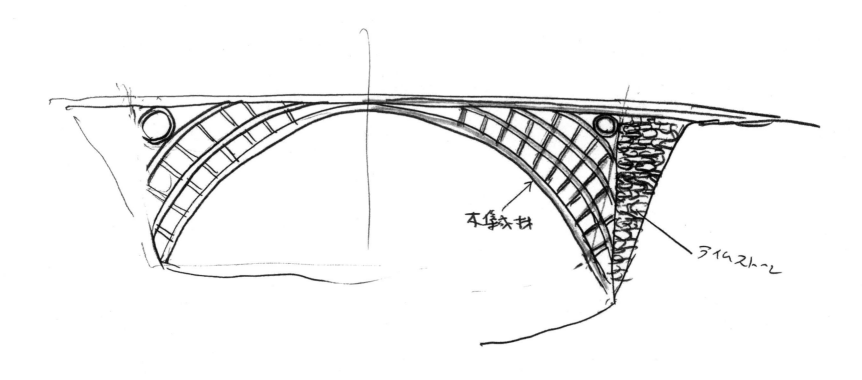

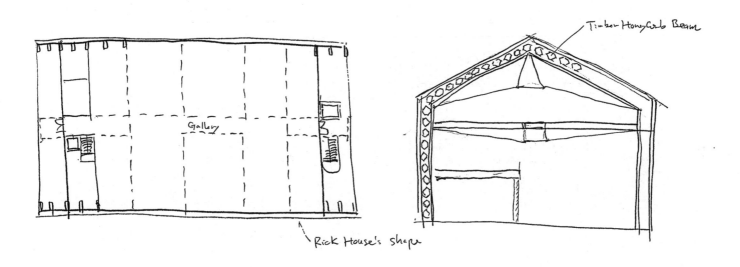

Timber HoneyComb Beam

Rick House's shape

Kentucky Owl Park 22/3/18
SB
Art Gallery

Kentucky Owl Park
ケンタッキー・アウル・パーク

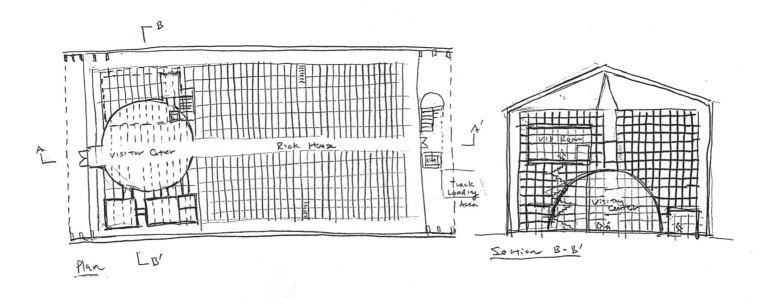
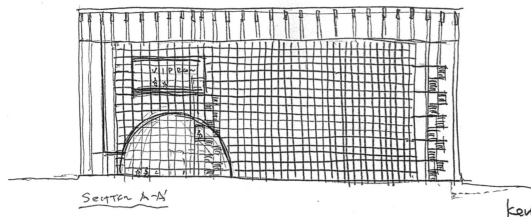

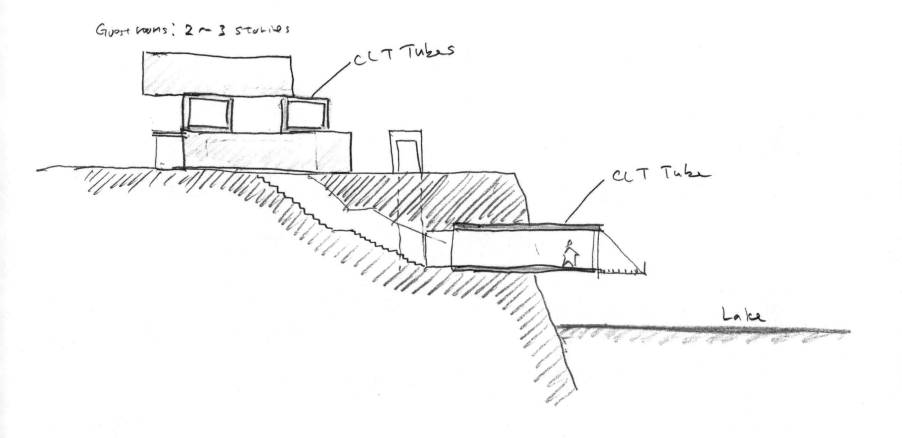

Kentucky Owl Park
ケンタッキー・アウル・パーク

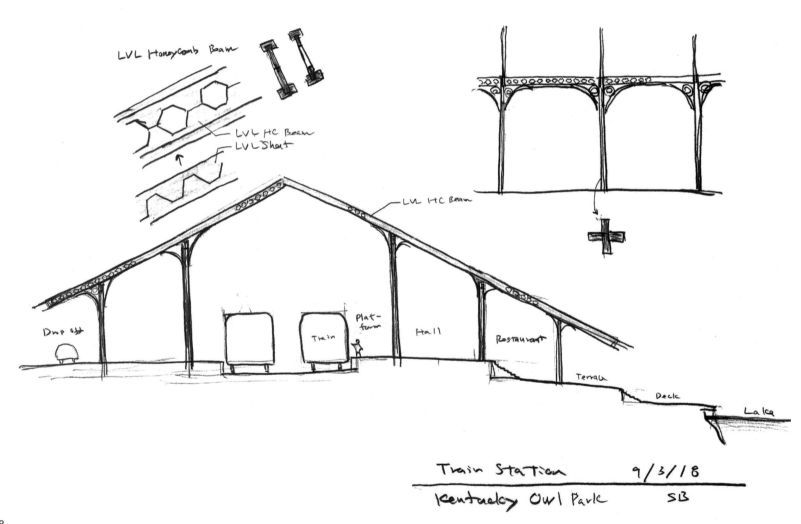

348

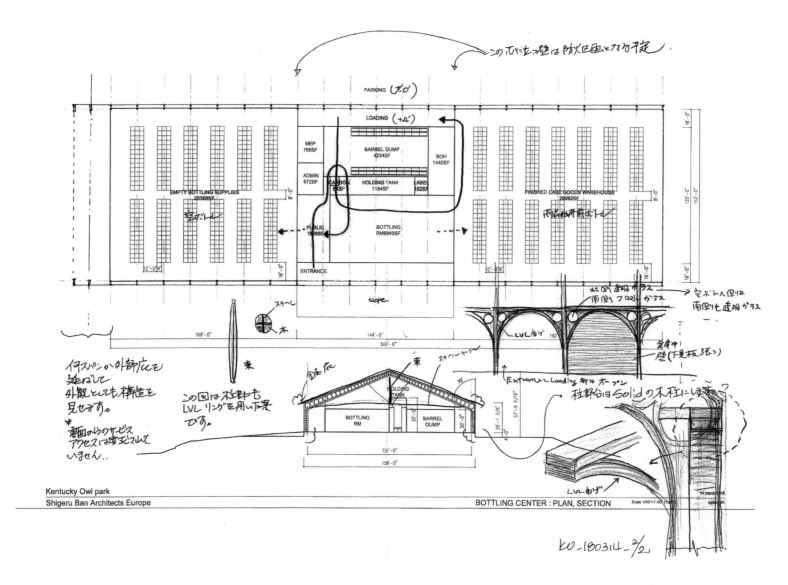

The Transparent Tokyo Toilet
ザ トウメイ トウキョウ トイレット

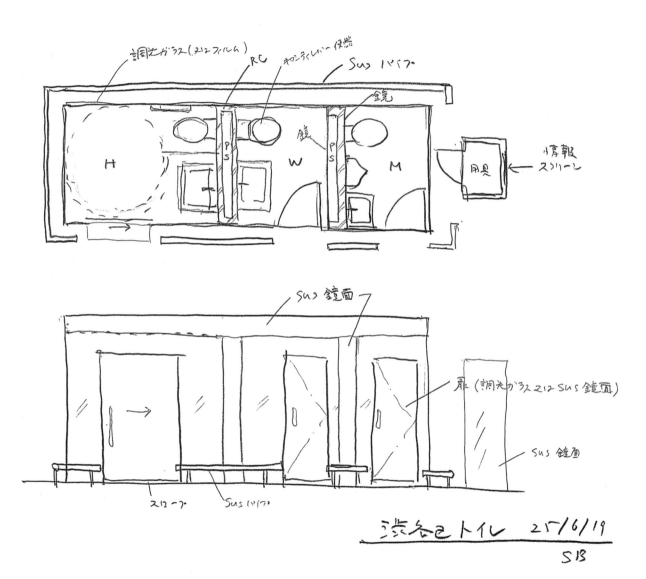

DMZ Passage
DMZ パサージュ

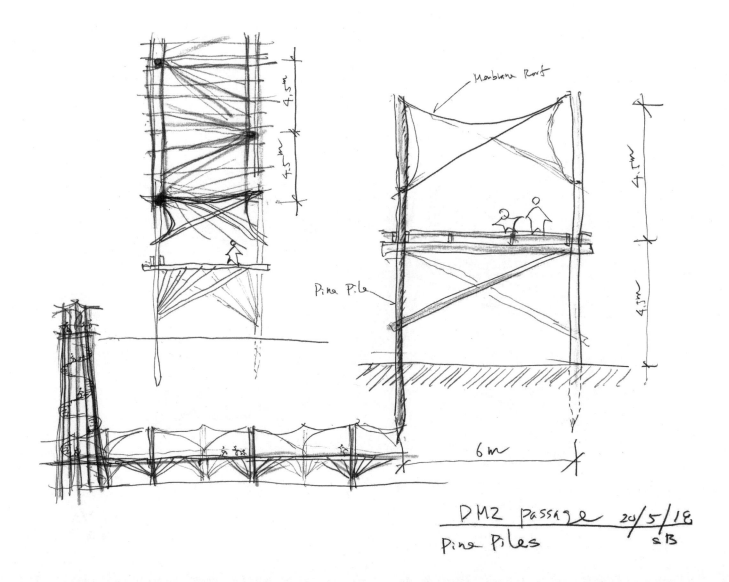

joints
ジョイント

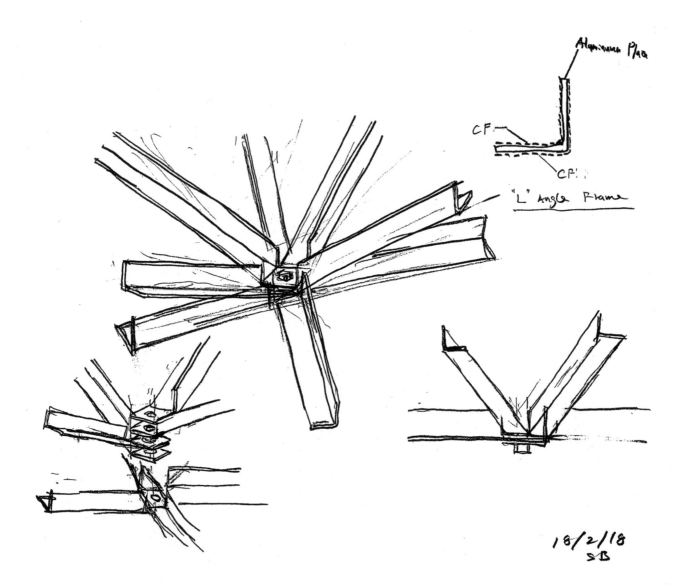

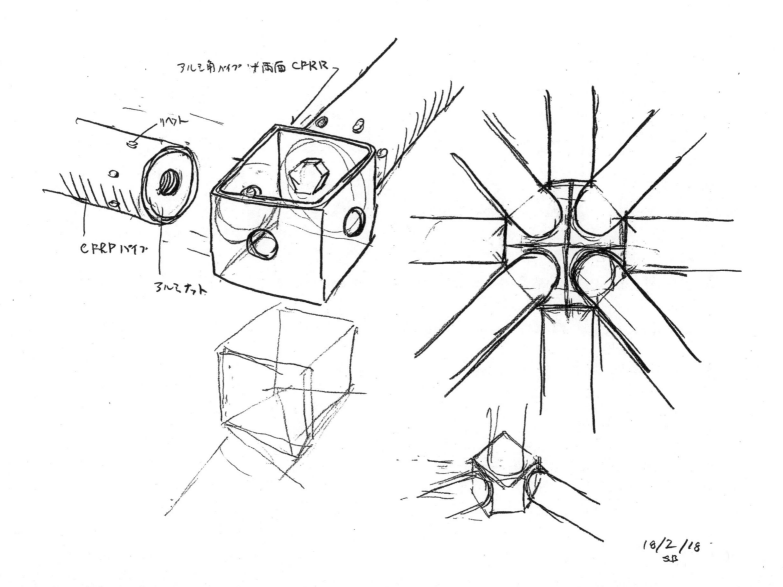

Tech Company Visitor Center
テック企業ビジターセンター

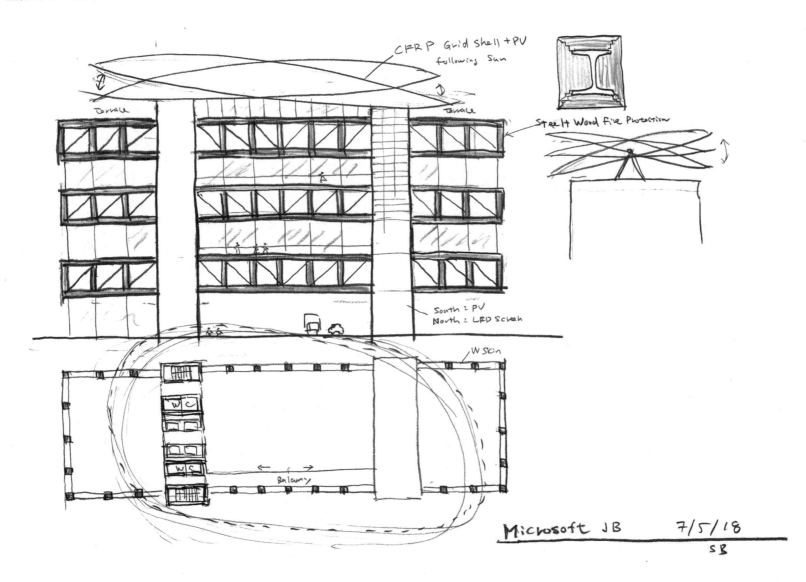

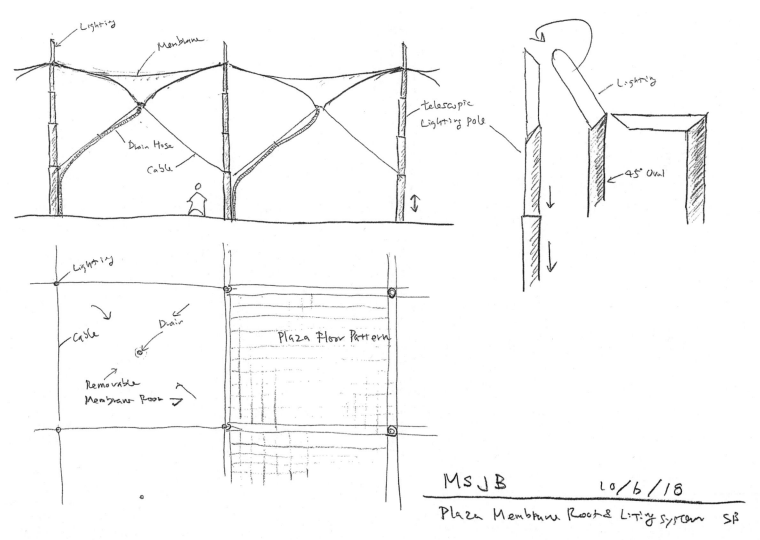

MSJB 10/6/18
Plaza Membrane Roof & Lighting System SB

Tech Company Visitor Center
テック企業ビジターセンター

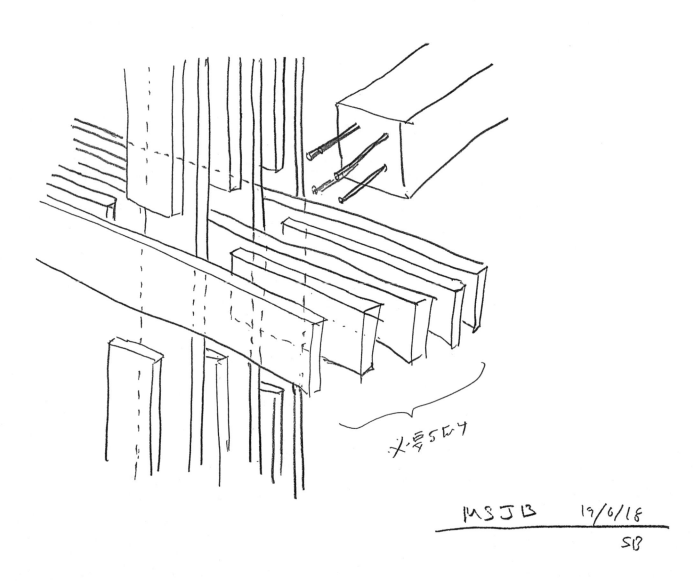

MSJB   19/6/18
SB

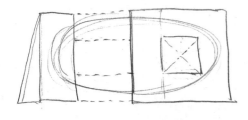
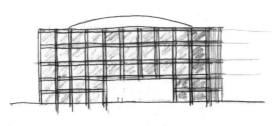
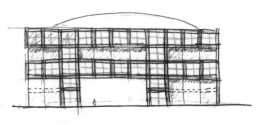

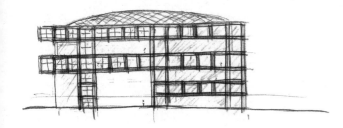

Microsoft 16/5/18
SB

Microsoft 16/5/18
SB

America's Cup Pavilion
アメリカズカップ・パビリオン

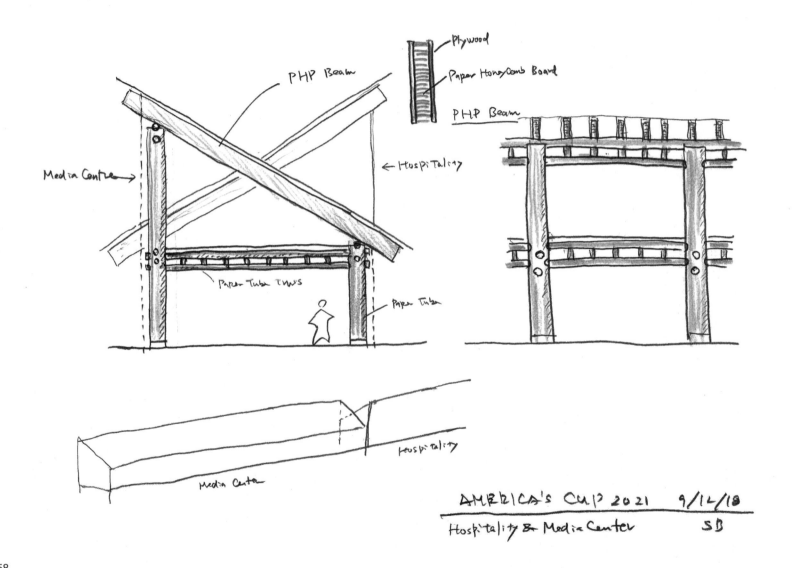

358

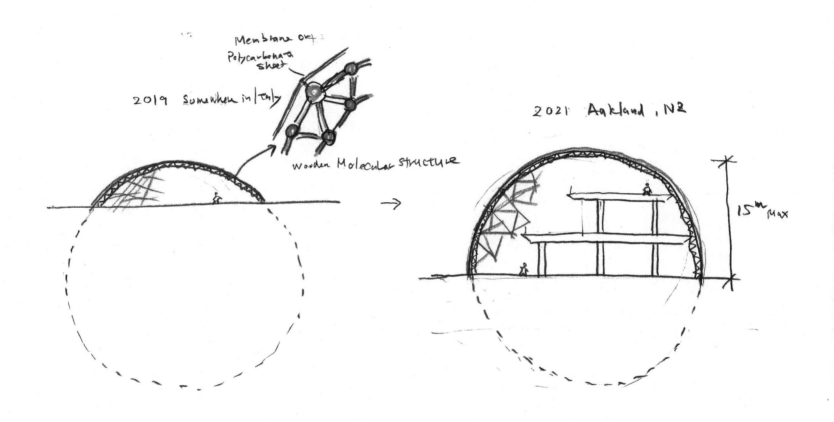

AMERICA's CUP 2019~2021   9/12/18
Luna Rossa Pavilion   S13

Chateau de Beaucastel
シャトー・ド・ボーカステル

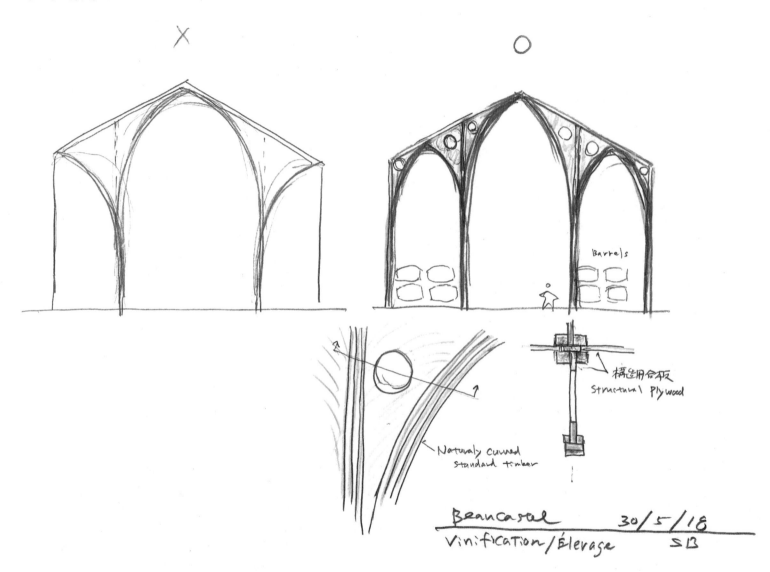

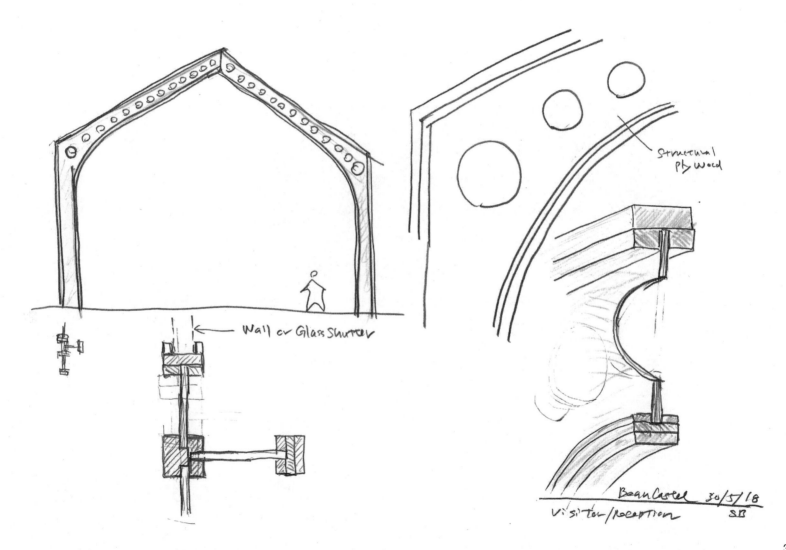
Wall or Glass Shutter

Structural Plywood

BeauCastel 30/5/18
Visitor/Reception   SB

Jack's Point Hotel
ジャックス・ポイント・ホテル

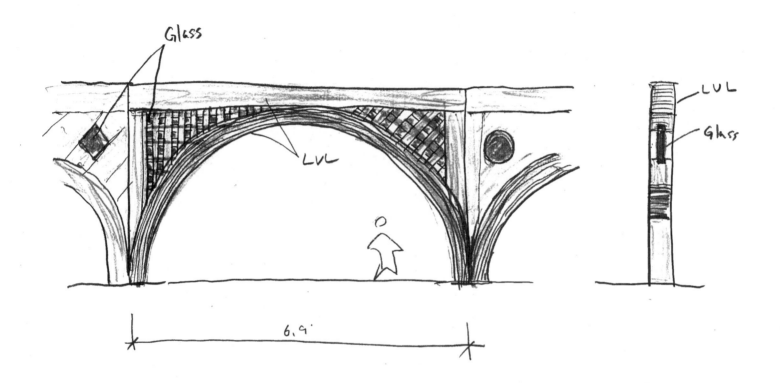

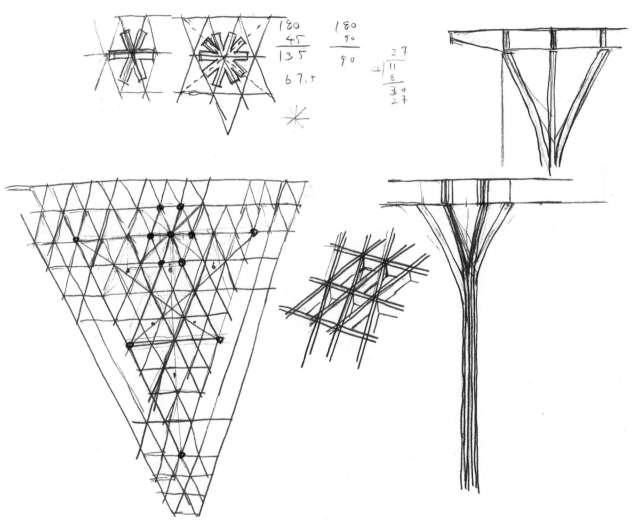

Jack's Point Hotel 24/3/19
SB

Oulu House & Pavilion
オウル・ハウス＆パビリオン

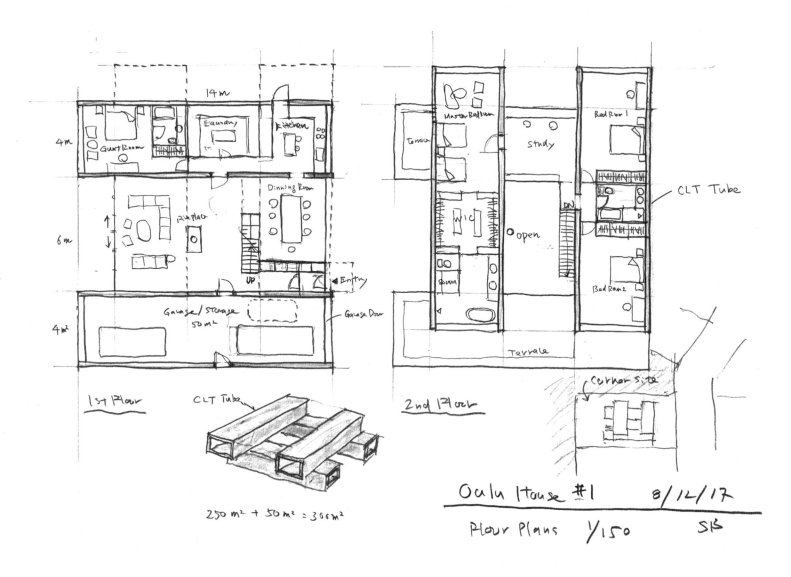

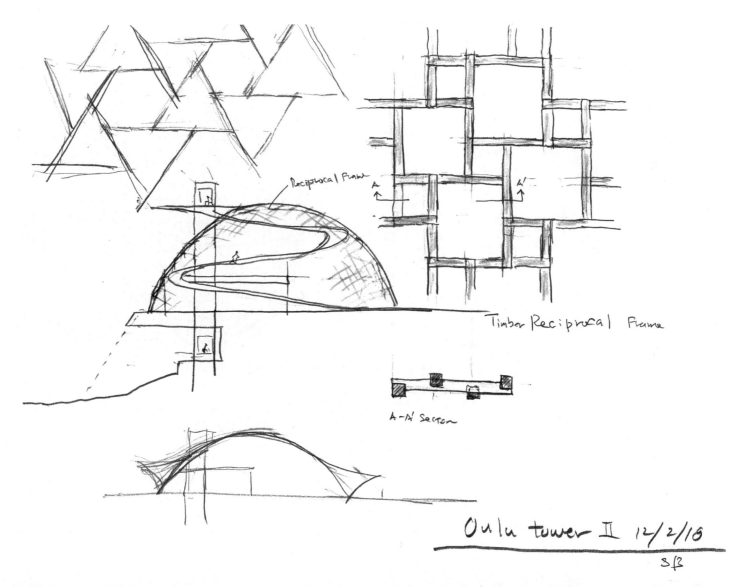

Oulu tower II 12/2/18

Swarovski Crystal Worlds Garden Pavilion
スワロフスキー・クリスタルワールド・ガーデン・パビリオン

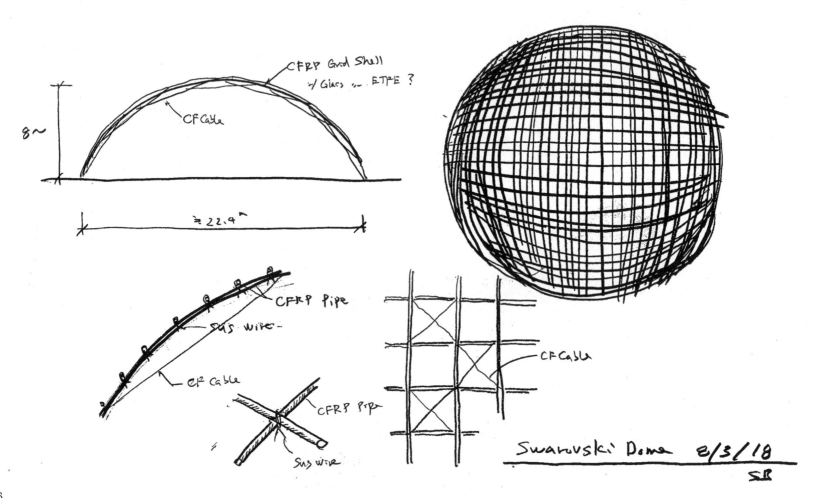

Swarovski Dome 8/3/18

The George Expansion
ザ・ジョージ 増築

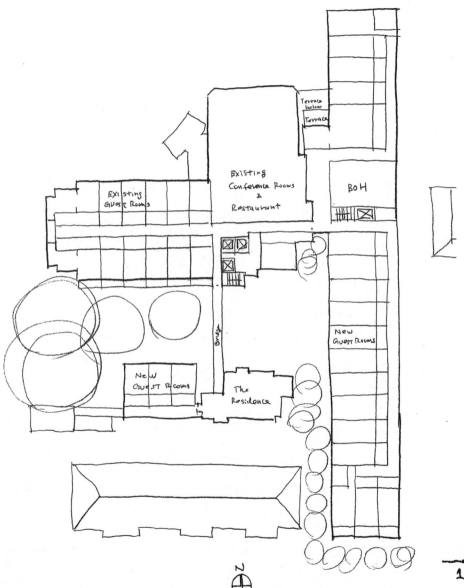

The George Expansion
1~3 Floor Plan 1/200 SB

The George Expansion
ザ・ジョージ 増築

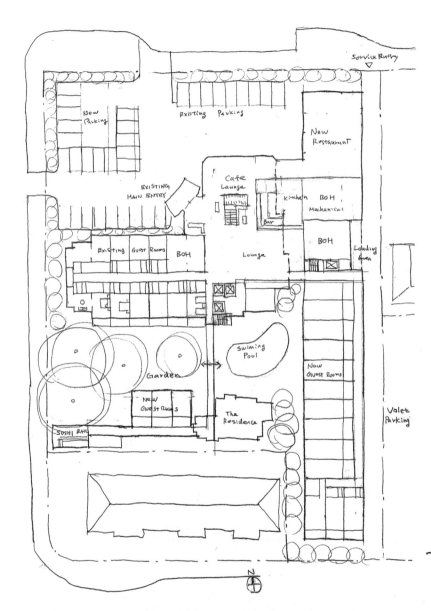

Parc Funeraire
パーク・フュネレール

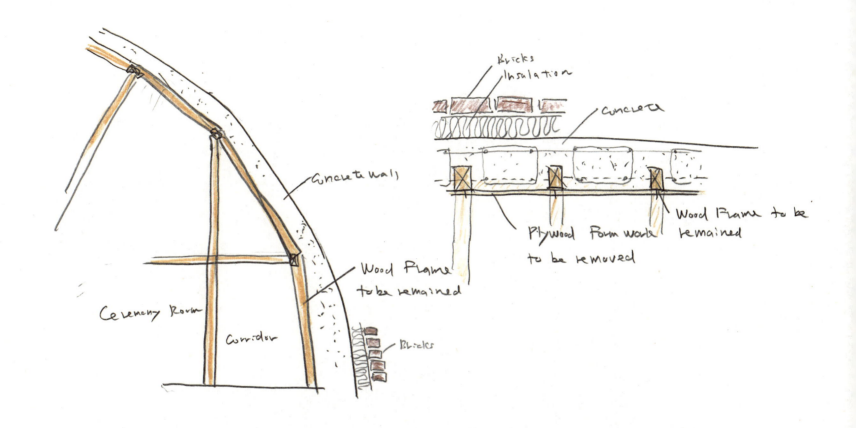

Parc Funéraire à Paris 18/6/18
Construction Detail   S13

Parc Funeraire
パーク・フュネレール

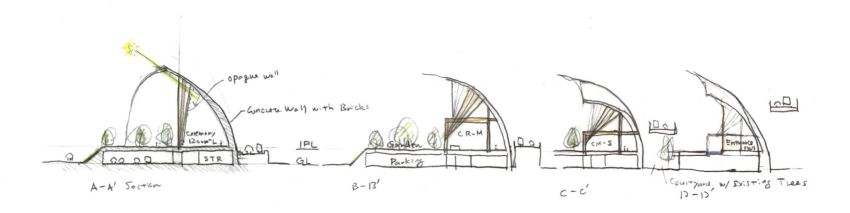

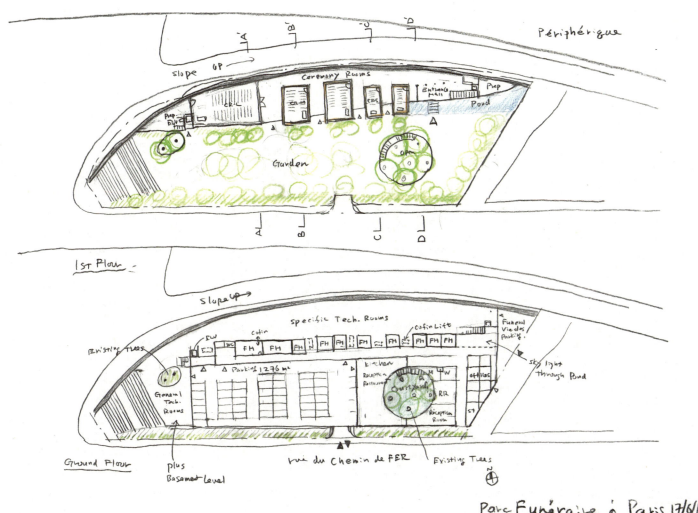

St. Vincent de Paul
聖ヴァンサン・ド・ポール

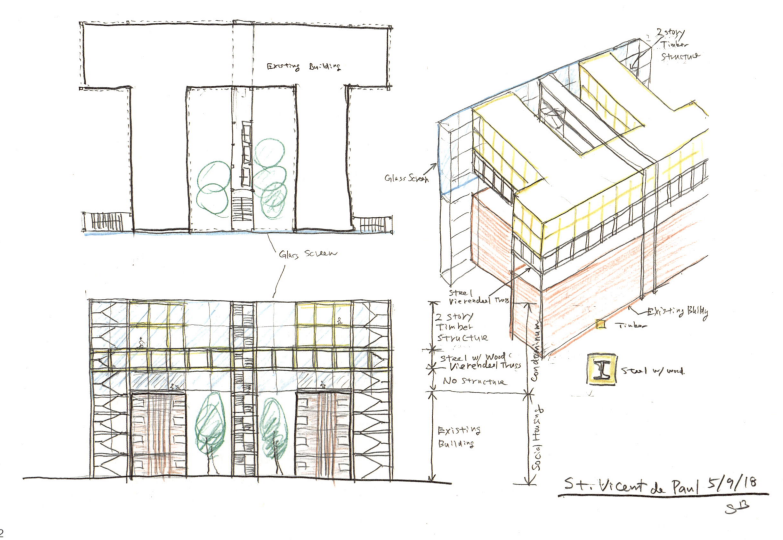

Toyota City Museum
豊田市博物館

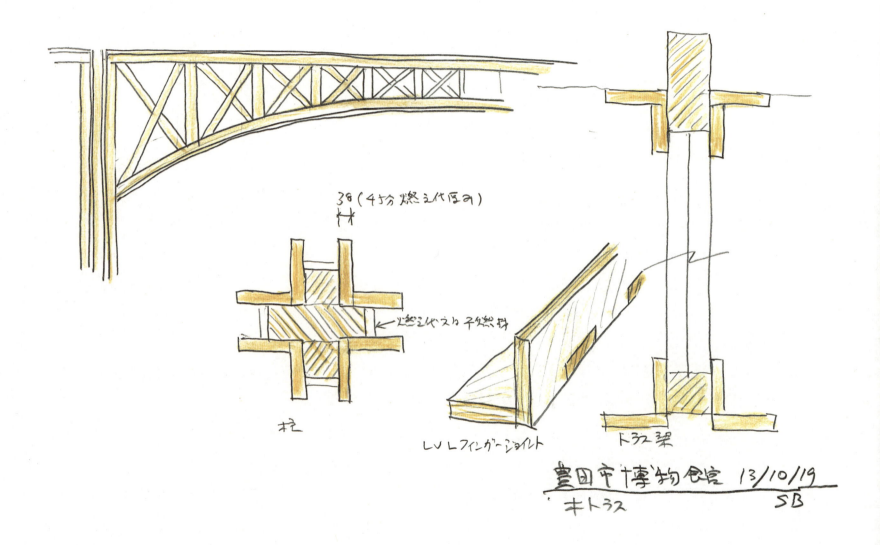

373

Toyota City Museum
豊田市博物館

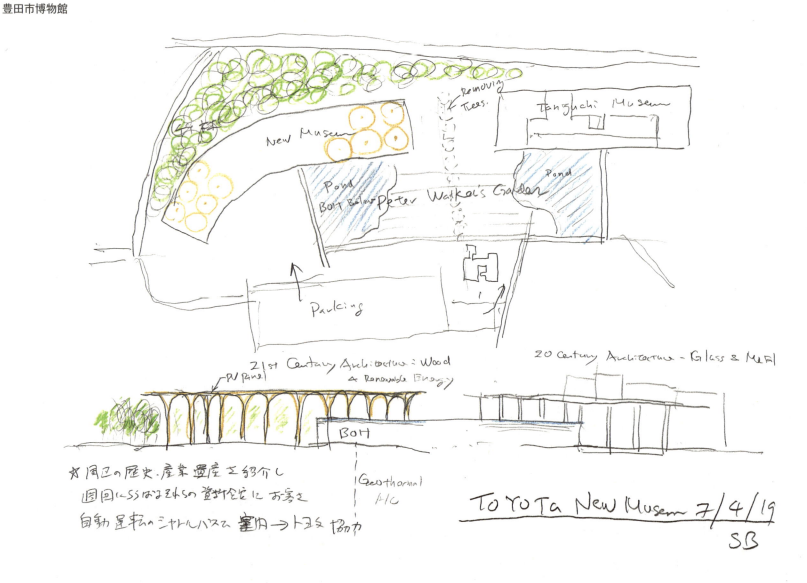

Wooden Rugby "Ball" Park
木造ラグビー"ボール"パーク

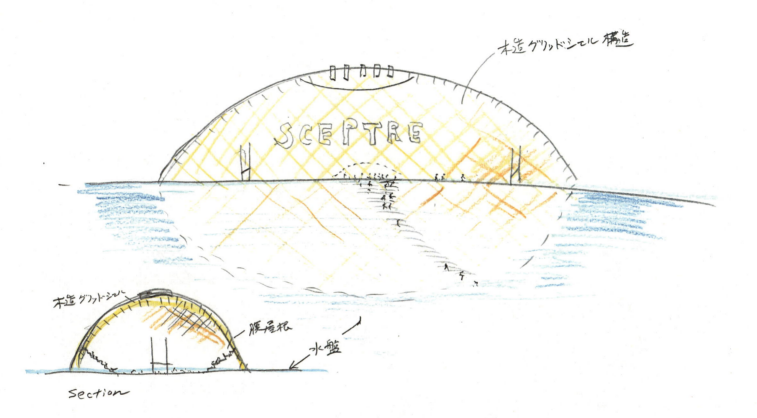

375

NWD K11 Art Mall & K11 ARTUS
NWD K11 アートモール & K11 アータス

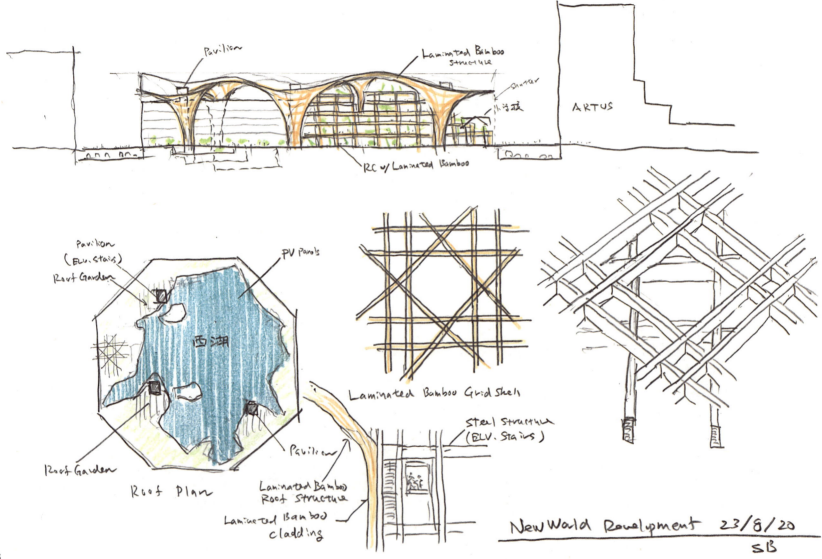

Park City House Event Pavilion
パークシティハウス・イベントパビリオン

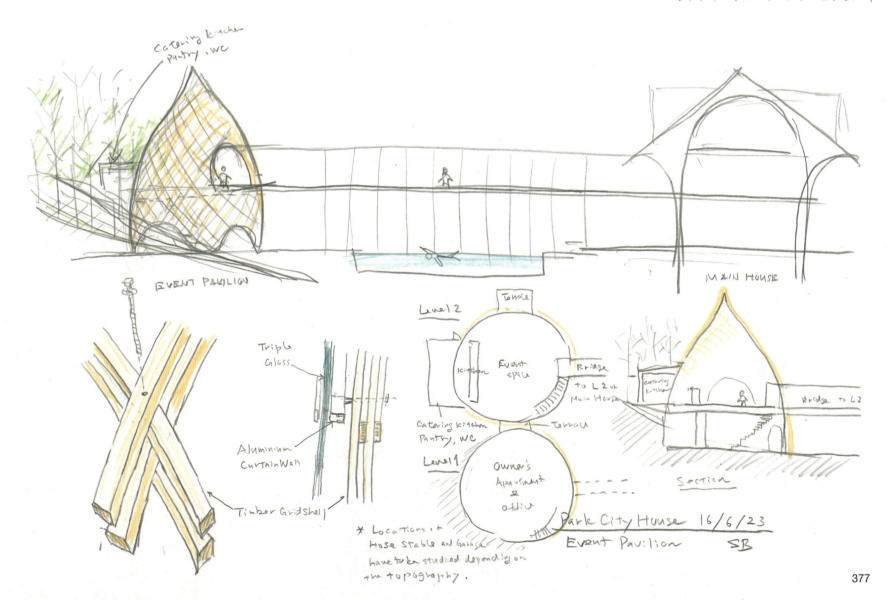

Penn State University Art Museum
ペンシルベニア州立大学美術館

Penn State Univ. Art Museum — 3
6/3/19   SB

3. Openable Flower (Mountain Laurel of State Flower of Pennsylvania)

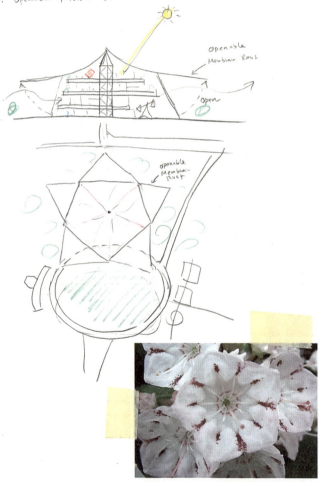

Openable Membran Roof

Open

Openable Membran Roof

Penn State Univ. Art Museum - 1
6/3/19   SB

1. Big Roof as Forest

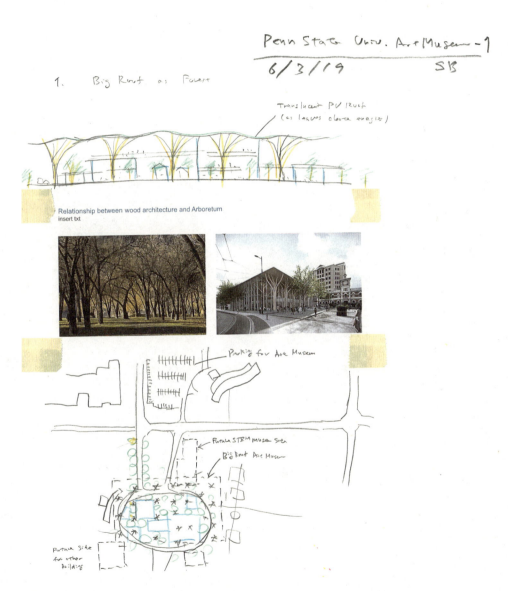

Hotel Iwaya
岩屋ホテル

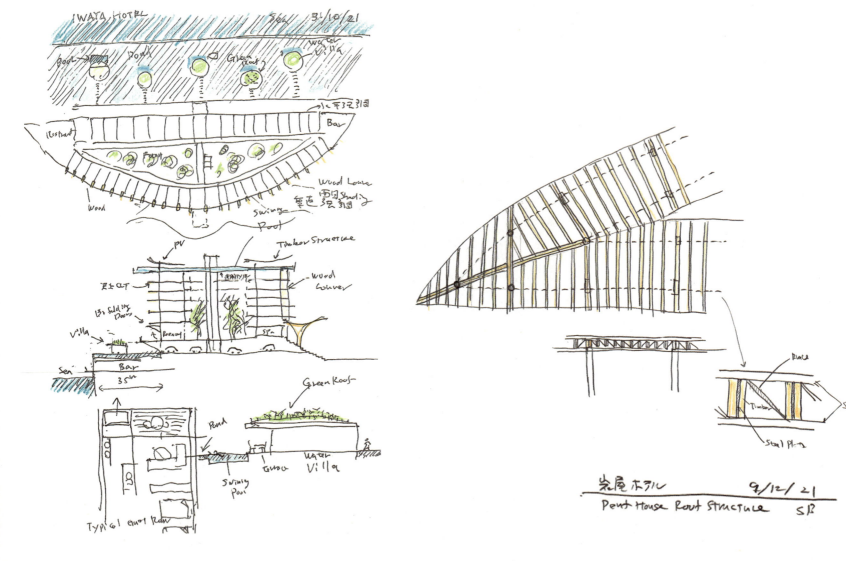

Jabal Ikmah Interpretive Centre
ジャバル・イクマ　ビジターセンター

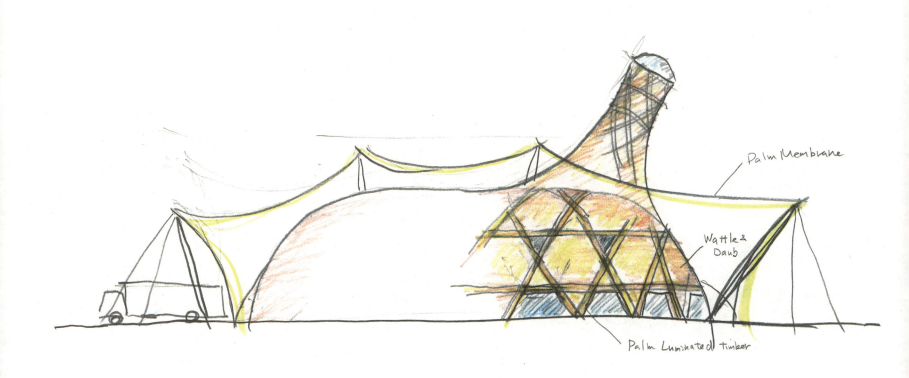

Dadan Interpretive Center
ダダン ビジターセンター

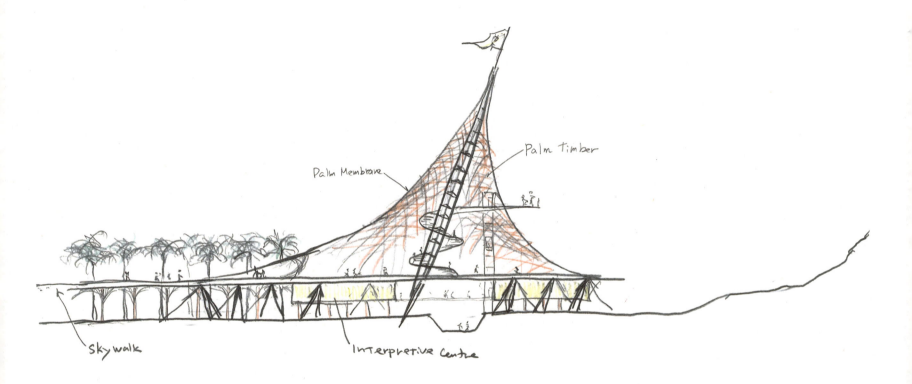

KONFiDA stand ITMA
KONFiDA 社ブース　ITMA 国際繊維機械展示会

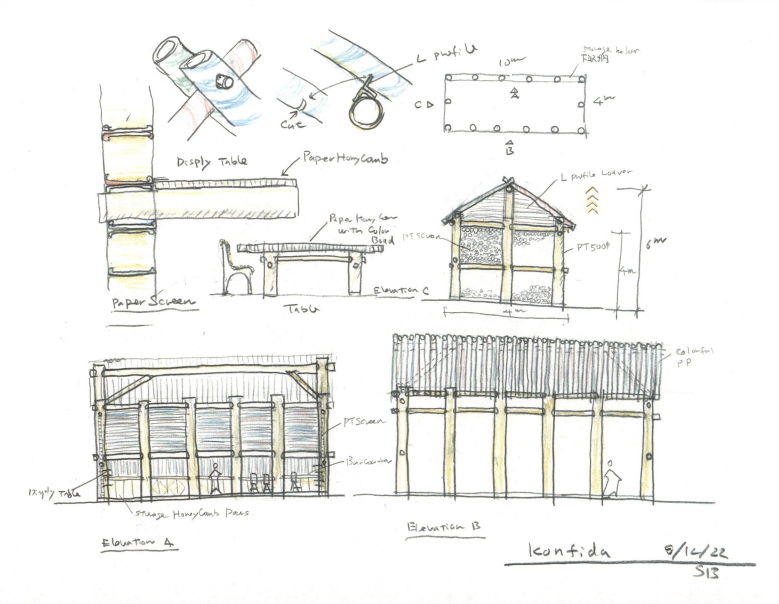

Paper Log House (Turkey/Syria)
紙のログハウス（トルコ / シリア）

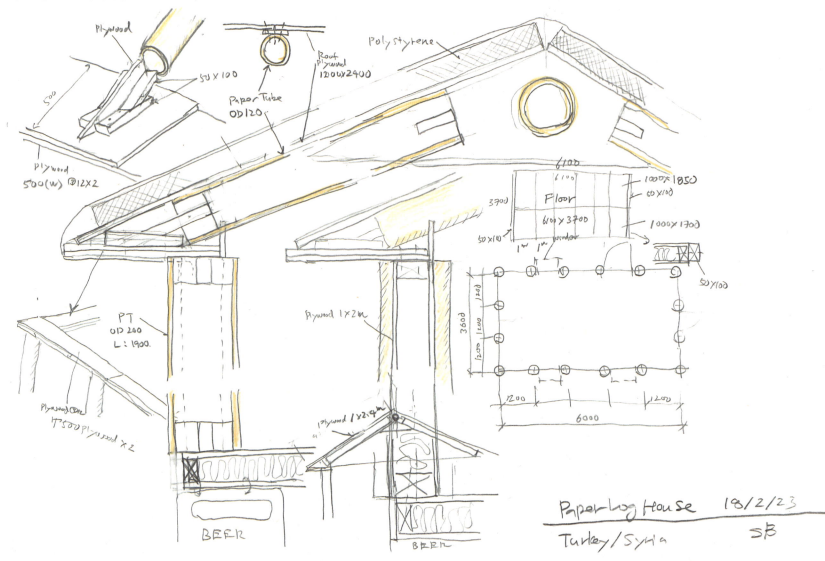

Bookshelf House
本棚の家

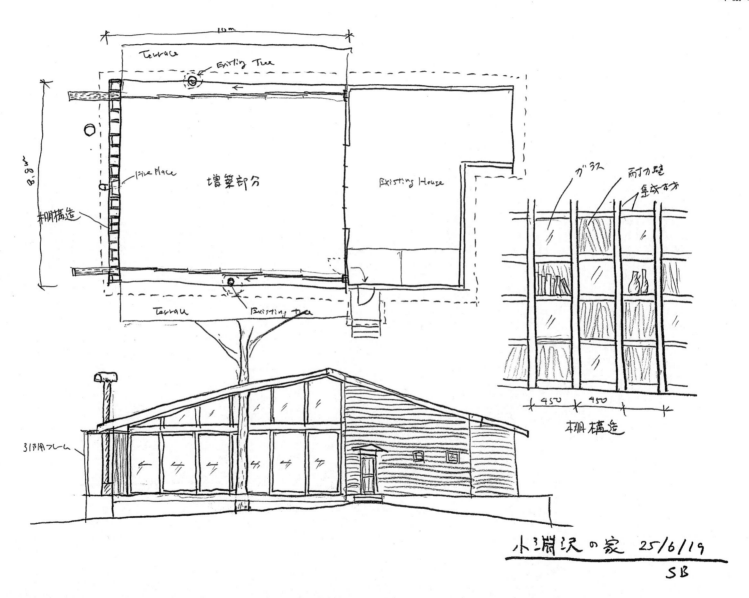

Culture and Art Center in Guizhou
文化センター・中国貴州省

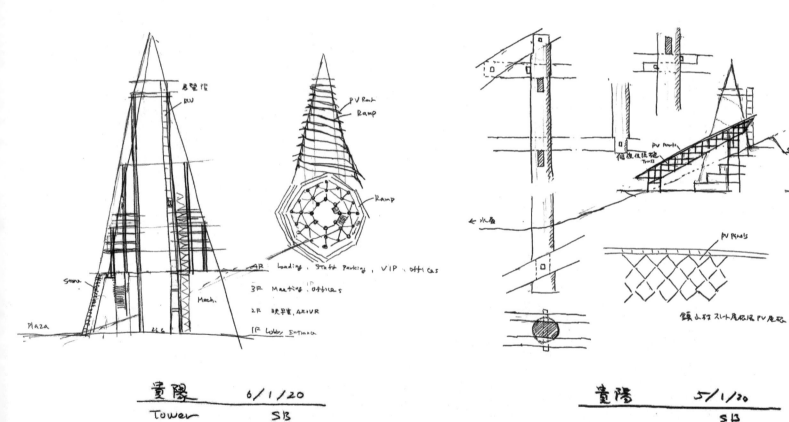

Farmer's Restaurant Haru San-San
農家レストラン 陽・燦燦

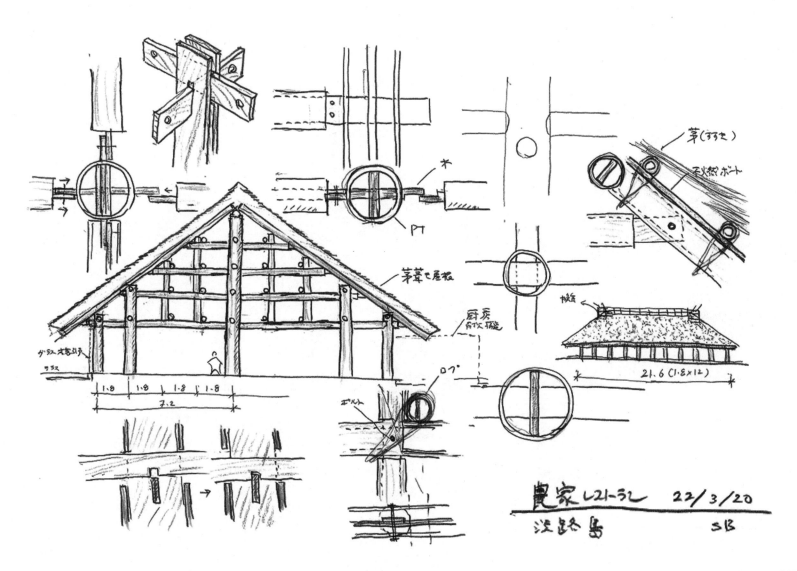

Birmingham
バーミンガム

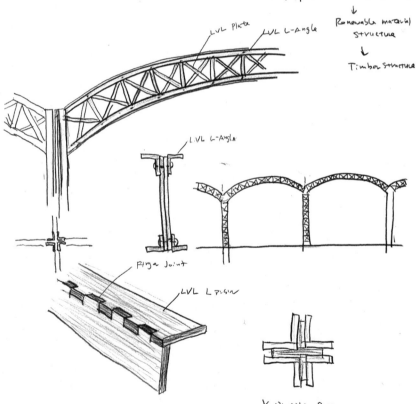

Grand Palais Ephemere
グラン・パレ・エフェメール

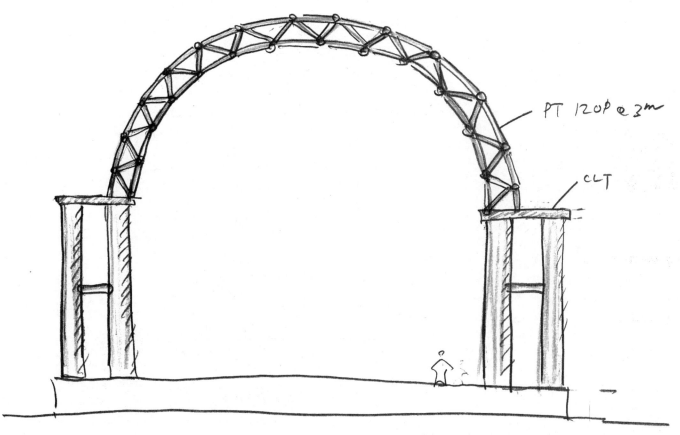

389

Grand Palais Ephemere
グラン・パレ・エフェメール

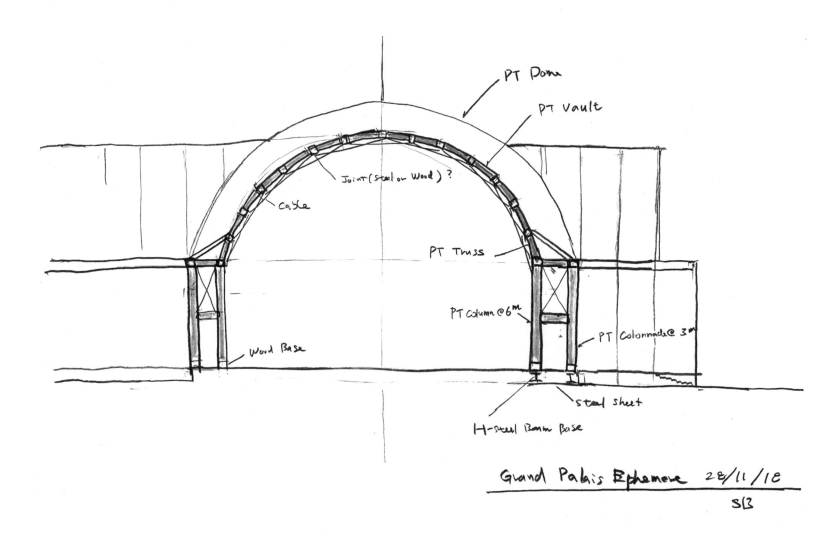

Renovation Project of the Former Architecture School in Nanterre
ナンテール旧建築学校リノヴェーション

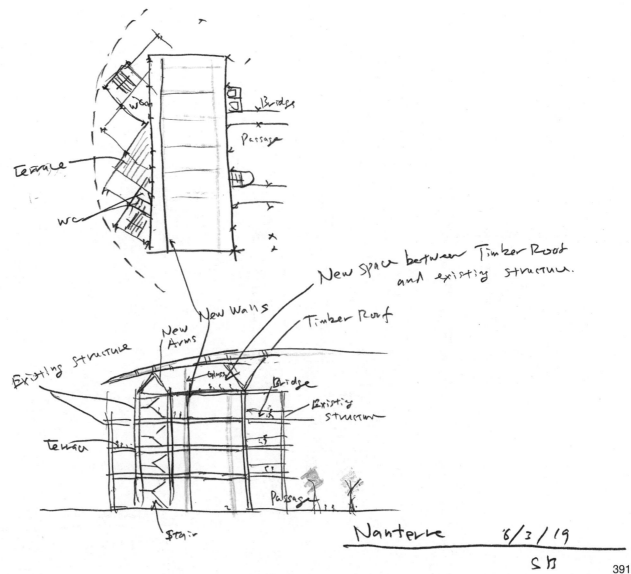

Temporary Pavilion for Notre-Dame de Paris
ノートルダム大聖堂のための仮設パビリオン

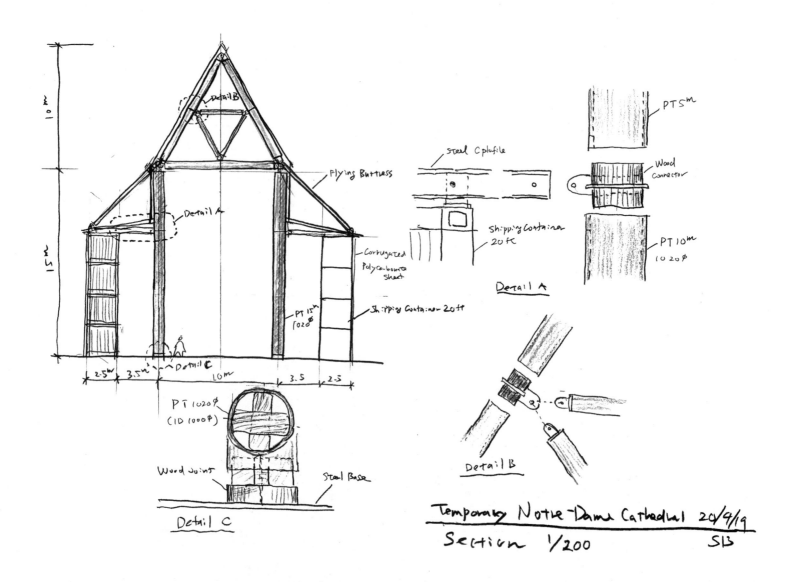

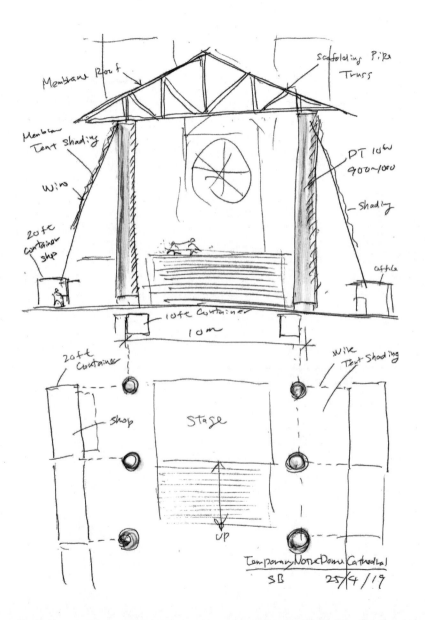

Temporary Pavilion for Notre-Dame de Paris
ノートルダム大聖堂のための仮設パビリオン

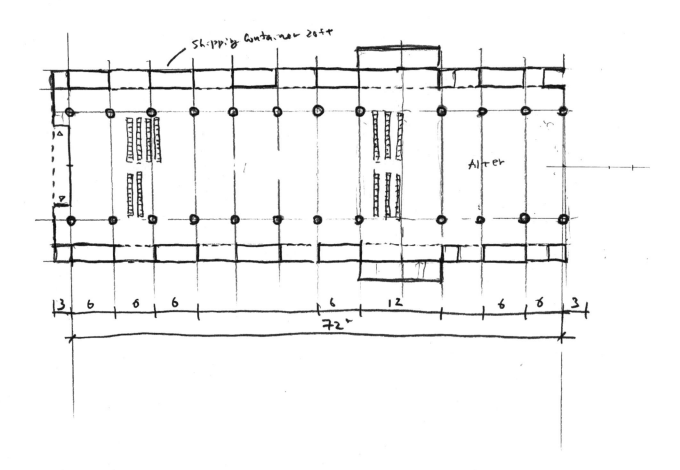

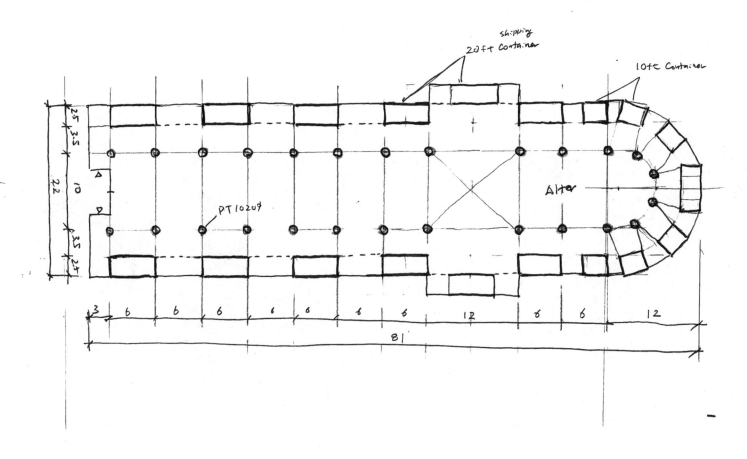

TULCHAN
タルカン

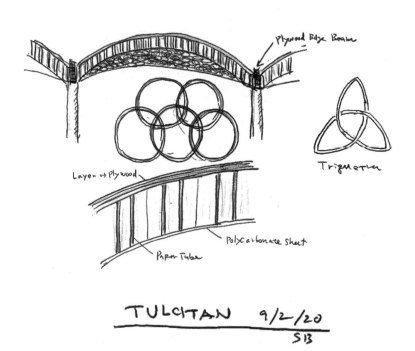

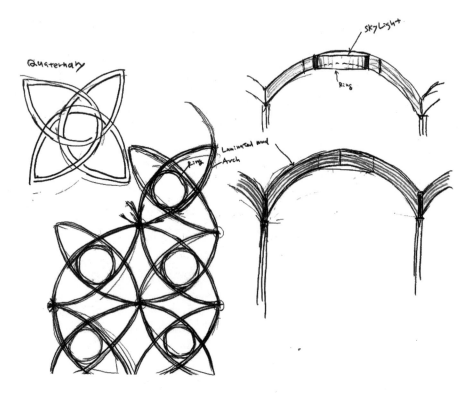

New memorial garden at International Committee of the Red Cross headquarters
国際赤十字委員会本部　新記念庭園

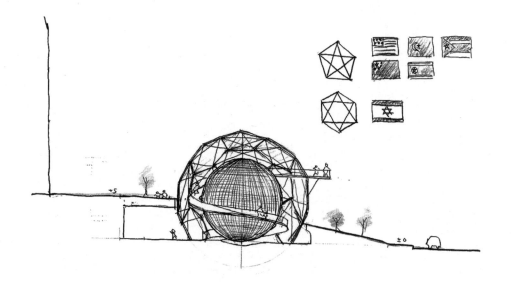
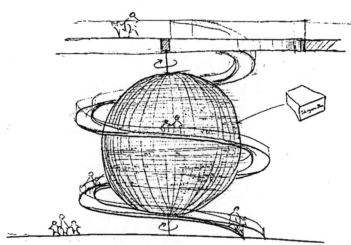

Farmer's Hut
農家の小屋

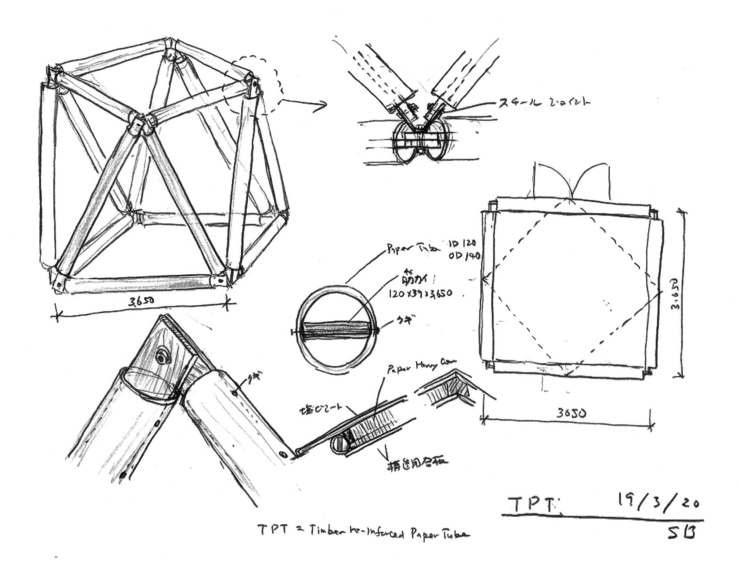

398

Isa City New Hall
伊佐市新庁舎

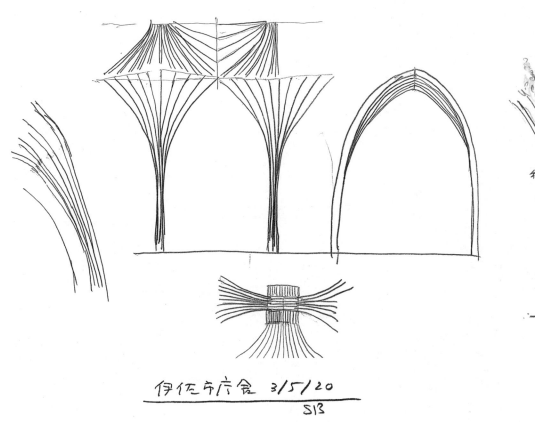
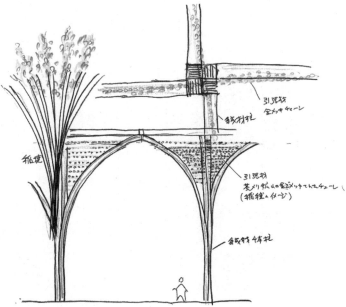

399

Atelier Gren
アトリエ・グレン

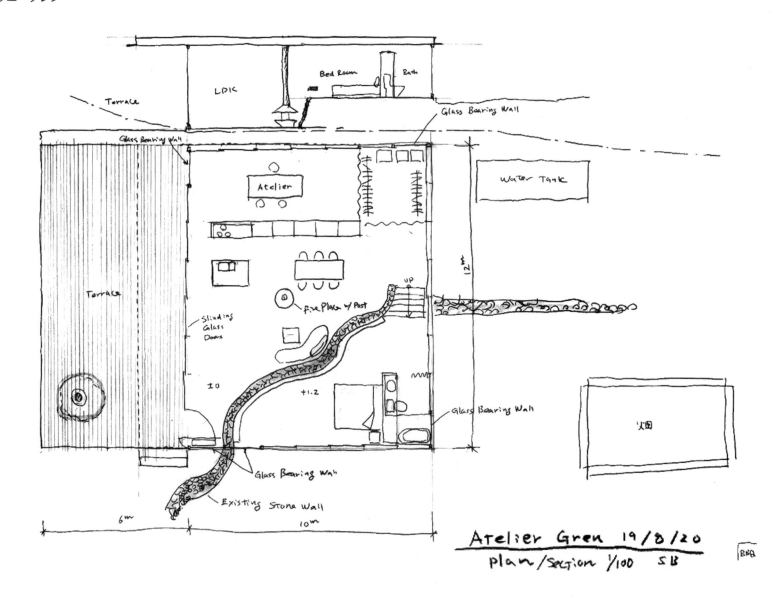

Zao Onsen
蔵王温泉

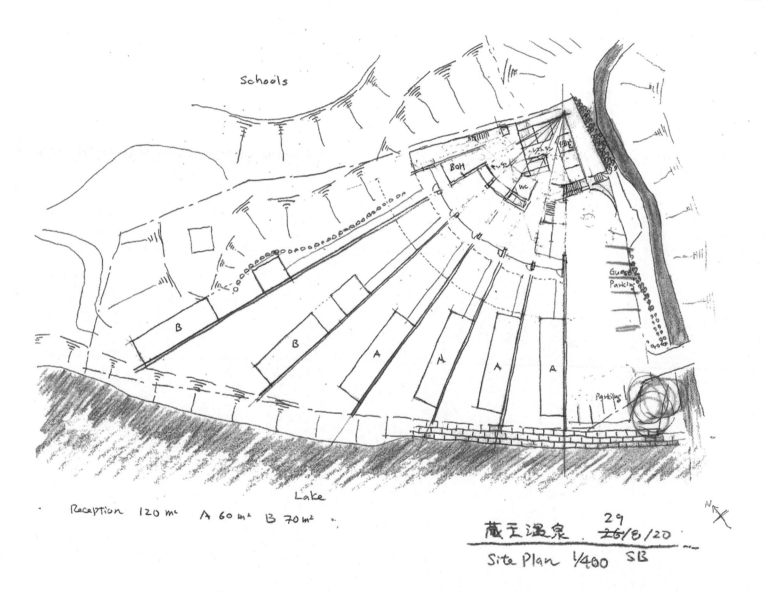

Duved
デュヴド

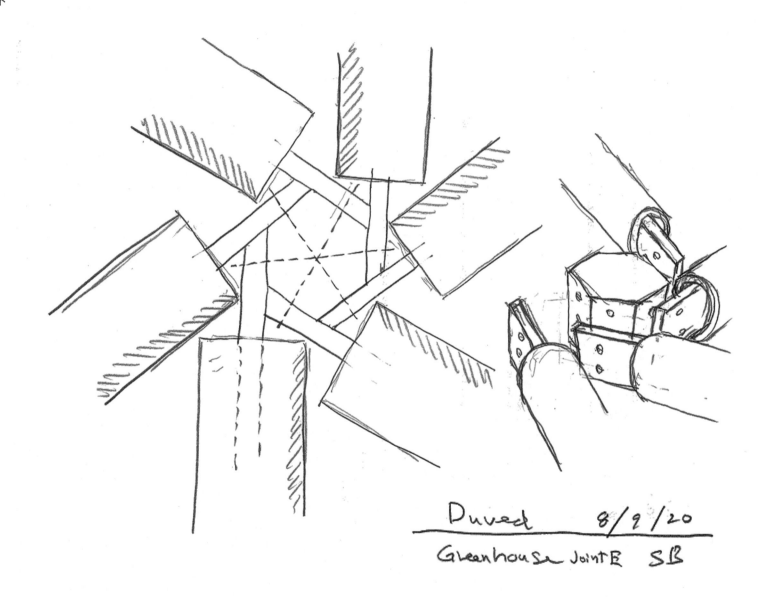

Duved 8/9/20
Greenhouse Joint E SB

Bridge design at Vanke Hangzhou 2022 Asian Games Athlete Village
万科杭州 2022 アジア競技大会選手村　ブリッジ案

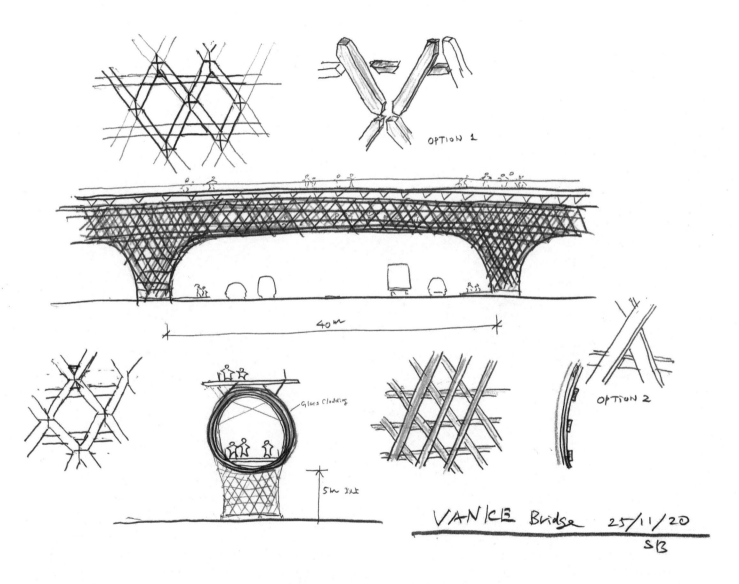

Lounge Furnitures
ラウンジ用家具

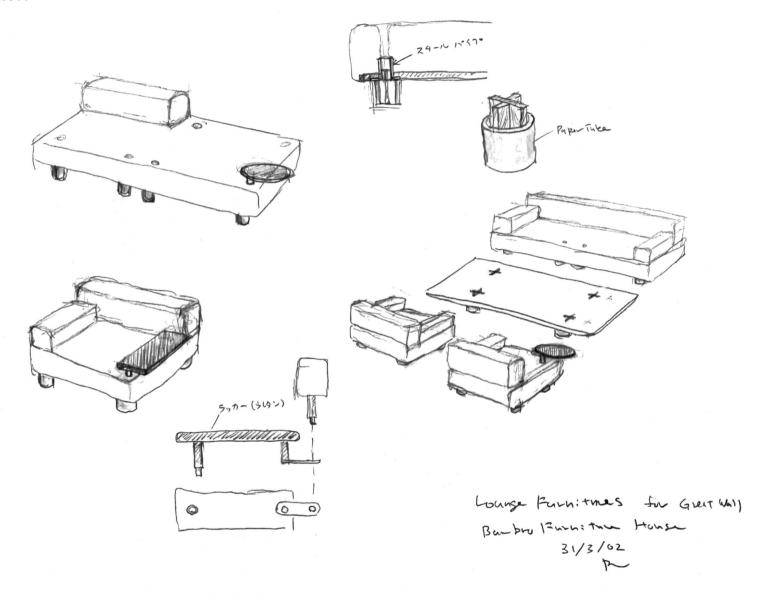

Karuizawa Town Hall
軽井沢庁舎

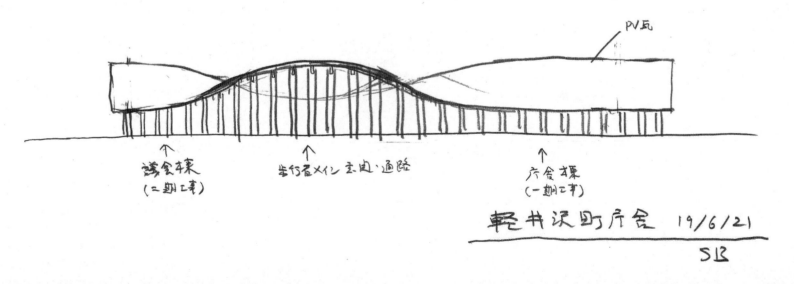

軽井沢町庁舎 19/6/21

Blue Ocean Dome
ブルー・オーシャン・ドーム

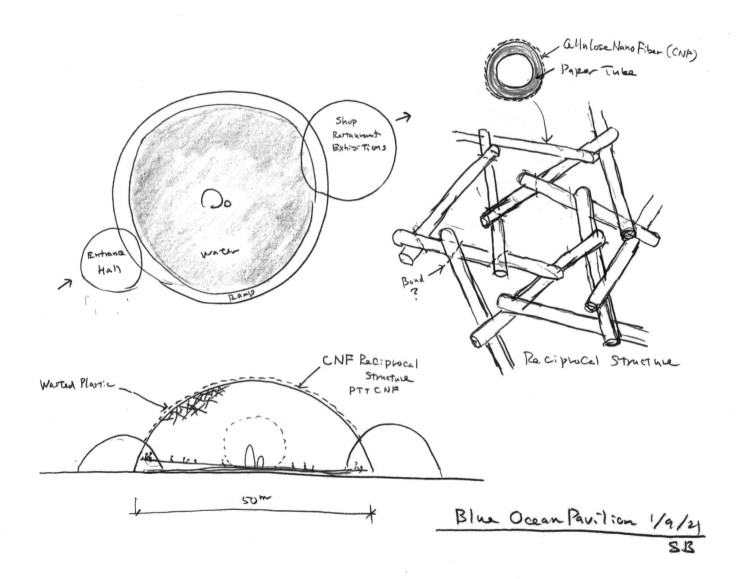

406

Hotel in Taikoo Li Xi'an
西安タイクーリ・ホテル

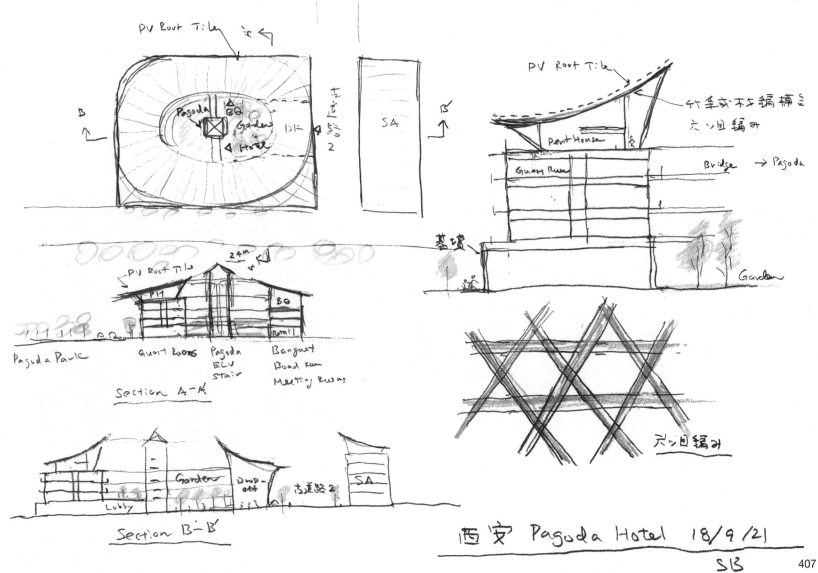

Shizuoka Central Library
静岡県立中央図書館

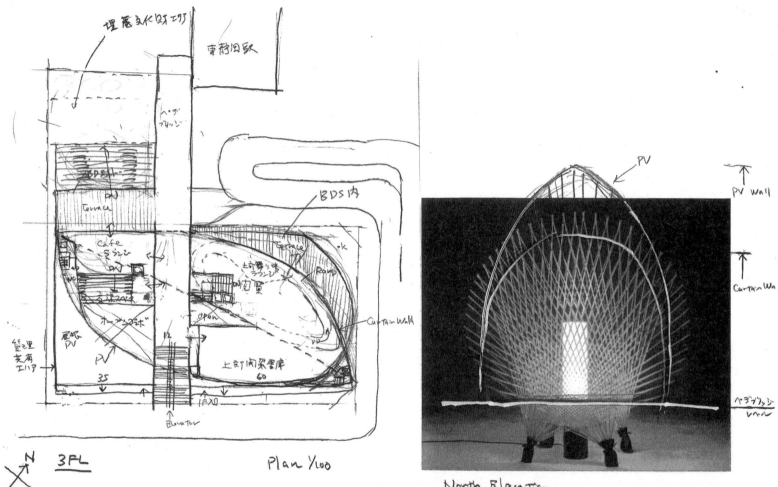

408

Guilin Pavilion
桂林パビリオン

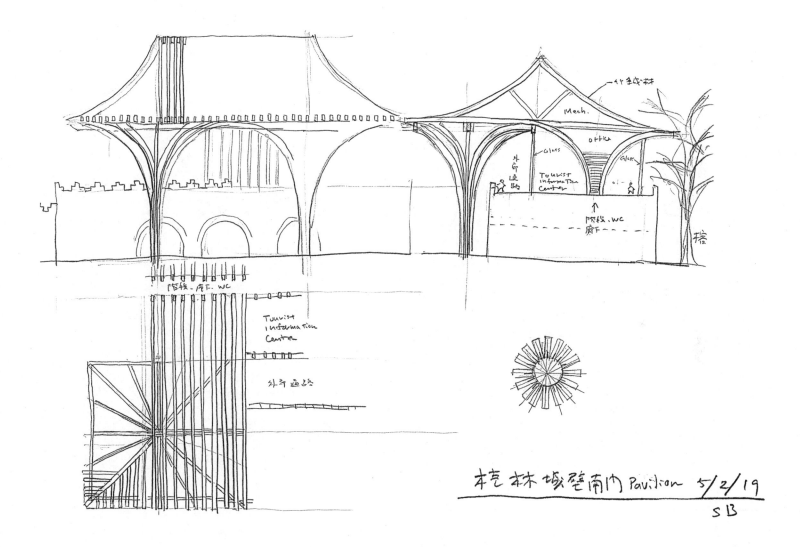

Guilin Pavilion
桂林パビリオン

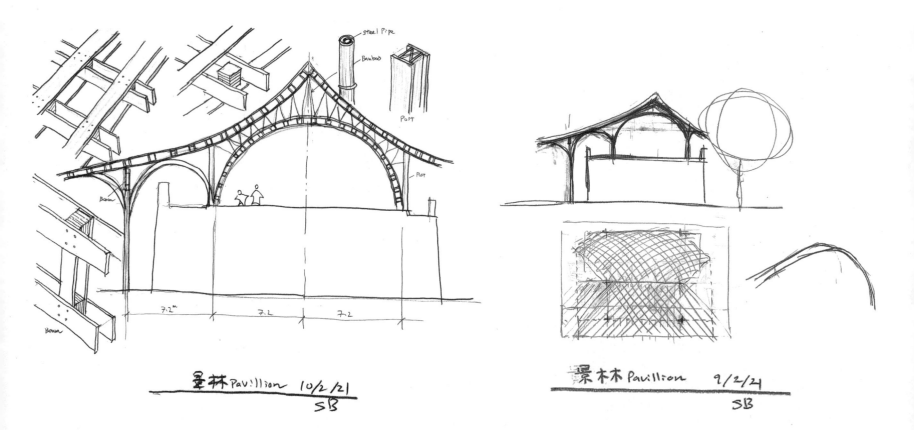

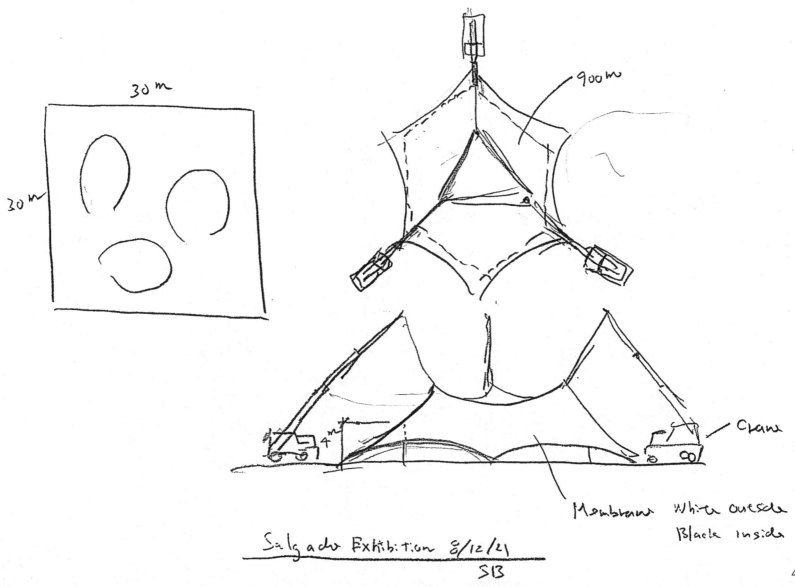

Wood-Steel Composite Truss
木スチール複合トラス

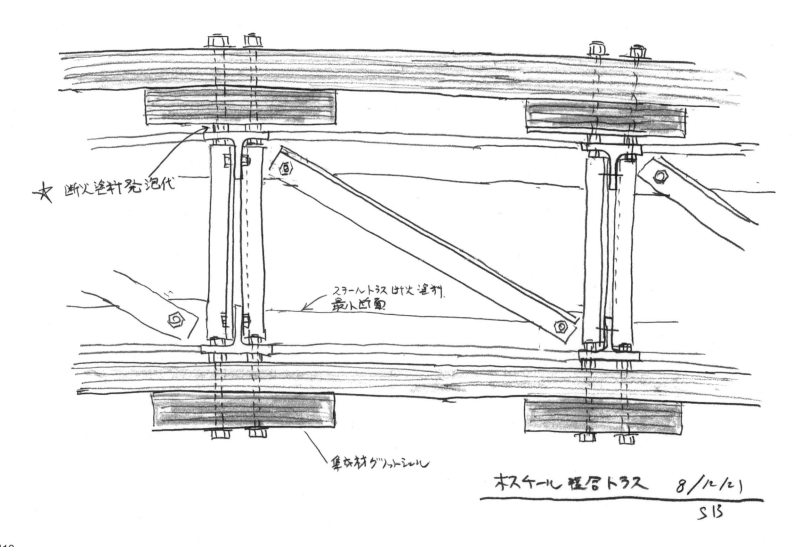

TIFFANY & Co Store Façade
ティファニー 店舗ファサード

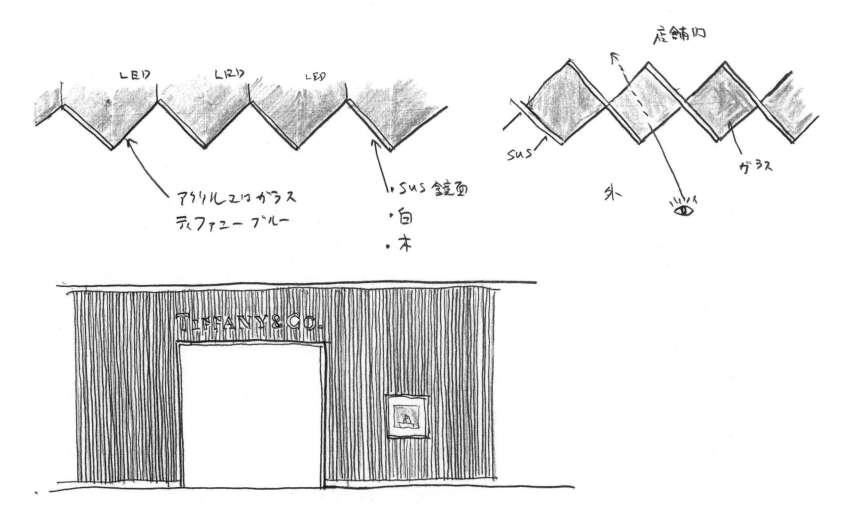

TIFFANY & Co.   20/12/21
Façade   SB

4G Wine Estate
4G ワイン・エステート

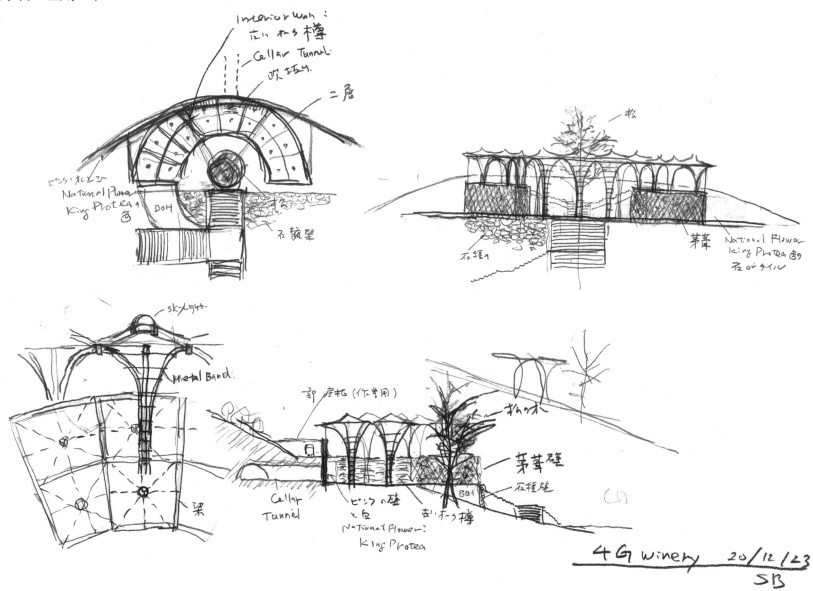

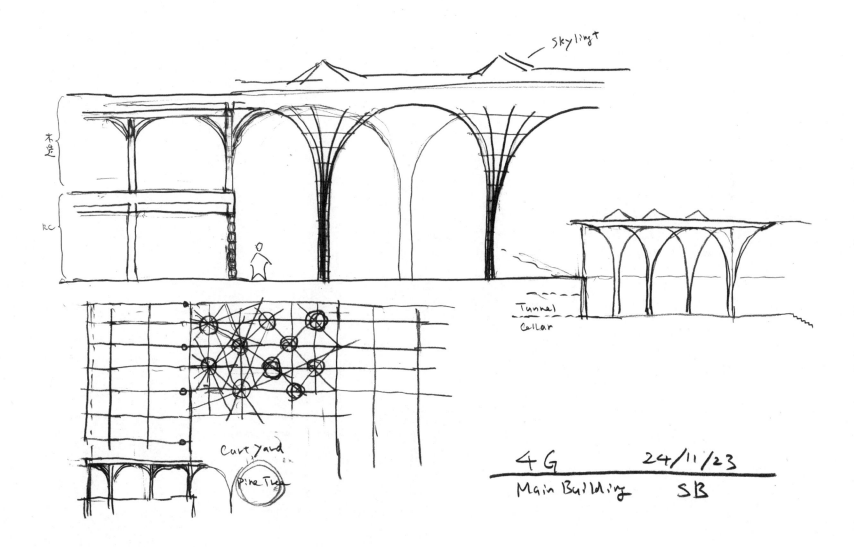

M Residence
M 邸

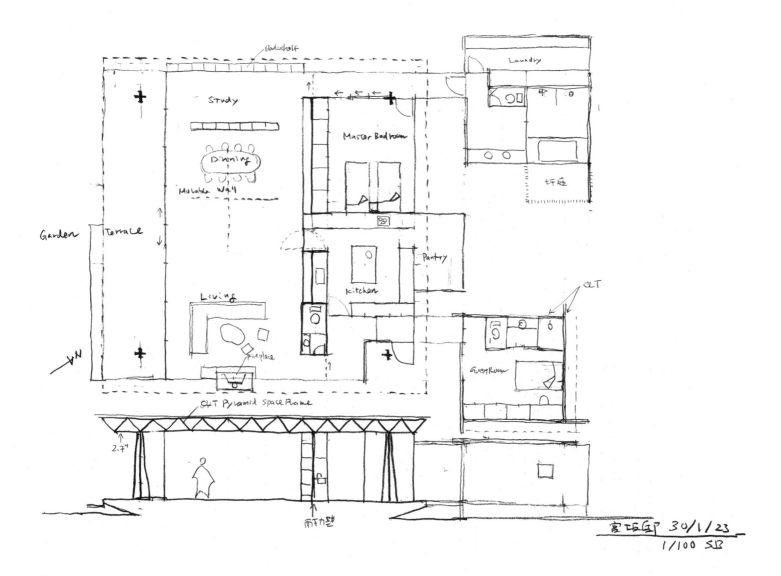

Breus Art Centre
ブレウス・アートセンター

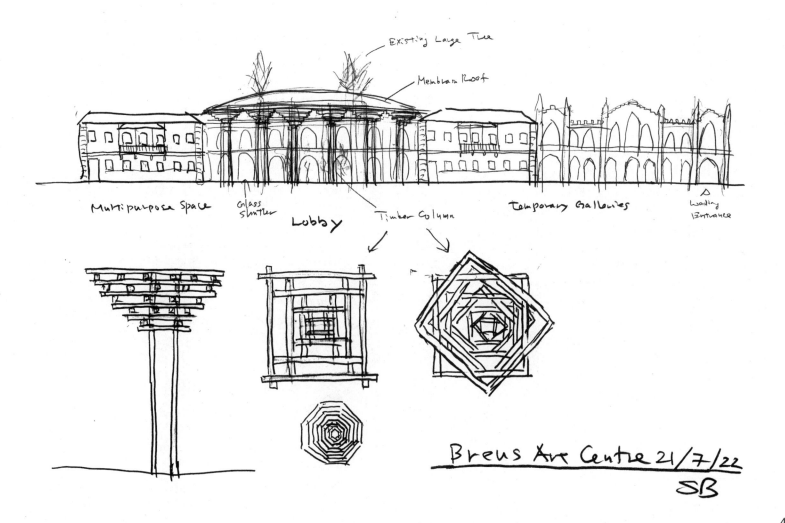

Lviv City Hospital
リヴィウ市病院

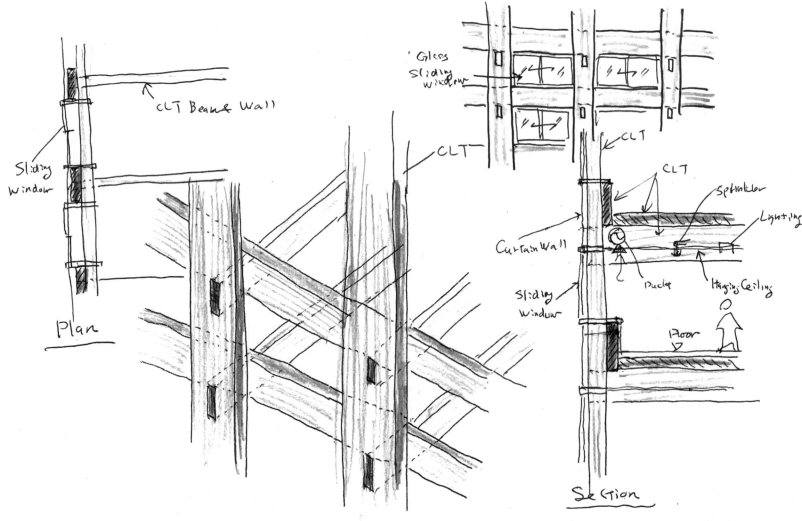

Shiosai Restaurant
潮騒レストラン

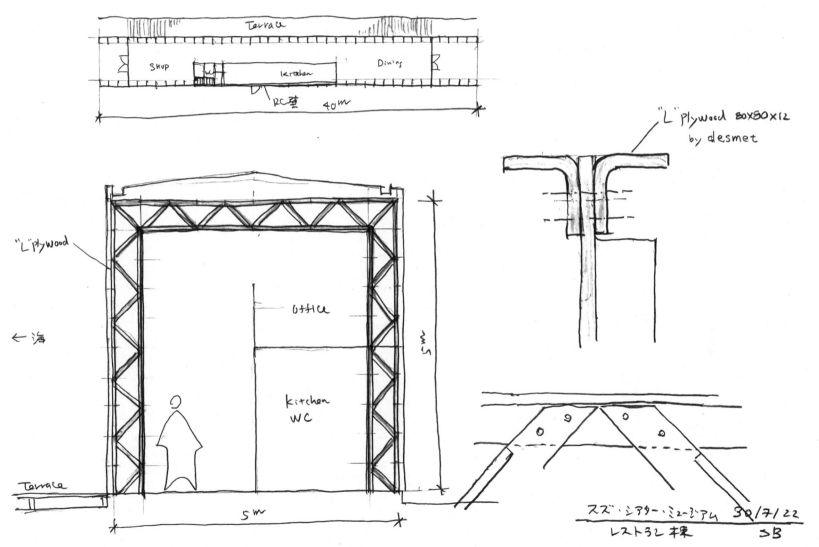

Index

Odawara Festival Main Hall　East Gate of Odawara Festival	小田原パビリオン　メイン会場東ゲート	8
Odawara Festival Main Hall	小田原パビリオン	9
Library of a Poet	詩人の書庫	10-11
Villa Kuru	ヴィラ　クル	12-14
MDS Gallery	紙のギャラリー	15
Paper House	紙の家	16-17
Dengyosha Factory at Hamura	羽村の工場　電業社	18
Studio for Vocalists	声楽家の家	19-20
House of Double-Roof	ダブル・ルーフの家	21
House for a Dentist	デンティストの家	22
Paper Temporary Studio	紙の仮設スタジオ	23
Maison E	メゾン　E	24
Papertainer Museum	ペーパーテイナー美術館	25
Sagaponac House	サガポナック・ハウス	26
Kennedys Bush House	ケネディーズ・ブッシュ・ハウス	27
House at Hanegi Park - Vista	羽根木公園の家 - 景色の道	28-29
Chenjia Town Clubhouse, Chongming Island	崇明島陳家クラブハウス	30-31
Japan Pavilion Hannover EXPO 2000	ハノーバー国際博覧会 2000　日本館	32-37
Paper Log House - Kobe	紙のログハウス - 神戸	38-39
Paper Church	紙の教会	40

2/5 House	2/5 ハウス	41
Tazawako Station	JR 田沢湖駅／田沢湖観光情報センター	42
Hanegi Forest	羽根木の森	43-45
Paper Dome	紙のドーム	46
Ivy Structure 1	アイビー・ストラクチャー1	47
Paper Emergency Shelter for UNHCR	国民難民高等弁務官事務所用の紙のシェルター	48-49
Nemunoki Children's Art Museum	ねむの木こども美術館	50
GC Osaka Building	GC 大阪営業所ビル	51
Imai Hospital Daycare Center	今井病院付属託児所	52
Shutter House for a Photographer	写真家のシャッター・ハウス	53
Picture Window House	ピクチャー・ウィンドウの家	54
Bamboo Furniture House	竹の家具の家	55
Sugar Muddler	砂糖のマドラー	56
Atsushi Imai Memorial Gymnasium	今井篤記念体育館	57
Takatori Catholic Church	膜の教会　カトリックたかとり教会	58
Nicolas G. Hayek Center	ニコラス・G・ハイエック・センター	59-60
Dormitory H	社員寮　H	61
Kirinda House – Tsunami Reconstruction Project	津波後のキリンダ村復興プロジェクト	62
Mul(ti)houses	マルチ・ハウス	63-65
Nomadic Museum New York	ノマディック美術館　ニューヨーク	66-70

Atelier for a Glass Artist	ガラス作家のアトリエ	71-73
Seikei Library	成蹊大学情報図書館	74-75
Haesley Nine Bridges Golf Clubhouse	ヘスリー・ナインブリッジズ・ゴルフ・クラブハウス	76-83
Paper Bridge, Remoulin	紙の橋	84-85
Sheikh Zayed National Museum	シェイク・ザイード国立博物館	86-95
Aspen Art Museum	アスペン美術館	96-104
Tamedia New Office Building	タメディア新本社	105
Paper Temporary School - Chengdu Hualin Elementary School	成都市華林小学校　紙管仮設校舎	106-107
Centre Pompidou-Metz	ポンピドー・センター　メス	108-142
EXPO 2012 Yoesu Thematic Pavilion	麗水国際博覧会 2012　テーマ館	143-144
Hong Kong- Shenzhen Bi-City Biennale Pavilion	香港深圳ビエンナーレ パビリオン	145
L'Aquila Temporary Concert Hall	ラクイラ仮設音楽ホール	146-147
Kazakhstan Drama Theater	カザフスタン国立劇場	148
Paper Emergency Shelters – Haiti	ハイチ緊急シェルター	149
Kaohsiung Port and Cruise Service Center	高雄　港クルーズ・サービスセンター	150
Haesley Condominium	ヘスリー・コンドミニアム	151
Hangzhou Golf Clubhouse	杭州市 ゴルフ・クラブハウス	152
AP Building	AP ビル	153
Cardboard Cathedral	紙のカテドラル	154
Skolkovo Golf Clubhouse	スコルコボ・ゴルフ・クラブハウス	155-159

Villa at Sengokubara	仙石原の住宅	160
Ristia Resort, Bali	リスティア・リゾート	161-164
Module H	モジュラー・アッシュ	165-166
National Library of Israel	イスラエル国立図書館	167
Ginza Façade Project	銀座ファサードプロジェクト	168
New Museum of Modern Art Toyama	新富山県立近代美術館	169-170
La Seine Musicale	ラ・セーヌ・ミュジカル	171-174
Oita Prefectural Art Museum	大分県立美術館	175
New National Stadium Japan	新国立競技場コンペ	176-177
Kyoto University of Art and Design Disaster Relief Center	京都造形芸術大学 災害支援センター	178
New Temporary House	新仮設住宅	179
Doshisha University Kyotanabe Campus Chapel	同志社大学　京田辺キャンパス礼拝堂	180
M+	エム・プラス	181
Onagawa Station / Onagawa Onsen Yupo'po	女川駅舎・女川温泉温浴施設ゆぽっぽ	182-183
Tech Company HQ Campus Pavilion	テック企業本社キャンパス・パビリオン	184-185
Garage Center for Contemporary Culture Temporary Pavilion	モスクワ仮設美術館　GARAGE	186-187
Madrid Paper Pavilion	マドリッド紙のパビリオン	188
Solid Cedar House	無垢杉の家	189
Abu Dhabi Art Pavilion	アブダビ・アート・パビリオン	190-192
Swatch / Omega Campus	スウォッチ・オメガ本社	193

Mt. Fuji World Heritage Centre, Shizuoka	静岡県富士山世界遺産センター	194-195
Mt. Fuji Shizuoka Airport	富士山静岡空港	196
Roman's Spa	ローマンズ・スパ	197
Shishi-iwa House, Karuizawa	ししいわハウス	198-199
Self-Build House in Nepal	ネパール震災復興住宅	200-201
DMZ Bamboo Passage	DMZ　竹のパサージュ	202-205
Terrace House	テラスハウス	206-207
Expo 2020 Dubai Mobility Signature Pavilion	ドバイ国際博覧会2020　モビリティパビリオン	208-210
Temporary Church for the Philippines	仮設の教会　フィリピン	211
Triangle House	三角の家	212
Tainan Art Museum	台南市美術館	213
Zenith	ゼニス	214-215
Shonai Hotel Suiden Terrasse	ショウナイホテル スイデンテラス	216-218
Monaco Cable Car Mid Station	モナコケーブルカー駅	219-226
Sully Morland's Concert & Performance Hall	シュリー・モルラン・コンサート＆パフォーマンスホール	227-230
Kur Park Nagayu	クアパーク長湯	231-232
Berggruen Institute	バーグルエン研究所	233
Paper Shelter for Nepal	ネパール復興住宅	234
Haesley Hamlet	ヘスリー・ハムレット	235-243
Art Biotop – Suite Villa	アートビオトープ・スイートヴィラ	244-245

Kentuck Knob Reception Pavilion	ケンタック・ノブ　レセプション・パビリオン	246
House in Auckland	オークランドの家	247
NSY/Victoria Street	NSY/ ヴィクトリア・ストリート	248-249
Le Monde Headquarters	ル・モンド本社	250-251
Yufu City Tourist Information Center	由布市ツーリストインフォメーションセンター	252-253
Chrystie Street Residences	クリスティー・ストリート集合住宅	254-255
Oita Prefectural Sports Arena	大分県立屋内スポーツ施設	256
Mokuzai/Bouscat	モクザイ / ブスキャ	257
Camper Mallorca	カンペール　マヨルカ	258
Varna One Table	ヴァルナ・ワン・テーブル	259-260
Potters Fields House	ポッターズ・フィールズ・ハウス	261
Sebastiao Salgado Exhibition	セバスチャン・サルガド展	262-264
SBC Dome (SFC)	SBC ドーム	265
Wooden Prefabricated Temporary Housing for Kumamoto	熊本地震木造仮設住宅	266-268
Europaris Tower	ユーロパリス・タワー	269-274
Maison du Peuple	メゾン・デュ・ププル	275-276
Team 7	ティームセブン新社屋	277-284
House Vision 2016	House Vision 2016	285-288
Human Future Pavilion	ヒューマン・フューチャー・パビリオン	289
Paper Tube Hut	紙管の小屋	290

Aubervilliers	オーベルヴィリエ	291
Novartis Pavilion	ノバルティス・パビリオン	292-294
Paper Temporary House Ecuador	紙の仮設住宅　エクアドル	295-297
Place Mazas	プラス・マザ	298
Morikami Museum	モリカミ美術館	299-302
Setagaya City Hall	世田谷区本庁舎	303-305
Kyoto City University of Arts Campus Relocation	京都市立芸術大学 移転整備	306-311
Mermaid Pavilion	マーメイド・パビリオン	312
Underwater Garden Restaurant	水中農園	313
Zenbo Seinei	禅坊 靖寧	314-315
SIMOSE	下瀬美術館	316-321
Taketa City Historical Museum & Community Center	竹田市歴史文化交流拠点施設	322-326
Pilot Houses for Kalobeyei New Settlement	カロベイエイ難民居住区のためのパイロットハウス	327
Triangle Lattice House	三角格子の家	328-329
Loro Piana Façade	ロロ・ピアーナ　ファサード	330
New Kagawa Prefectural Sports Arena	新香川県立体育館	331
Kumoi-dori District Redevelopment	雲井通5丁目地区再開発	332-333
Japan Security Union	日本連合警備本社	334-335
Shishi-iwa House2	ししいわハウス2	336-337
Paper Green House	紙の温室	338

LV Pavilion	LV パビリオン	339-343
Kentucky Owl Park	ケンタッキー・アウル・パーク	344-349
The Transparent Tokyo Toilet	ザ トウメイ トウキョウ トイレット	350
DMZ Passage	DMZ パサージュ	351
joints	ジョイント	352-353
Tech Company Visitor Center	テック企業ビジターセンター	354-357
America's Cup Pavilion	アメリカズカップ・パビリオン	358-359
Chateau de Beaucastel	シャトー・ド・ボーカステル	360-361
Jack's Point Hotel	ジャックス・ポイント・ホテル	362-363
Oulu House & Pavilion	オウル・ハウス＆パビリオン	364-365
Swarovski Crystal Worlds Garden Pavilion	スワロフスキー・クリスタルワールド・ガーデン・パビリオン	366
The George Expansion	ザ・ジョージ　増築	367-368
Parc Funeraire	パーク・フュネレール	369-371
St. Vincent de Paul	聖ヴァンサン・ド・ポール	372
Toyota City Museum	豊田市博物館	373-374
Wooden Rugby "Ball" Park	木造ラグビー“ボール”パーク	375
NWD K11 Art Mall & K11 ARTUS	NWD K11 アートモール & K11 アータス	376
Park City House Event Pavilion	パークシティハウス・イベントパビリオン	377
Penn State University Art Museum	ペンシルベニア州立大学美術館	378-379
Hotel Iwaya	岩屋ホテル	380

Jabal Ikmah Interpretive Centre	ジャバル・イクマ ビジターセンター	381
Dadan Interpretive Center	ダダン ビジターセンター	382
KONFiDA stand ITMA	KONFiDA 社ブース ITMA 国際繊維機械展示会	383
Paper Log House (Turkey/Syria)	紙のログハウス（トルコ / シリア）	384
Bookshelf House	本棚の家	385
Culture and Art Center in Guizhou	文化センター・中国貴州省	386
Farmer's Restaurant Haru San-San	農家レストラン 陽・燦燦	387
Birmingham	バーミンガム	388
Grand Palais Ephemere	グラン・パレ・エフェメール	389-390
Renovation Project of the Former Architecture School in Nanterre	ナンテール旧建築学校リノヴェーション	391
Temporary Pavilion for Notre-Dame de Paris	ノートルダム大聖堂のための仮設パビリオン	392-395
TULCHAN	タルカン	396
New memorial garden at International Committee of the Red Cross headquarters	国際赤十字委員会本部 新記念庭園	397
Farmer's Hut	農家の小屋	398
Isa City New Hall	伊佐市新庁舎	399
Atelier Gren	アトリエ・グレン	400
Zao Onsen	蔵王温泉	401
Duved	デュヴド	402
Bridge design at Vanke Hangzhou 2022 Asian Games Athlete Village	万科杭州 2022 アジア競技大会選手村 ブリッジ案	403
Lounge Furnitures	ラウンジ用家具	404

Karuizawa Town Hall	軽井沢庁舎	405
Blue Ocean Dome	ブルー・オーシャン・ドーム	406
Hotel in Taikoo Li Xi'an	西安タイクーリ・ホテル	407
Shizuoka Central Library	静岡県立中央図書館	408
Guilin Pavilion	桂林パビリオン	409-410
Salgado Exhibition	サルガド写真展	411
Wood-Steel Composite Truss	木スチール複合トラス	412
TIFFANY & Co Store Façade	ティファニー 店舗ファサード	413
4G Wine Estate	4G ワイン・エステート	414-415
M Residence	M邸	416
Breus Art Centre	ブレウス・アートセンター	417
Lviv City Hospital	リヴィウ市病院	418
Shiosai Restaurant	潮騒レストラン	419

坂　茂
SHIGERU BAN

プロフィール

1957年東京生まれ。77-80年、南カリフォルニア建築大学（SCI-Arc）在学。84年クーパー・ユニオン建築学部（NY）を卒業。82-83年磯崎新アトリエに勤務。85年坂茂建築設計を設立。東京、パリ、ニューヨークに事務所を構える。95年から国連難民高等弁務官事務所（UNHCR）コンサルタント、同時にNPO法人ボランタリー・アーキテクツ・ネットワーク（VAN）を設立し、世界各地で災害支援活動を行う。2010年ハーバード大学GSD客員教授、コーネル大学客員教授。2001〜08年、15〜23年慶應義塾大学環境情報学部教授。代表作に、「紙の教会　神戸（1995）」、「ハノーバー国際博覧会日本館（2000）」、「ポンピドー・センター メス（2010）」、「紙のカテドラル（2013）」、「大分県立美術館（2014）」、「静岡県富士山世界遺産センター（2017）」、「ラ・セーヌ・ミュジカル（2017）」、「スウォッチ・オメガ（2019）」、「禅坊　靖寧（2022）」、「SIMOSE（2023）」、「豊田市博物館（2024）」などがある。これまでに、日本建築学会賞作品部門（2009）、フランス国家功労勲章オフィシエ（2010）、芸術選奨文部科学大臣賞（2012）、フランス芸術文化勲章コマンドゥール（2014）、プリツカー建築賞（2014）、JIA日本建築大賞（2016）、紫綬褒章（2017）、マザー・テレサ社会正義賞（2017）、アストゥリアス皇太子賞（2022）、高松宮殿下記念世界文化賞　建築部門（2024）など受賞。現在、ニュー・ヨーロピアン・バウハウス委員、芝浦工業大学特別招聘教授。

PROFILE

Born in Tokyo in 1957. After studying at the Southern California Institute of Architecture (SCI-Arc) in 1977–1980, Ban graduated from the Cooper Union with a Bachelor of Architecture in 1984. In 1982–1983, he worked at Arata Isozaki Atelier. In 1985, he established Shigeru Ban Architects and set up an office in Tokyo, Paris, and New York. In 1995, he began serving as a consultant for the United Nations High Commissioner for Refugees (UNHCR). In the same year, he founded a nonprofit organization named Voluntary Architects' Network (VAN) to engage in disaster relief efforts worldwide. In 2010, he served as Visiting Professor at Harvard University Graduate School of Design as well as at Cornell University. In 2001–2008 and 2015–2023, he served as Professor at the Faculty of Environment and Information Studies, Keio University. His major works include Paper Church – Kobe (1995), Japan Pavilion Expo 2000 Hannover (2000), Centre Pompidou-Metz (2010), Cardboard Cathedral (2013), Oita Prefectural Art Museum (2014), Mt. Fuji World Heritage Centre Shizuoka (2017), La Seine Musicale (2017), Swatch Omega (2019), Zenbo Seinei (2022), SIMOSE (2023), and Toyota City Museum (2024). He is the recipient of Grand Prize of Architectural Institute of Japan (2009), le grade d'officier for L'Ordre des Arts et des Lettres, France (2010), the Minister of Education, Culture, Sports, Science and Technology's Art Encouragement Prize (2012), le grade de commandeur for L'Ordre des Arts et des Lettres, France (2014), Pritzker Architecture Prize (2014), JIA Grand Prix (2016), Medal with Purple Ribbon, Japan (2017), Mother Teresa Social Justice Award (2017), and Princess of Asturias Award for Concord (2022), Praemium Imperiale for Architecture (2024). Currently, he serves as a High-Level Roundtable member for the New European Bauhaus and Special Guest Professor at Shibaura Institute of Technology.

建築家・坂 茂 スケッチ集

令和6年11月19日　初版一刷発行

著　者　坂 茂

発 行 人　山下和樹
発　　行　カルチュア・コンビニエンス・クラブ株式会社
　　　　　光村推古書院書籍編集部

発　　売　光村推古書院株式会社
　　　　　〒604-8006
　　　　　京都市中京区河原町通三条上ル下丸屋町407-2
　　　　　ルート河原町ビル 5F
　　　　　PHONE　075 (251) 2888
　　　　　FAX　　　075 (251) 2881
　　　　　http://www.mitsumura-suiko.co.jp

印　　刷　株式会社シナノパブリッシングプレス

© 2024　Shigeru Ban
Printed in Japan
ISBN978-4-8381-0627-1

本書に掲載した写真・文章の無断転載・複写を禁じます。
本書のコピー、スキャン、デジタル化等の無断複製は著作権法上
での例外を除き禁じられています。本書を代行業者等の第三者に
依頼してスキャンやデジタル化することはたとえ個人や家庭内で
の利用であっても一切認められておりません。

乱丁・落丁本はお取替えいたします。